THE ROAD TO ISANDLWANA

PHILIP GON

THE ROAD TO ISANDLWANA

The Years of an Imperial Battalion

JONATHAN BALL PUBLISHERS
Johannesburg

All rights reserved. No part of this publication may be
reproduced, stored in a retrieval system, or transmitted in any
form or by any means, electronic, mechanical, photocopying,
recording or otherwise, without the prior permission
of the publisher.

© Philip Gon 1979

First published 1979 by Ad. Donker (Pty) Ltd

This edition published 1992 by
Jonathan Ball Publishers (Pty) Ltd
P O Box 2105
Parklands
2121

ISBN 0 947464 40 9

Maps drawn by Crawford Hay and Associates, Johannesburg
Typeset by National Book Printers, Goodwood, Cape
Cover design by Michael Barnett
Cover painting by courtesy of the Africana Museum, Johannesburg – 'Dying to save
the Queen's Colours' – the death of Lieutenants Melvill and Coghill, 24th Regiment,
Battle of Isandlwana.

To the memory of my father

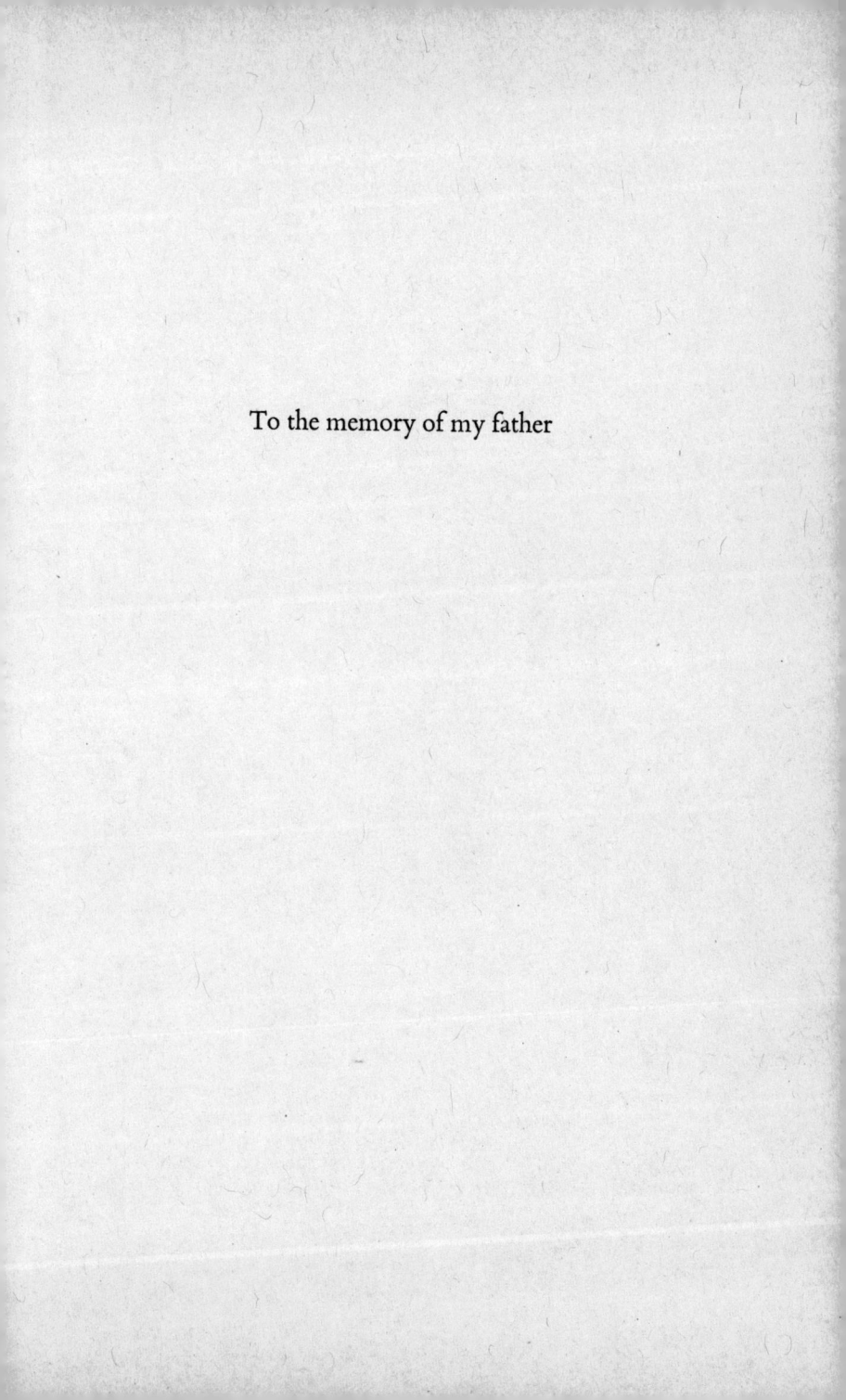

Contents

Preface	11
Prologue: 1874	17

Part One: January 1875 to August 1877

1	The Cape of Good Hope	27
2	A tale of diamonds	31
3	The road to 'Eldorado'	41
4	For the sake of Confederation	50
5	Diamond days	58
6	A troubled state	64
7	Carnarvon takes action	73
8	Boers and blesbok	79

Part Two: September 1877 to August 1878

9	A wedding-feast in the Transkei	91
10	Frontier War	101
11	The Ngqika Rebellion	116
12	Nyumaga and Centane	129
13	The old order changes	141
14	War in the Amatholes	152
15	Frontier settlements	164
16	The Mounted Infantry	170

Part Three: September 1878 to August 1879

17 September days ... 183
18 All roads lead to Natal ... 193
19 The Central Column ... 203
20 The 'Little Sphinx' ... 212
21 Wednesday 22 January ... 222
22 The final months ... 249
Epilogue ... 256
Bibliography ... 261
Index ... 267

List of maps

The Eastern Frontier	95
The Battle of Centane	138
Scene of operations in the Eastern Amatholes	162
Scene of operations of the Central Column	220
Battle at Isandlwana	244–246

Preface

Some years ago, a photograph album compiled by the Bandmaster of the 1st Battalion, 24th Regiment of Foot, came into my possession. The photographs, though not of great historical interest, did constitute a record of four years residence in South Africa of a member of the battalion that was massacred in Zululand on 22 January 1879. Establishing the fate of the Bandmaster proved much more difficult than I had anticipated and I found myself caught up in the wider drama of the years that led to the battalion's annihilation. My search, which lasted almost five years, began in the newspaper room of the Johannesburg Public Library and took me to Cape Town, Kimberley, King William's Town, the Transkei, Durban, Zululand, Sekhukhuneland, the Kalahari, London and Brecon in Wales. In following the fortunes of the 1/24th I delved into events that had received scant mention in history books, in particular, the 'Black Flag' Rebellion and the Ninth Frontier War.

This frontier war was won by a relatively small number of troops and at a low cost in white lives – facts which must have been carefully weighed up by Sir Bartle Frere when he set in motion a train of bloody events in the furtherance of Lord Carnarvon's confederation dream. This forgotten war offers a great deal that is of interest to the military historian. The battle at Centane, in the Transkei, was hailed, at the time, as a model action against numerically superior but inferiorly armed forces. It resulted in a euphoric overestimation of the potency of disciplined infantry armed with the Martini-Henry rifle, an error which, indubitably, played a part in the terrible mismanagement, a year later, at Isandlwana.

The climax of the story of the 1/24th is the battle at Isandlwana. I have not detailed the meanderings of Lord Chelmsford's column on that day, but concentrated on the more shadowy (to this day) events that took place in the camp. My attempt at reconstructing the massacre was guided by F.W.D. Jackson's excellent analysis. Nevertheless, I found it necessary to read the available testimonies, memoirs and reminiscences of survivors and witnesses from both armies, for myself. Four visits to Isandlwana were undertaken, the fugitives' trail was followed and the reported positions of recognisable corpses were carefully analysed in an endeavour to reconstruct the likely course of events *after* the last of the survivors had fled the field of battle. By closely studying the activities of the members of the 1/24th over the four years preceding the Anglo-Zulu War, I came across snippets of information that lent some insight into the character of Major Henry Pulleine; and as a result permitted myself a certain amount of conjecture as to his likely behaviour on the day of battle. A similar liberty was taken in respect of Colonel Anthony Durnford.

The connecting thread on the battalions road to destruction is Carnarvon's confederation policy. Its beginnings coincide with the battalion's advent on the South African scene and its end begins with the massacre at Isandlwana.

I have avoided detailed references to the bibliography on the grounds that this book is not aimed at the academic but at the general reader with an interest in South Africa's past, and that in most instances, the authors of quotations are self-evident. I wish to emphasise that the 'protagonist' of this narrative is an imperial infantry battalion, and that where possible the perceptions of its members, however fanciful, have been incorporated – a useful source has been the lively comments of Lieutenant Nevill Coghill. I have relied, largely, on contemporary or near-contemporary, written evidence augmented by on site inspections. Documented accounts, impressions and memoirs of the Battalion's antagonists received equal consideration. Accounts recorded many years after the events described, however, have been treated with great circumspection.

The task of tracing the footsteps of the 1/24th was made considerably easier by the consistent patience and helpfulness of the staff of the Africana Library in Johannesburg. I must make special mention of the co-operation I received from Major G.J.B. Egerton of the 24th Regiment Museum, Mr Brian Randles of the Kaffrarian Museum in King William's Town and Dr A.M. Lewin Robinson of the South African Library, Cape Town, who permitted me to study the Merriman and Molteno Papers. I must acknowledge the National Army Museum, Chelsea, for allowing me to quote extensively from the Coghill Papers, and the kindness of Sir Patrick Coghill in sending me his memoir of his uncle Nevill Coghill.

I owe a debt of gratitude to Norman Holme of Bolton, Lancashire, for some preliminary research undertaken on my behalf, to Fiona Barbour of the McGregor Museum, Kimberley for useful advice, and to the University of Fort Hare Xhosa Dictionary Project for assistance with the spelling of Xhosa names. In the spelling of place names I followed the more recent 1:50 000 Trigonometrical Survey Office maps.

Amongst the friends who gave of their time and lightened my burden, I thank Harry Green, Peter Joubert and David Liknaitzky. Here I must include Stanley Coghan who introduced me to the photograph album of Bandmaster Burck and, unwittingly, started off an obsessive search.

Heartfelt thanks are offered to Jacqueline Marks for giving up so much of her free time to produce a near perfect typescript.

I am grateful to Christine Suzman, my editor, for patiently uncovering errors that persistently eluded me, and to my publisher for the enthusiastic co-operation which has made the preparation of this book a pleasurable experience.

Last but not least I thank my daughters Sara and Josephine for accepting, uncomplainingly, a part-time father for five years.

Confederation will involve, we hope, self defence, which will remove the liability under which we labour of spending our blood and money upon these wretched Kaffir quarrels in South Africa.

> Lord Cadogan
> Hansard, 3rd Series CCXLIV
> 25 March 1879

Prologue

1874

The Rock was half hidden by heavy dark clouds when the P & O steamer *Peshawar* entered the Bay of Gibraltar. She carried fifty-seven passengers, almost half were young subalterns sent to replenish the imperial garrisons in the Mediterranean. Of those who disembarked at Gibraltar that morning, seven had been posted to the 1st Battalion of the 24th Regiment of Foot. Their names were Edgar Oliphant Anstey, James Patrick Daly, Nevill Josiah Aylmer Coghill, William Edward Day Spring, George Frederick John Hodson, Wilfred Heaton and Charles John Atkinson. The date was 2 June 1874; less than five years later only two of them would still be alive.

The regiment these men had been commissioned in had a proud reputation for bravery and a less enviable one for misfortune. It was raised in 1689 to fight for William and Mary against the Jacobites. Thirteen years later under the colonelcy of John Churchill, Duke of Marlborough, the regiment began its collection of battle honours. 'Ramillies', 'Blenheim', 'Malplaquet' and 'Oudenarde' were later emblazoned on the Regimental Colours.

In 1741, in a costly campaign waged in the West Indies to determine whether England or Spain would have dominance in trade with the New World, the 24th lost four-fifths of its strength from bloody fighting and sickness. In the next thirty years it was compelled to surrender twice to enemy forces. The first time to the French in the war that broke out over the commercial exploitation of North America and ended with General Wolfe's capture of Quebec; the second time to the Colonists in North America, when the 24th formed part of General Burgoyne's army. During the Napoleonic Wars the regiment was enlarged to two battalions. The new battalion took the brunt of the French attack at Talavera and lost half its strength in a single day's fighting. In 1810, three 'East Indiamen' while transporting the 1st Battalion to India, were attacked by a French flotilla off the coast of Madagascar. Two of the British ships were captured and to prevent the Colours falling into enemy hands, the Commanding Officer of the battalion ordered them thrown into the sea. Almost forty years later, the Colours featured in a battle which came to be regarded as the regiment's most glorious disaster.

On 13 January 1849, during the Second Sikh War, an unexpected advance of the enemy guns at Chillianwala provoked a hastily organised attack by the British line. The Right Brigade, of which the 24th formed the centre, was thrown against the enemy with an injunction to carry the guns with the bayonet. The sheer bravado of the assault through dense jungle carried them through to the guns; but a furious Sikh counter-attack drove them back. The fighting that followed was heavy and confused. The Commanding Officer was killed and the Colour Party of the 24th shot down. The Regimental Colour was recovered but the Queen's Colour was never found. Some thought that it had been buried concealed on the body of a private soldier who had ripped it off its broken staff. When rain and failing light brought the fighting to an end, one hundred and thirty-eight men of the 24th lay dead in the wet grass. One of the wounded was a young soldier called William Charters. In 1874 he was the Quartermaster of the 1/24th – its living link with that hard-fought day at Chillianwala.

Most of the senior officers in the battalion had joined the army in the fifties. A few had seen action in the Crimean War and the Indian Mutiny. The oldest officer was the forty-five-year-old Paymaster, Major Francis Freeman White. He had joined the regiment in 1850.

Uppermost in the thoughts of Nevill Coghill as he stepped ashore at Gibraltar was the worry about what status his rank would enjoy; he was one of 'those new creations known as sub-lieutenants, whose Social standing is not yet, and I doubt whether it will ever be, properly understood . . .' Coghill and his contemporaries had joined the army at a time of transition. For the past six years the British Army had been convulsed by an unprecedented number of changes and reforms. Sub-lieutenant had replaced ensign, the time-honoured title for a fledgeling officer; commission by purchase had been abolished (since 1870 direct commission had been by examination only); supply and medical services had been radically re-organised; flogging for peace time infringements of regulations had been prohibited; no longer was the soldiers' meat and bread deducted from his shilling a day; and efforts were being made to increase literacy among the men: the 1/24th even had a schoolmaster on its staff. The improvements in the soldiers' lot had been quite remarkable for an age more sentimental than sensitive, and men like Sergeant James Pullen, who had joined the regiment before the Crimean War, had seen more changes than the army had known in a hundred years.

The years of reform, gleefully described by one sub-lieutenant as a 'Reign of Terror' when every soldier 'lived from day to day in a fever of apprehension as to what was going to happen to him next', was largely due to the efforts of Edward Cardwell, the Whig Secretary of State for War. The outstanding success of the Prussian reserve system in the Franco-Prussian War had forced him to re-examine the relationship between Britain's permanent army and its militia. To provide the nation with a large trained reserve Cardwell decided to introduce short-service enlistment; twelve years with the Colours was changed into six in service and six in reserve. The regulation had provoked considerable controversy. And while the officers railed against the demise of the purchase system, the NCOs – the men largely responsible for the training of recruits and maintenance of discipline in the Queen's Army – attacked short-service enlistment. In their experience it took six years to transform a raw recruit into a useful soldier. The new regulation, they feared, would turn the regiments of the line into training schools for the nation's reserve, leaving the Empire to be policed by green troops. The non-commissioned officers of the 1/24th, however, were grateful, that its ranks at least, were filled with long-service men who had enlisted before 1870. Affluence had adversely affected recruiting and to promote recruitment, Cardwell proposed the creation of closer ties between militia units and regiments of the line. Territorial brigade districts consisting of two militia battalions, and one regular battalion, were established all over the country. The 24th Regiment, which for ninety-one years had carried the county title of '2nd Warwickshire', had been assigned a brigade district made up of four South Wales border counties. A permanent home had yet to be established in Brecon. The 1st Battalion, which for the past eight years had been stationed in Mediterranean garrisons had, at best, only a tenuous connection with Wales.

This period of reform and re-organisation had also coincided with a far reaching improvement in the infantryman's arms. In 1868 the 1/24th had been issued with its first breech-loading rifles. The days of the muzzle-loader, of old 'Brown Bess', were over. New musketry techniques had to be introduced and different tactics devised. In the 1st Battalion the man responsible for this duty was its senior subaltern, thirty year old Frederick Carrington. His assistant in this task was James Pullen, the Sergeant-Instructor of Musketry. By 1874 the men were drilling with the British Army's second generation of breech-loaders, the Martini-Henry.

While Cardwell was endeavouring to provide Britain with a large army for the unlikely event of a Continental war, the British Empire for the past decade had furnished the young military careerist with fewer and fewer opportunities for brevet promotions. It had become politically fashionable in the sixties to regard the colonies as an expensive burden on the mother country. The Whig Government under Gladstone had tried to lessen Britain's commitment to colonial defence whenever possible. All the colonies that could undertake their own protection had been offered responsible government, and the imperial garrisons in Canada, Australia and New Zealand had been drastically reduced. In 1873, however, Gladstone's government had been provoked, by an Ashanti invasion of the unofficial protectorate which Britain had established on the shores of the Gold Coast, into an imperial adventure in Africa. An expedition had been hastily mounted under the command of Sir Garnet Wolseley, the egotistical and talented young general who had been Cardwell's associate in army reform. In less than two months, Wolseley had taken three battalions through fever-ridden jungles to Kumasi, the Ashanti capital village, burnt it, and returned to the coast. The campaign had been conducted with vigour and enterprise and a band of war correspondents had given it good coverage. Gladstone's little war had focused the interest of the British public on Africa and the army, and a delighted nation had showered honours on Wolseley and his staff (the Ashanti Ring) when they returned home. Gladstone's ministry, however, had been denied the opportunity of capitalising on the happy outcome of the war. By the time the victorious troops came home the Tory Party under Benjamin Disraeli occupied the government benches.

Disraeli, himself, was largely uncommited on imperial direction, but the return of the Tory Party to power had brought to the Colonial Office a very positive Secretary of State for Colonies. Henry Howard Molyneux Herbert, Fourth Earl of Carnarvon, also known as 'Twitters', was an ambitious man with an obsessive interest in his work. He had acquired a taste for colonial affairs seven years before as a member of Derby's Cabinet, and few doubted that under his direction the Colonial Office would feature prominently in national politics. The most important pointer, perhaps, to an imminent change in imperial policy was the competitive economic outlook which had resulted from the growth of the United States and the rise of powerful industrial states in Europe, especially Germany, whose victory against France had pushed her to the forefront of potential rivals for colonial markets. Wolseley's foray into Ashantiland had given the nation a taste for inexpensive but dazzling colonial adventures. The Tory Government was likely to provide occasion for many more.

Within a few weeks of their arrival in Gibraltar the new subalterns learnt that the 1/24th was in line for a distant colonial posting. There was much speculation as to where it would be, but southern Africa was considered the most likely. In October Captain William Degacher arrived in Gibraltar with a large draft of men. The 1/24th was being brought up to an establishment of eight hundred and twenty rank and file, the strength at which a battalion about to depart for overseas service was kept; it was to be moved to the Cape of Good Hope within a few weeks.

Africa, since the abolition of the slave-trade, had ceased to hold any exploitive interest for the governments of Europe and the continent had been largely forgotten by a Europe obsessed with its own industrial destiny. Curiosity had returned with the age of African exploration. The explorers had furnished a sentimental age with the noble heroes it yearned for, and they in turn, repayed the acclaim they received with lurid tales of witchcraft and unmentionable (by Victorian standards) barbaric rituals. It was, however, the recently opened Suez Canal in the north and the precious mineral discoveries in the south that in 1874 attracted the serious attention of the European world. Britain by then had the biggest stake in Africa, and to the young subaltern Africa meant Napier's expedition against the mad Emperor of Abyssinia, the Ashanti campaign and David Livingstone. In April 1874 the mortal remains of the great explorer, missionary, doctor and opponent of the slave-trade had been brought back from Africa for internment in Westminster Abbey. The eulogies that were heaped on the man who had symbolised the virtues for which mid-Victorian youth had been exhorted to strive, produced in the subsequent months a nostalgia sufficient to make a visit to the continent where he had breathed his last seem like a pilgrimage. The year before, South Africa too, had featured briefly in War Office bulletins. Some of the officers might have remembered reading about a rebellious Zulu chief called Langalibalele who for a few months had given the settlers of Natal a run for their money.

The country was renowned for its small, fierce 'Kaffir Wars' and its large herds of game. There had not been a 'Kaffir War' for an incredible twenty-three years, but the prospect of filling the family mansion with hunting trophies engendered an air of great excitement in the Officers' Mess at the Buena Vista Barracks. The biggest beneficiaries of the forthcoming move were the gunsmiths; money saved and money borrowed was spent on the latest in sporting guns. The merits of the different pieces were argued over for weeks at the mess table, but economy in the end forced some to re-appraise the virtues of the regulation Martini-Henry. If hunting became the obsession of the officers, diamonds were the preoccupation of the battalion rank and file. Stories of wealth scooped from rivers, of fortunes gathered from the dust of Kimberley in a single day by men like themselves, men from the industrial slums of Europe, circulated continuously in the barracks.

Some of the older soldiers had passed through Cape Town on their way to and from India. They spoke of a particularly potent brandy that was readily available and inexpensive; then they proceeded to describe the Cape Colony's coloured women in similar terms.

First to leave Gibraltar was a detachment of one hundred and seventy-two men under the command of Major Henry Degacher in the *Elizabeth Martin*, a steamer chartered from Mr Donald Currie's line. Next to leave was the Headquarters of the Battalion. Departure day was Saturday 28 November. The battalion had been stationed in Gibraltar for three years and its members were well known to the community. The *Gibraltar Chronicle* recorded their imminent departure with some regret: 'on parade they were second to none, and in the hunting fields, on the race-course or in the ballroom, it required a good man to get in front if the 24th had a representative present ...' Embarkation was preceded by a colourful parade which helped brighten an otherwise dismal winter day. Colonel Richard Thomas Glyn, who had commanded the 1st Battalion for eight years, was congratulated by the General Commanding on the appearance of his men. He seemed particularly impressed by the fact that there were no absentees and no 'unsteady men' on parade. Despite Cardwell's attempts to make the army more democratic and to enlist a better type of recruit, in the General's eyes, and indeed in the popular imagination, the army of 1874 was still the refuge for vagrants and social misfits, more an extension of Britain's prison system than the valued guardian of its empire. The era of public adulation had still to come.

Five hundred soldiers embarked on Her Majesty's Troopship *Simoon*, a ship of less than three thousand tons burthen. Their wives and children were crowded into one large cabin which was locked at night. When the fully laden *Simoon* sailed, two companies under Major Henry Burmester Pulleine were left behind. They were to follow within a few days in the larger *Himalaya*, the troopship that was to transport the Headquarters of the 1/13th (Prince Albert's Light Infantry) from Malta to South Africa. Last to leave Gibraltar was Sub-lieutenant Nevill Coghill; he was returning to the new regimental depot in Brecon for further instruction.

Part One

January 1875 to August 1877

I

The Cape of Good Hope

'... We dropped anchor in Table Bay and gazed up delighted at Table Mountain, and drank in the scented breeze which blew off to us from the land.' Thirty-five days of cramped tedium and indifferent food were over. It was New Year's day, the second-last day of the extended Christmas holidays that annually turned Cape Town into a deserted city, but on this occasion a fair-sized crowd had gathered on the jetty to watch the *Simoon* dock. Major Henry Degacher, Captain William Mostyn and Lieutenant Anstey, who had arrived aboard the *Elizabeth Martin* three days before, were there, and the band of the 86th (Royal County Downs), was waiting to escort the newcomers to the Main Barracks. Critical eyes appraised Colonel Glyn's men as they marched down Dock Road. The comments were favourable. 'They are mostly fine, stalwart, well built men', recorded one onlooker, but he did not consider them as smart a regiment as the 86th, which had been at the Cape so long that it had become an institution. Three days later the *Himalaya* docked, and room had to be found for Pulleine's detachment. The city, recovering from its holiday stupor, came to resemble a 'miniature Aldershot'.

The disembarkation contrasted with a day sixty-nine years before when a flotilla of sailing ships entered Table Bay in rough seas and was forced to turn about to attempt a landing sixteen miles to the north under the guns of a hostile army. The 1/24th, then, had been part of the expeditionary force which had been dispatched to occupy the Cape of Good Hope after that temporary lull in the war with Napoleonic France known as the Peace of Amiens.

The 86th finally left South Africa on 2 February. Two days later the 1st Battalion took possession of the Castle and the Main Barracks in Cape Town. Its South African tour of duty had begun.

The two-hundred-year-old Castle, which housed the Headquarters of the Imperial Command in South Africa, was a low, thick-walled, pentagonal edifice with a bastion on each corner. It was surrounded by a moat which had, over the years, become a muddy trap for the garbage and effluence of Cape Town and gave off a memorable stench on windless days. Colonel Glyn, as the Castle's new Commandant, occupied quarters in the wing that had once formed part of the Dutch Governor's residence and which still retained some of its former stateliness. But the soldiers' quarters, with few exceptions, were cramped and gloomy. The windows mostly faced onto stone walls where moss grew in the crevices. The rooms were either uncomfortably stuffy in summer or cold and damp in winter. The section allocated to the unmarried officers was particularly cheerless. The advent of steam transportation had added the racket of passing trains to the discomforts of life in the Castle. The builders of the railroad had run their line past the two sea-facing bastions. Most of the soldiers, however, were accommodated in the nearby Main Barracks, a commodious if cheerless complex less than a hundred years old.

From the Castle ramparts, the buildings of Cape Town presented a monotonous vista uninterrupted by any distinctive architecture. The area between the Castle and the docks presented a particularly decayed and unkempt appearance. It was the industrial part of town, and contained tanneries, flour-mills, soap factories, wood-processing plants, boat-building yards and the gas-works. The buildings were mostly two-, occasionally three-storied structures of plastered brick showing the ravages of time and weather. The few that had been highlighted by a fresh coat of whitewash only emphasised the impression of a town well past its first flush of youth.

A closer inspection of Cape Town confirmed most new arrivals in their first impression: an unremarkable town overshadowed by the grandeur of Table Mountain and its attendant peaks. Anthony Trollope, who visited South Africa the following year, remarked that 'though Cape Town as a City is not lovely, the Capetowners have as good a time of it as the inhabitants of more beautiful capitals'. A good time, but as they soon found out, at a price. The inexpensive life-style, which the 1/24th had heard about, dated from the depressed sixties, when a visitor of modest means could live in comparative luxury amongst colonists whose livelihood depended on a languishing agricultural economy. But the discovery of diamonds and a fashion for ostrich feathers had changed all that; for the first time since its founding, Cape Town was enjoying prosperity and experiencing inflation. Since the opening of the diamond fields, prices in some instances, had increased by four hundred per cent. A pound of prime beef had quadrupled to ninepence. An acceptable riding horse fetched nearly £50. A few years before, its equivalent could have been bought for a quarter the price.

The officers of the Queen's Army, who had grown up in the middle years of Victoria's reign, had been inculcated with a code of sexual disavowal that required an extraordinary amount of self-confidence and a considerable denial of upbringing to flaunt. But rigid class distinction neither demanded nor expected the ordinary soldier to exhibit the same moral scruples, and for his supposedly different needs, Cape Town catered more than adequately. As a major sea-port with a naval base and a permanent garrison, it was capable of satisfying all tastes in vice and dissipation. Canteens and bars were plentiful, while gambling houses and brothels were tolerated. A large number were situated in Harrington Street and Primrose Square, conveniently close to the Castle and the barracks. The district was described by a contemporary newspaper as 'the constant scene of a saturnalia of protitutes and thieves of the worst description'. The men could avail themselves of whores in a range of colours that few comparable towns could offer, with prices inversely proportional to the degree of pigmentation. Some years later, when an outcry was raised against Cape Town's rampant vice, and the matter was brought up in Parliament, a police report was quoted which divided Cape Town's six hundred official prostitutes into four hundred Continentals, twenty-five British, seventy-five Colonials and one hundred Cape Coloureds.

The Cape Colony was the largest and richest province in southern Africa and almost two-thirds of the country's white population lived within its borders – a quarter of a million people dispersed on large farms and in small towns and villages that were separated from each other by great distances and poor roads. Populous by South African standards it might have been, but Trollope tried to place it in perspective when he pointed out that the settler population of the entire colony was slightly smaller than that of the twenty-five year old city of Melbourne, Australia. Most of the colonists confined themselves to the coastal strip that stretched from Cape Town to the Kei River (the eastern border); beyond lay the Transkeian territory, commonly referred to as 'Kaffirland' – a veritable Balkans of independent tribes and tribes under nominal colonial protection.

In 1875 the political spectrum of the geographical entity known as South Africa included black despotic kingdoms, colonies at different stages of development, and democratic republics which bestowed their freedoms on their white citizens only. The two white groups in the country were divided by language, culture and past conflict, but both feared the black majority more than they disliked each other. Common to all the states, with the exception of the Colony of Griqualand West, was an economy based on stock farming and agriculture, sources of livelihood which promoted competition for lands and herds, and, sometimes, led to war.

Cape Town was happily isolated from the trouble spots of southern Africa. The imperial garrison was there to protect the installations at Simonstown from the remote possibility of a sea-borne attack by a hostile Continental power; but guarding the sea-route to the 'Empire in the East' was an imperial responsibility which did not concern the good burghers of Cape Town. They were much more interested in the spending power of the Garrison and what contribution its officers would make to the social and sporting life of the community. A battalion that possessed an accomplished band was also appreciated in a city without a resident orchestra. In this department the 1st Battalion was particularly strong. Its band had thirty-two active members, a very comprehensive assembly of brass and a large fife section. Military bands were the property of their battalions and were maintained from regimental and mess funds. If a band proved sufficiently popular with the colonial community it could bring in an income from public appearances. Competent bandmasters were, consequently, much in demand, and in Herr Carl Burck, the 1/24th had such a man.

2

A tale of diamonds

Life in Cape Town changed radically when it became the gateway to the diamond fields. Every week the black-hulled mail-ships of the Union Line and the dove-grey steamships of Mr Currie's Line disgorged their cargoes of fortune-seekers onto Cape Town's dockside. They scrambled out of steerage and into the city's over-crowded hotels and rooming houses. Most were short of funds and all were anxious to get to the diamond country, but few had realised that they had to travel seven hundred miles into the interior to reach the mines. Compelled to hang around Cape Town, waiting for transport, the new arrivals cursed the heat when there was no wind, the 'South-easter' when it choked them with dust, their bug-ridden beds, the inedible food, and the high prices they were forced to pay. But wherever men met the talk always came back to the diamonds, and the most favoured topic was the wondrous 'New Rush' mine, the Kimberley kopje that was being turned into a mammoth hole. That it had made rich men out of paupers in less than a week was well known; less cheerful were the recent reports of landslides and flooding. Men who had yet to find their first, small, flawed stone agonised about unregulated overproduction and an imminent slump in the world diamond market. By 1875, there were fears that the best years were over and that newcomers had missed their chance.

Nevertheless, the South African mineral revolution charged Cape Town with an air of excitement that infected old settlers and newcomers alike. Within three months of their arrival, eight men from the 1st Battalion had deserted. But by April, rumours of a different kind were emanating from Griqualand West; instead of diamonds, the talk was of rebellion.

Eight years had gone by since the stone was found that focused the attentions of a sceptical world on the interior of South Africa, momentous years that had jolted a poor, backward land into the nineteenth century and stimulated an unexpected prosperity. The subsequent rush into the interior had provided the incentive to improve communications, which for centuries had moved at the pace of the trek-ox. The construction of a telegraphic network had become a matter of priority, the country's embryonic railway system received an impetus which even the isolationists could not ignore. The diamonds had brought a complexity of social, economical and political problems that were challenging the old order in South Africa.

The diamond fields were situated in a district with ill-defined and disputed borders where lived Griquas (emigrant mixed breeds from the Cape Colony), Tswanas, Koranas, Boers and Bushmen. The diamond discoveries had led to territorial claims and a jostling for political influence, particularly on the part of the two Boer republics; and an influx of determined fortune-seekers and land-jobbers from the two English Colonies had compounded the land claim mayhem.

When at the close of 1870, Sir Henry Barkly arrived to take office as Governor of the Cape Colony, he found himself flooded with appeals for protection, arbitration and guidance from bewildered Tswana chiefs and Griqua captains. Barkly had been assigned the task of preparing the Cape Colony for responsible government, but the chaos in Griqualand West was made his immediate concern. Objecting strongly to responsible government, because he believed that the non-whites would be denied fair treatment by colonial legislators, and urging vigorous action in Griqualand West, was Barkly's chief advisor on South African affairs – the Colonial Secretary.

Richard Southey was a man of inflexible philanthropic principles who firmly believed that the interests of Africa and its peoples were best served by the dissemination of British liberalism through imperial expansion. He had seen in the confusion in Griqualand West a situation that had to be exploited to stop the Boer Republics with their oppressive native policies from acquiring a valuable asset.

Before a year had passed, Barkly had accepted the allegiance of Waterboer (the most important Griqua leader), proclaimed the Griquas British subjects and made the diamond territory a crown colony. The annexation had been greeted with dismay in both Cape Town and Westminster. The bitterness it produced in the Boer republics and in the hearts of the 'Old Colonists' (the descendants of the Dutch settlers living in the Cape Colony), was to affect subsequent Colonial Office policy and was to haunt Barkly for the remainder of his career. The act was widely regarded as a piece of political chicanery and John Molteno, the Cape Colony's Prime Minister, who drew a large measure of his support from the 'Old Colonists' had been unable, under the circumstances, to agree to the incorporation of the new Colony of Griqualand West into the Cape Colony.

In the months following annexation conditions on the diamond fields became progressively more unsettled. President Brand of the Orange Free State had refused to accept the boundaries and retained a magistrate at the diggings. With two authorities claiming control of the road to the diamond fields, clashes were bound to occur, particularly as the arms traffic to Kimberley moved along this road. The arms trade was a prime source of contention. Payment with guns attracted black labour to the mines, and the trade in arms provided the Griqualand West administration with revenue. Selling arms to blacks was to the Boers a concept so outrageous that it verged on blasphemy. Furthermore, internal discontent had been aggravated by the desultory dealings of the Colony's caretaker administration. This situation had decided Barkly to institute constitutional rule as quickly as possible and establish a permanent administration in Griqualand West. In December 1872, Richard Southey was appointed Lieutenant-Governor of Griqualand West. Barkly had rewarded him for his role in the annexation of that territory and had removed from Cape Town a dedicated opponent of responsible government.

The Lieutenant-Governor and his retinue had received a great welcome from their subjects when they reached the diamond fields. Disenchanted by a year of half-hearted rule from Cape Town, the whole community had made an occasion out of Southey's arrival. Men on horses, wagons packed with diggers and their ladies, and hordes of near-naked labourers had lined the road into Kimberley. Joseph Benjamin Robinson, the territory's first millionaire, had loaned his fine carriage and horses for the formal entry. The party had been received in the dusty Market Square by a cheering crowd and a loud brass band. The celebrations had carried on well into the night with a fireworks display that was brilliantly augmented by the accidental explosion of a barrel of gunpowder.

Southey's first disappointment had been the corrugated-iron cottage which had been set aside for a 'Government House' and which was already overshadowed by the premises being erected for the representatives of the international diamond merchants. His second disappointment must have been the boisterous community he had come to govern. The thousands of professional diggers, the shrewd diamond-buyers, the hotel and canteen proprietors, the entertainers, prostitutes and traders, who made up the polyglot population of many nationalities, was, with a few notable exceptions, a self-seeking horde that cared little about a greater British Africa and less about his concern for civilising the native peoples. It was a far cry from the dedicated community he had hoped to see established there.

The honeymoon was quickly over. Southey was an experienced administrator, but lacked the wiliness and political sophistry to govern such a querulous community. Although the colony was little more than a large mining camp, its problems would have taxed the most experienced economists and sociologists. Backed by a hopelessly inadequate constabulary and an incompetent, if over-worked, civil service, he was forced to rely heavily on the support of his Colonial Secretary. John Blades Currey was an arrogant man who relished the power of his position and, in a competitive and speculative society, had the ill-sense to acquire a reputation for favouring friends with contracts and licences. He made many enemies and his unpopularity reflected on the Governor whose own autocratic inclinations were a sufficient handicap.

The disputes over land before the annexation had resulted in a multitude of titles and options granted by chiefs and headmen to land speculators. Some of the titles were genuine; many were imaginary. The resultant confusion was further compounded by unscrupulous agents who sometimes sold or ceded titles to more than one party. To try and solve the very fundamental problem of land ownership, Southey established a land commission. The investigations meant unravelling a monumental web of claims and counterclaims that were far beyond the limited talents of his staff. The problem was intensified by powerful speculating syndicates from the Cape Colony's Eastern Province who obstructed any detailed examination of their titles.

It was not long before he was at odds with the owners of land on which mines and business premises were situated. These men had bought the original farms at inflated prices, and not being permitted to derive any profit from the diamond finds, tried to extract it from rentals and claim licences. Southey denied their claims to mineral rights by insisting that these belonged to the Crown. To get better control over the landowners, he proposed certain ordinances in the Legislative Council which would limit mineral rights and give the colonial government power to regulate rentals. One of the major shareholders in Vooruitzicht, the farm on which the 'New Rush Mine' was located, was John Paterson, the unofficial leader of the Eastern Province bloc in the Cape Legislative Assembly. A wealthy man with influence in London, he successfully instigated an opposition to Southey's ordinances which were disallowed by the Home Government. The temptation to hold claims and mine their own ground was so great that the landowners intensified their efforts to make mining uneconomical for the small digger. A proposed monthly rental of £10 was too much for Southey. He stepped in with Ordinance 10, which Westminster had accepted, forbidding the acquisition by any individual or company of more than ten claims.

The financiers and landowners in turn began to buy up claims under fictitious names, falsified the records of ownership, and surreptitiously took over abandoned claims. As the conglomerates grew bigger and mining more costly, the small digger began to disappear. Tension and confusion developed as the divisions between capital and labour began to manifest themselves. Insecurity added racism to the brew of discontent. The complexities of deep mining made every digger dependent on a steady supply of cheap labour. Fortunately for them, tribesmen from all over the country were attracted to the diamond fields. Drought and starvation in the tribal lands were powerful recruiting agents, as was the unheard-of custom of being paid for their services with guns. Labourers came from Basotholand, Natal, Zululand, the Transkei and the Transvaal, and when they returned to their kraals, they took back guns and a knowledge of white industrial society. As long as they were prepared to work in the mines for low wages, the diggers forgave them their bouts of drunkeness and their periodic outbursts of violence. Those who stayed on soon learnt that there was more money in diamonds than in digging, and some aspired to become claim owners in their own right (the laws of Griqualand West under Southey made no distinction between white and black in this respect). They also discovered that a stolen diamond readily found a buyer.

In times of prosperity a certain amount of pilfering could be tolerated, but as the cost of mining escalated, so did the demand for illicit diamonds. Fears of a recession in the diamond market led to a hardening in the attitude towards thieving and a suspicion towards blacks. As few white men, it was argued, would stoop so low as to buy stolen diamonds, the obvious recipients of the illicit stones were the labourers' compatriots.

The calls for stricter laws and harsher penalties against illicit diamond buying became more insistent. The diggers wanted more rigorous application of the vagrancy laws and quicker convictions. Southey had neither the police nor the judiciary to deal with the many charges that were laid. He regarded most of them merely as manifestations of racial prejudices. He was incapable of disguising his strong feelings about colour prejudice and they sometimes led him to make accusations of racism where none was involved. His attitude led to a yearning for the good old days when the harsh native laws of the Orange Free State were enforced on the diamond fields. They wanted the black man endowed with the status of a temporary sojourner, whose only privilege was the sale of his labour. Southey was condemned as a 'nigger-lover' and his detractors, diggers and financiers, began to coalesce around this one emotional issue.

Diggers, landowners, mining syndicates, racists, and exponents of republicanism found common cause in bringing about Southey's downfall. They had begun, towards the end of 1874, to co-ordinate their aims through the Diggers' Protection Association, an organisation created to thwart illicit diamond dealing and keep surveillance over the blacks. Its chairman was Henry Tucker, a respected supporter of the small diggers' rights. He had represented Cradock in the Cape Legislative Assembly before coming to the diamond fields and had developed a taste for the political hurly-burly. The Griqualand West administration was an easy target for his detractions which were made even more formidable by his talent as a cartoonist. The Association, as originally formulated, was not subversive, but Southey considered it an affront to his authority and lost no time making his disapproval known. Official condemnation made the Association more attractive to a number of socially and politically unreconciled personalities. The most important was Alfred Aylward, whose militant republicanism helped the Association acquire a revolutionary character.

Aylward's past history was hidden behind a veil of lies, contradictions, and aliases. He was an educated man who combined an unpredictable temper with a talent for inflammatory oratory and a taste for the dramatic gesture. He had involved himself in Fenian affairs, and had made his way to South Africa when Ireland and England became too dangerous for him. A free-living, politically unstable territory like Griqualand West proved too strong an attraction for his contumacious instincts. On the basis of some experience on a New York newspaper, he succeeded in persuading the new owners of the *Diamond Fields* to give him an appointment. After a few months, his journalistic career was interrupted by a year's imprisonment for common assault. When he returned to society, he was more violently anti-British than before and more confirmed in his republicanism. Under his guidance, the *Diamond Fields* became the official mouthpiece of the anti-government factions and found place for Henry Tucker's most vitriolic cartoons.

The handsome and dashing Conrad von Schlickmann was another unusual individual attracted into the Diggers' Protection Association. His past too was shrouded in rumour and mystery, but popular belief held that he was an ex-Prussian army officer and a hero of the Franco-Prussian War who had been driven to the diamond country by an unhappy love affair. Whatever the truth, he admirably fitted the role of adventurer and mercenary. Both men saw opportunities in discontent. They contributed rabble-rousing speeches and urged the creation of an armed wing in the Association. The dissent gradually changed to a mood of rebellion, and every action of the Lieutenant-Governor, no matter how well intended, seemed only to heighten the tension.

The militants in the Diggers' Protection Association began to have their way. The enrolment of men for armed rebellion gained momentum. Rifle-practice and drilling were openly flaunted. Reports came in of a squadron of 'cavalry' with revolvers and new Martini-Henrys parading in front of Henry Tucker, of a detachment of 'infantry' mustering on the cricket ground at De Beers, and of a company of German miners demonstrating their disciplined drill in the middle of Market Square. Inspector Gilbert Percy, Commander of the Griqualand West Police, was perturbed by this show of force. He warned the Lieutenant-Governor that should a clash occur, the administration would not survive without military help.

On 19 March, Southey published a proclamation in the name of 'Her Most Gracious Majesty', warning the populace against the 'evil disposed persons' who were spreading rebellion, the taking of illegal oaths, the assembling with arms, and the drilling without lawful authority. 'They shall answer the same at their peril', was his final threat. To Barkly he wrote asking for 'the presence as soon as possible of such a force as would convince the disaffected that resistance to constitutional authority was hopeless'.

Southey had officially acknowledged the threat of rebellion, and the Associationists wasted no time answering his warning. The next day they accused him of scandalous lies against loyal subjects. Carefully emphasising their devotion to the Queen they proceeded to censure him for reducing the administration to a contemptuous object in the eyes of the neighbouring states and tribes. They pledged 'to adopt all measures for the security of life and property which through feebleness and incapacity of the local government had been jeopardised'. A few days later a public meeting was called by the Associationists. Aylward was in great form, and in the middle of a rousing speech dramatically produced a piece of plain black cloth. When publicly hoisted the 'Black Flag' was to become the signal for an armed uprising.

Southey refused to be intimidated. He would risk violence rather than see the laws of the territory flaunted. It had become an open secret that the canteen of a certain William Cowie served as an arms store for the rebels, and a warrant was issued for his arrest. On 12 April, the day of his trial, a crowd gathered near the Court House demanding his release. The small, stuffy courtroom was packed with his fellow conspirators, and the proceedings were rushed through. No one was more surprised than Cowie when a sentence of £50 or two months was delivered. He was quickly hustled through a back door, while his outraged friends scrambled out of the building to prevent his removal to prison. Halfway to the gaol, prisoner and escort found themselves surrounded by a threatening mob. Further progress was made impossible. At that moment an armed police reinforcement arrived and took up position in front of the gaol. There were armed men in the crowd, and the sound of guns being loaded was heard. The slightest miscalculation could have precipitated an attack on the police and the escorting party; that the insurrection did not take the irretrievable step was entirely due to the cool action of the resident magistrate and the responsible instincts of Henry Tucker. The former attracted the crowd's attention by loudly asking who its leaders were. Tucker came forward and placed the blame for the crisis on the Governor's obdurateness, but agreed to negotiations provided they took place immediately. The magistrate offered to take him personally to Southey's office, and Tucker in turn appealed to the crowd to remain calm until his return.

They had not been gone long, when a pistol was discharged (some thought it was fired by von Schlickmann), but the crowd heeded Tucker's injunction. It was then that everyone saw the 'Black Flag' of rebellion fluttering on Mount Ararat, Kimberley's biggest waste dump. The moment for insurrection, however, had passed.

At Government House Southey remained totally contemptuous of the threatened rebellion and insisted upon correct formalities being observed before he received any representation. Tucker's business was with a conviction of the court, and he was referred to the Attorney-General. The latter was more realistic. He persuaded Tucker that legalities could be maintained and the prisoner freed, if he issued a personal cheque for the £50 fine. He assured him that it would not be cashed until Cowie's case was reviewed. But Southey refused to give assurances that no action would be taken against any person involved in the afternoon's affair. Convinced that agreement could never be reached with the Governor, an exasperated Henry Tucker, nevertheless, returned to announce Cowie's release. The diggers began to disperse. Tucker was no revolutionary firebrand, the Associationists were hesitant about committing the diamond fields to bloodshed, and even Alfred Aylward had failed to put in an appearance after the 'Black Flag' was raised.

Despite the peaceful outcome of what might have been an ugly incident, Southey seemed set on provoking his enemies. He was not prepared to overlook the threats made by the mob and issued another proclamation. It stated that 'by attempting to resist the execution of a sentence passed by a court of justice, certain persons had gone into rebellion against the Queen'. At the same time, it called for the enrolment of 'all loyal and well-disposed persons' for the maintenance of law and order until the Imperial Forces arrived. Southey was willing to divide the Colony into loyalists and rebels for the sake of his principles.

At this juncture, a new party which claimed to represent three-quarters of the population announced its existence. Its members described themselves as 'Moderates', and its leaders were drawn from the prestigious Mining Board. They allegedly wanted the government to rectify its errors, but were against illegal acts. To demonstrate their reasonableness, they proposed sending a deputation to Barkly to explain the diggers' grievances. The men nominated to the deputation were closely linked with J. B. Robinson. Southey interpreted the move as a devious attempt to lend respectability to rebellion. His suspicions were reinforced when a petition signed by other prominent business and professional men denied that the deputation, 'a bare quorum of the Mining Board', represented the views of the community. A more outspoken criticism of the deputation was signed by over a hundred blacks and coloureds. They expressed alarm that the persons appointed to seek an interview with Sir Henry Barkly intended 'to deprive your Petitioners and all other coloured persons of the right of mining and searching for diamonds'.

Southey forwarded both petitions to Barkly with an earnest request not to receive the four deputants. Robinson in turn sent a personal letter to Molteno urging him to use his influence with the High Commissioner on their behalf. Despite Southey's official disapproval, the deputants left Kimberley on 18 April, and the scene for decision-making shifted to Cape Town.

3

The road to 'El Dorado'

By the end of March, the unrest in Griqualand West was common knowledge in Cape Town. The newspapers had seized on Southey's proclamation and featured it prominently together with the diggers' manifesto and descriptions of armed preparations against the regime. Within days the city was rife with rumours about an imminent expedition to the diamond fields. Barkly had alerted General Cunynghame, the Commander of Her Majesty's forces in South Africa, about the official request for military reinforcements, and the matter was communicated to Colonel Glyn. None in the 1/24th could have imagined that their first adversaries might be white subjects of the Queen, but then the rebels were described as alien Germans, Fenians, and an unfamiliar political group which the *Grahamstown Journal* referred to as 'Communists, devil-may-care enough for anything'. The battalion rank and file were delighted with the prospect of a visit to the diamond country at Her Majesty's expense. They heard that three hundred men would be dispatched to Griqualand West and that negotiations for transport were in progress. Excitement mounted, but nothing happened.

Every successive report from Kimberley stressed how disturbed the insurgents were by the news that troops were on their way and that only this knowledge prevented bloody rebellion. One newspaper authoritatively stated that two hundred men would start within ten days and that Major Henry Degacher was to command the expedition. The next day the *Diamond News* reported a different version with equal authority. In this welter of contradictions, and with no official announcements forthcoming from the High Commissioner, the *Cape Argus* hit out at the 'lamentable weakness and vacillation' of the imperial authorities, and blamed General Cunynghame and Barkly for 'all their huckstering dealings' with transport tenderers. They were accused of wanting to cancel all the arrangements for the dispatch of troops because prices quoted for transportation were too high. Most disturbing to the soldiers in Cape Town was the observation made by the *Daily News* that the route would be easier and the distance shorter if troops stationed in the Eastern Province were sent.

To all appearances the military were more involved in ensuring a successful day at the Green Point Autumn Races than in mounting an expedition. Barkly, too, seemed frantically occupied with matters social and ceremonial. He was, in fact, anything but unconcerned over the crisis in Griqualand West. Reprimanded for saddling the Crown with an unwanted colonial burden, he, more than anyone, was liable for censure if that burden were to be made any heavier. Now, less than four years after annexation, the Colonial Office was about to be faced with a bill for transporting a military force across five hundred miles of desert to suppress a rebellion of Her Majesty's white subjects. If only Southey would exercise more diplomacy Barkly was prepared to be conciliatory in the hope that tension would subside. Instead of promising troops, he advised Southey to rely on 'moral influence', and when Aylward threatened violent action, he expressed satisfaction because he could now be dealt with by the normal processes of the law. But when Southey indicated that he was willing to enrol and arm blacks against the diggers, Barkly could not procrastinate much longer. Lord Carnarvon was informed that 'the presence of regular forces is absolutely necessary for the maintenance of Her Majesty's Government', and General Cunynghame was instructed to mount an expedition in support of the Griqualand West Government.

The General saw the disturbances in more basic terms. In his opinion the diggers had been duped by German officers and Irish Fenians to haul down the British flag and establish a republic of their own or join the Orange Free State so that 'every man could thrash his nigger as he liked', a phrase he borrowed from the newspapers. In 1869, while in command of the Northern Ireland garrison, Cunynghame had suppressed an ill-timed Fenian rising. It had earned him the thanks of the British Government, a KCB and promotion to Lieutenant-General. In the light of his experience he readily accepted the notion that Fenians and their fellow-travellers were responsible for the troubles in Griqualand West.

Arthur Thurlow Cunynghame, at sixty-three, was still a handsome figure of a man. An excellent horseman with a fine military bearing, he looked like the popular image of a British general. In forty-five years with the army, Cunynghame had seen service in the First Opium War, the Crimean War and India. His detractors, however, were convinced that his career had been advanced by his father-in-law, Viscount Hardinge, Wellington's successor as Commander-in-Chief of the British Army. When in 1873 he was sent to take command of the forces in South Africa, one of his ADCs described him as 'a highly enthusiastic soldier' but 'of the old school'. His years of service had taught him the value of sound organisation and he set about mounting the expedition to the diamond fields with an obsessive eye on costs that resulted in long bargaining sessions with transport contractors.

The Kimberley newspapers served as his intelligence. They published the planned composition of Aylward's rebel army. The force was estimated at seven hundred drilled men and an unknown number of sympathisers. Cunynghame decided to oppose the rebels with three hundred infantry and two 7-pounders but bemoaned the fact that there was no cavalry attached to the imperial command. In past frontier wars colonial horsemen had helped correct this deficiency; but when he approached Molteno for a troop of mounted police, the Prime Minister refused because white miners were not the same as 'insurgent Kaffirs'. Cunynghame then proposed a new innovation, he would turn forty selected men from the 1/24th into a troop of mounted infantry.

On Tuesday 4 May, while Barkly was holding talks with the delegates from the 'Moderate Party', an order was published detailing the departure within two days of three officers and one hundred men for Griqualand West. They were to be followed within a few days by another two companies of infantry and twenty-six artillerymen with two 7-pounder Armstrong guns.

At dawn on Thursday, the advance detachment assembled at the Main Barracks. Captain Edward Sawbridge, who had served with Napier in Abyssinia, was in command of the force. His subalterns were Edward Curteis and James Patrick Daly. Their long journey began with a comfortable forty-five mile ride on the 7 : 16 train to Wellington, the terminus of the Colony's planned railroad to Kimberley. The second detachment could not leave Cape Town until the conclusion of an important ceremonial occasion – the laying of the foundation stone of the Colony's first Houses of Parliament. The 1/24th was to supply a Guard of Honour and men to line the approaches to the chosen site.

Colonel Glyn was to command the expeditionary force to Griqualand West. Major Henry Degacher was his second in command, and the company commanders were Henry Harrison and the younger Degacher. The subalterns, Fred Carrington, John Dickinson and Edward Browne were selected for their equestrian skill. It would be their task to turn forty footsoldiers into a troop of cavalry. The selected men were fitted with corduroy trousers and leggings and were issued with saddles, but their mounts would be purchased later. The Battalion Sergeant-Major had died a month before and Colour-Sergeant James Pullen was given the acting rank for the expedition. Command of the Cape Town Garrison passed to Major Henry Pulleine.

At midday on 12 May, a Royal Salute from the Castle guns followed by lusty singing of the 'Hallelujah Chorus' announced to the startled gulls of Table Bay that the foundation stone of the first Parliament in Africa had been laid. Three days later the Army of the Vaal (the name given to the expeditionary force by the newspapers) crowded into the Wellington train. A last-minute addition to Glyn's column was a party of eight civilians headed for the diamond fields. It included two women and a young man named Lionel Phillips, who was hoping to make his fortune in the employ of J. B. Robinson.

The long march began before sunrise, on a cool, wet morning. In front of the expeditionary force stretched the mountain barrier that separated the settled 'Old Colony' from the arid hinterland. Bain's Kloof, the pass over the nearest range, had been hailed as a great feat of road-making when it was first opened, but early winter rains had turned the road to mud. The heavily-laden wagons made painfully slow progress up the steep climb to the summit. Every man was called upon to help the straining mules move their load. It was an exhausting day's work that brought the troops to the top. Ahead was a steep, tortuous descent to the Breede River and the welcome halt at Mr Tubbs's inn. From there, the little Army of the Vaal, dwarfed by towering mountains which became progressively more barren, wound its way north for almost two hundred miles before it ascended the vast plateau to which the Hottentots had given their word for 'dry'.

The Great Karroo was hundreds of miles of shale and sandstone, a dreary monotony more emphasised than relieved by isolated, flat-topped hills and starkly eroded peaks. The vegetation was small bushes, grey, brittle and sapless, which when wrenched by sudden fierce winds from the sandy soil, would tumble about in all directions – providing a temporary excitement in the tedious emptiness. Withered trees were sometimes found near the shallow beds of dried-out rivers. Occasionally their grey branches displayed an unexpected crop of green leaves, proof that the roots were still alive and had found moisture beneath the baked sand. In the dry air the dazzling winter sun would produce shimmering waves and weird optical illusions from mid-morning onwards.

On this parched, ash-grey and dun plain, the Army of the Vaal, covered in dust, streaked with sweat, and pestered by an ever-present swarm of flies, plodded on at a steady twenty miles a day. Tunics that were hot encumbrances in the day proved hopelessly inadequate in the bitterly cold nights. Wood was scarce, and the men grew accustomed to huddling under the wagons over low fires made of dried dung. The extremes of temperature and the dehydrating air blistered and cracked the exposed skin, producing painful lesions that were aggravated by the penetrating duststorms which the Karroo provided by way of diversion. Old Karroo dwellers attributed the soldiers' epidermal torment to their foolish practice of regularly washing their hands and face.

In the past, remoteness and isolation had made the Karroo farmers welcome the passing traveller, but their hospitality had worn thin after six years of the diamond rush. Now, they were either hostile or at best indifferent to the motley procession of would-be prospectors that knocked on their doors. The red-coated soldiers were less welcome than most. Despite repeated denials, the Karroo Boers remained convinced that the expedition was directed against the Republics: '... nothing could make them believe us ... and they naturally look upon any information they receive with the same suspicion as that which they give generally deserves'. Colonel Glyn and Lieutenant Carrington, in their search for horses for the mounted infantry, acquired first-hand experience of this antagonism. Driving ahead of the troops, they had the misfortune one evening of running into a ditch and badly damaging their cart. When they tried to obtain shelter for the night at a nearby farmhouse, the owner directed them to the shanties where his 'Hottentots' slept, with the reassurance that they would feel more at home there.

The column reached Hopetown on 12 June. A camp for refitting and recuperating had been established near the ferry on the south bank of the Orange River.

The three hundred and fifty mile journey had taken twenty-six days. The General and his staff had overtaken the troops and were already lodged in Smith's Hotel. Hopetown, founded twenty years before, had prospered for a while as a convenient centre for hunters and traders, but within five years of the discovery of diamonds it had been reduced to a stopover on the road to Kimberley. The soldiers thought it a 'miserable place' where everyone tried hard to recover from them the prosperity they had lost to Kimberley. Camped in the open, the troops suffered from nights so cold that sleep was almost impossible. Some of the men reported sick with 'rheumatism' and a minor epidemic of diarrhoea and conjunctivitis broke out. The medical officer had to prevail on Cunynghame to buy them extra warm clothing despite the exorbitant rates demanded by the local traders.

A week had been allowed for the formation of a mounted troop, and when Carrington and an artillery captain, who had been scouring the countryside for horses, returned with some passable animals (bought at inflated prices), training got underway with a vengeance. At the end of a week, the six NCOs and thirty-seven privates of Cunynghame's cavalry could stay in the saddle and fire from horseback. Because the regulation Martini-Henry was too long and its recoil too vicious for use on horseback the men were issued with Snider carbines. The latter had a less efficient breech, but it was the more comfortable gun to fire.

The men soon tired of the inconspicuous delights of Hopetown. Even the novelty of gazing at a river that actually flowed wore off. They were in good shape, and a little proud of having confounded the colonial critics who had prophesied that the expedition 'would end up in smoke'. Most of them were ready to tackle the rebels and look at last upon the South African Golconda. There was one snag, however, the latest reports from Griqualand West intimated that their journey no longer had any purpose. Barkly, it seemed, had all but settled the quarrel from Cape Town.

When Barkly met the Kimberley deputation he had insisted that the prerequisite for considering their complaints was the immediate disbandment of the Association and the surrender of all arms. He had promised in return, a general amnesty for everyone except the ring-leaders. The Associationists had held a meeting in Kimberley and agreed on dissolution by a majority of three. They had added two qualifications: the amnesty should apply to all the members and Barkly must undertake to redress their grievances. They also refused to surrender their arms 'in the presence of so many armed niggers'.

Despite the conditions, it was clear that the fight had gone out of the Association. A week after the decision was taken to disband, Alfred Aylward, with his considerable experience of Her Majesty's prisons, left the diamond fields. Southey, in the interests of peace, had restrained himself from having him arrested, even though he had known in advance about his intended departure. Barkly's next move was designed to foil the ambitions of the 'capitalist' conspirators. He had agreed all along with Southey that the principal cause of unrest was 'the exorbitant demands of the proprietors of Diamondiferous Farms'. They had obstructed the passage of protective ordinances and had used the law 'to commence a series of exactions calculated to confiscate the property both of claim-holders and stand-holders and drive them off the Farms'. His own observations had confirmed Southey's allegations that the agitation against the administration had been fomented by wealthy men who wanted to become the owners of the 'New Rush', and were 'vain and foolish enough to imagine that if the present Government were overthrown the Diamond Fields would be ruled by a Commercial Company'. His solution was for the government to purchase Vooruitzicht, the farm on which Kimberley had sprung up. He felt that by keeping rentals low and selling land at fair prices the diggers would be pacified. By the same stroke the mine would be permanently secured against the monopolist ambitions of rich men.

John Paterson and the principal shareholders of Vooruitzicht had realised earlier that they had overplayed their hand with their exorbitant rentals and were willing to rid themselves of the contentious property. Barkly had opened negotiations with a warning that he 'was not going to use British bayonets for the purpose of making their speculations more profitable'. To Carnarvon, he had pointed out that military intervention would cost more than the farm, 'the alternative for the Government of Griqualand West would be between maintaining the Proprietors' rights by force, or buying them out on the lowest terms practicable'. He got the farm for £100 000.

The hurried departure of the deputants for Cape Town may well have been a desperate attempt by J. B. Robinson to forestall government ownership of Vooruitzicht. He probably knew that negotiations were taking place in Cape Town that would permanently remove the diamond-studded farm from his reach. He had placed a special messenger in Colesburg (the nearest telegraph office to Kimberley) to rush all telegrams from the deputation directly to him. The day after Southey heard that the farm had been purchased, the *Mining Gazette*, the mouthpiece of Robinson's 'Moderate Party', came out into the open with a blistering attack on the government. The crisis was virtually over. As the troops prepared to cross the Orange River into Griqualand West, a notice appeared in the

Government Gazette announcing that Vooruitzicht had become government property and inviting offers from the present tenants for the purchase of stands.

After crossing into Griqualand West the Army of the Vaal set out for the Modder River. Rumours had reached the General that 'the Fenians' planned to oppose his crossing, and despite confirmed reports that the rebellion had all but collapsed, Cunynghame intensified his precautions. The mounted infantry scouted far in advance of the main body during the day, and at night picquets and vedettes were posted in the freezing veld. They found the banks of the Modder deserted, and after wading through knee-deep water, took possession of the unoccupied northern bank. The only setback was the loss of eight mules that took a notion to desert, and the only shots fired were directed by his officers at some large game-birds which made an excellent supper.

The General's plan was to by-pass Kimberley and march to the river-diggings at Barkly, a course that would take him away from the nearby Free State border and avoid any incidents with President Brand's police. He also had a notion that the presence of soldiers in Kimberley might provoke the rebels to violence. But a very ebullient Southey drove out to meet him and quickly brushed aside all his ideas of sneaking past Kimberley. As far as the Lieutenant-Governor was concerned such a move would be interpreted as a sign of weakness. The rebels and their instigators were in disarray and with half a battalion of infantry at hand, he felt himself to be 'in a position to legislate with a view to the permanent stability of the place and the benefit of the inhabitants'. Nothing less than a formal entry of the Army of the Vaal into Kimberley would satisfy him.

On Tuesday 29 June, two months after leaving Cape Town, the advance detachment escorted the General and his staff into Kimberley. All business was immediately suspended, and every available cart and carriage took the Old De Beers road along which the troops were approaching. Africans rushed out from the mines 'like so many black ants from out of the ground when hot water had been poured in upon them', shouting 'the rooi baadjies [red-coats] are come!' But when the troops marched by, they stood completely transfixed, incapable of uttering a sound. A public parade for the entire force was scheduled for eleven o'clock the following morning in the Market Square. A huge crowd gathered to watch the show, but certain prominent ex-Associationists were conspicuous by their absence. Also missing were several loyal and respected members of the community who had deserted from the British army during the Eighth Frontier War, almost twenty-five years before.

One of Cunynghame's staff officers did not share in the joy of the peaceful outcome; he recorded, 'to our disgust, the rebellion had subsided and the force was received with great enthusiasm by the inhabitants'. Their long haul from Cape Town had not been entirely in vain. Richard Southey at last felt strong enough to take action. The following morning, at dawn, Tucker, von Schlickmann and three others were arrested and charged with sedition and riot. The charge, as read to the magistrate, had been prepared four weeks before. Southey would have loved to have seen arraigned in front of the magistrate the rich men 'who supplied money and materials to the insurrectionists'. But Barkly had advised him earlier not to waste his time indicting the wealthy supporters of rebellion because no jury would convict them. Bail for Tucker and his fellow conspirators was fixed at £1 000 and two persons were required to stand surety for each of the accused. The money was quickly put up by members of the 'Moderate Party'.

Cunynghame preferred to keep his men some distance from Kimberley, in case the 'unbounded riches near at hand' should tempt them to desert. At Barkly, on a flat piece of ground, close to the Vaal River, the troops made their encampment and settled down to await the High Commissioner's third visit to the diamond fields.

4

For the sake of Confederation

Barkly had been detained in Cape Town by an important parliamentary debate. The issue had arisen out of a Colonial Office directive to the Cape Government to rescind an act it had passed the previous year. The man who gave rise to the contentious act, was Langalibalele, the hereditary chief of the Hlubi clan. He and his followers had fled Zululand many years before and had settled in the Drakensberg foothills under the jurisdiction of Theophilus Shepstone, the Natal Secretary for Native Affairs.

After the opening of the diamond fields many of his followers were drawn to the diggings by the firearm lure. In time, a small arsenal had accumulated in the amaHlubi kraals. Black ownership of guns was not illegal in Natal, but as a form of safeguard, the jittery white minority had insisted that all guns in the Colony be registered. When the authorities in Pietermaritzburg heard about the Hlubi hoard, they became alarmed and ordered Langalibalele to register his people's guns. The Chief had at first chosen to ignore the directive; and the Government messenger, who had brought the order, was mishandled. More noted as rainmaker than as a warrior, Langalibalele, on reflection, had grown anxious about his act of disobedience and had made preparations to move his tribe and cattle to neighbouring Basotholand. The settlers, in turn, had feared that their prestige with the 300 000 blacks who lived on reservations in Natal would be adversely affected by any act that diminished the authority of the Government. Theophilus Shepstone was a pround man and jealous of his achievements in the field of native affairs. He had viewed Langalibalele's defiance as a personal affront and a threat to his native reserve system. Fear on both sides, injured pride, and over-reaction had transformed the Hlubi emigration into an act of rebellion and an expedition against the amaHlubi had been hastily mounted under the authority of Sir Benjamin Pine, the Lieutenant-Governor of Natal.

On 2 November 1873, a small force of volunteers and black levees commanded by Anthony Durnford, a Major in the Royal Engineers, stumbled on a detached Hlubi rearguard in the Drakensberg near the Bushman's River Pass. A skirmish had taken place and three volunteers were killed; one of them was the son of the Natal Colonial Secretary. Durnford, who received a thrust in his left arm which severed a nerve, had managed to extricate his patrol from what might have been a massacre, but the honours, that day, had gone to the tribesmen.

The setback had provoked a furious reaction in Natal. The main body of troops had laid waste the Hlubi location and killed over two hundred people. Langalibalele, who had taken refuge with a 'friendly' Basotho chief, was betrayed to the Cape police, and they had handed him over to the Natal authorities. By mid-December, the 'rebellion' was over.

Shepstone had made up his mind to try the captive chief in a manner approximating native customary law. The judges had been Sir Benjamin Pine (in the role of Supreme Chief), a magistrate, four tribal chieftains, and Shepstone himself. The composition of the court had been neither tribal nor colonial. Langalibalele had been refused permission to cross-examine the witnesses, no defending counsel had been found for him, and two of the judges (Shepstone and Pine) had participated in the expedition against him. The verdict had been a foregone conclusion, and the only appeal had been to the 'Governor-in-Executive-Council', which included two of the trial judges and the bereaved Colonial Secretary.

The sentence had been life imprisonment; but Natal had no facilities for long-term political detainees. Robben Island, the wind-swept leper colony in Table Bay, had seemed the most appropriate place. The Lieutenant-Governor of Natal did not have the power to detain Langalibalele in another colony, and the Cape Parliament was prevailed upon to pass an act authorising his detention on Robben Island. This act, No. 3 of 1874, was the one that Carnarvon wanted Molteno to rescind.

In the normal course of events the chief would have been forgotten within a few years by settlers and tribesmen alike, but the energetic protestations of John William Colenso, the Bishop of Natal, had thwarted this convenient outcome. He had taken the matter to London and confronted the recently appointed Secretary of State for Colonies with South Africa and its problems. Lord Carnarvon's vigorous attention had had two consequences: a secret agent had been sent to South Africa to investigate the feasability of confederation, and a decision had been taken to have Langalibalele returned to the mainland.

The request that Act No. 3 be repealed had arrived in Cape Town in the first week of 1875. Its publication had provoked an immediate uproar in the Cape Colony and Natal. Molteno, concerned with the Cape Colony's rights under responsible government, had seen Carnarvon's instruction as peremptory interference in Cape government. The disallowance of a measure passed by his Parliament only six months before, had looked very much like an upbraiding from Downing Street. His immediate response was a flat refusal.

General Cunynghame had appointed a court of enquiry to investigate the Bushman's River Pass affair, and the findings, which had been published shortly after the 1/24th arrived in South Africa, had met with the unreserved approval of the regular army. Major Durnford was exonerated of all blame and commended for his bravery. The report had disapproved of the many authorities in command, the poor organisation of supply lines and the volunteers had been found to be greatly deficient in discipline and steadiness. It had also added the pertinent reminder that the amaHlubi were, after all, part of the Zulu nation and, as such, quick to take advantage of any order which permitted them to come in close before opening fire.

By the time Colenso returned to Natal, the colonists had something new to ponder over. Sir Benjamin Pine had been recalled and his successor had turned out to be a most surprising choice. Natal was to be dignified with Britain's hero of the moment – Sir Garnet Wolseley. The Colony was overwhelmed by the honour. The wives and daughters of the settlers, thrilled by the prospect of having in their midst that 'delicate, high-bred face', lit by 'brilliant dark eyes', could hardly contain their excitement. But the more sceptical suspected that the motives for sending so famous a personality to an obscure colony went much deeper than the official announcement admitted.

The Langalibalele affair and the despatches from the secret agent he had sent to South Africa, gave Carnarvon a false impression about the likelihood of a widespread native insurrection in Natal. He decided to replace Pine with a man who could determine the best means for preventing uprisings and who could gather information about 'the military topography of the country' for the 'future formulation of imperial policy'. And with the British Government shouldering the responsibility for Natal's safety, Carnarvon wanted greater control over Natal's internal affairs in order to guide the Colony into a southern African confederation. This could only be achieved by changing its constitution. The settlers would have to be persuaded to accept diminished autonomy.

Sir Garnet, with his experience of Canada at the time of confederation and his vigorous settlement of the Ashanti affair, had seemed well suited for the task. Wolseley's motives for accepting the commission were the chance to ingratiate himself with the Tory government and the belief that war with the Zulus was imminent. He had insisted on a command completely independent of Cunynghame and authority to raise all available troops in South Africa and Mauritius should circumstances demand it. To add lustre to his mission in Natal, he demanded a large staff – his devoted assistants from the Ashanti affair were the obvious choice.

Sporting a powdered French imperial, the army's youngest general arrived in Cape Town on 20 March. 'On no previous occasion', raved the newspapers, 'has a commission composed of such eminent officers been appointed to the administration of affairs anywhere in South Africa'. The *Grahamstown Journal*, further from the scene and more reflective, remarked, 'Sir Garnet succeeds Sir Benjamin Pine. Success over barbarians sends one man home in disgrace; a similar success, attended with vastly more bloodshed and fifty times as much expense, elevates the other into his place, amidst the plaudits of a whole people'. Cunynghame felt unable to share Cape Town's excitement; he confined himself to his Rondebosch home with a severe cold. Wolseley met with Molteno, and found the Prime Minister much to his liking. He transmitted Carnarvon's views on Langalibalele, but confided to Molteno that it would suit his purpose if the chief was kept on Robben Island until his own mission in Natal was completed.

John Charles Molteno had been a member of the Cape Parliament since the institution of representative government. For twenty years he had represented the sheep-farming district of Beaufort West and had earned the sobriquet 'The Lion of Beaufort'. It well fitted his appearance, his indisputable integrity, and his righteous stubborness. He had been a strong advocate of responsible government and was particularly intolerant of any attempts by either the Colonial Office or the Governor to influence Cape affairs. In his bid for the Premiership he had received the support of Saul Solomon, the liberal proprietor of the *Cape Argus* and the Member for Cape Town. But Solomon had demanded assurances that he would follow a just native policy. When he turned down Carnarvon's request to lay the matter of Langalibalele's imprisonment on Robben Island before Parliament, the *Argus* attacked him with hard-hitting editorials. In the end, his debt to Solomon and his respect for Barkly, had made him comply with Carnarvon's wishes.

The motion to transfer Langalibalele to the mainland provoked even more argument than Barkly had expected. 'Resist Imperial meddling!' became the rallying cry and the familiar bogey about encouraging black militancy by appearing conciliatory was revived. Molteno almost threatened resignation before the measure was passed. The decision was for the chief to be brought to the mainland when practicable and settled on a farm in the desolate Cape Flats under a form of 'house arrest'. He could keep his sons with him and a reasonable number of wives.

By the end of May, Barkly could look back on his achievements with some satisfaction. He had averted a rift between the Cape Government and the Colonial Office, and, by acquiring Vooruitzicht, had spared the diamond fields a struggle between capital and labour. He was at last in a position to follow Cunynghame's troops and complete the job with a few necessary changes in the Griqualand West Administration. Only the chill he had caught in the bad weather that marred the Queen's birthday celebrations, delayed his immediate departure for Kimberley.

On 2 June, while still confined to bed, Barkly received a despatch from Lord Carnarvon that drove all thoughts of Kimberley from his mind. He was confronted with a situation of such delicacy that it made the Langalibalele business seem like a children's squabble. The despatch instructed him to arrange as quickly as possible a conference of delegates from all the South African states to discuss the 'widely differing systems of native treatment' and 'the present position of Griqualand West'. There was an unmistakable hint at the end of the letter that the real objective was confederation of the country. The issues were contentious in themselves, but what made them explosive was Carnarvon's recommendation that Molteno should represent the Western Province and John Paterson the other half of the Colony.

Barkly was appalled at having to confront an already bruised and smarting Molteno with the news that the Secretary of State wanted him to represent only part of the Colony at an important conference. He was amazed that Carnarvon could be so oblivious of the sensitive nature of the 'separation' controversy in the Colony as to propose the very divisions that the Premier refused to recognise. Barkly knew that Molteno was primarily interested in a united Cape Colony and had little enthusiasm for a greater South African union. In Molteno's view, any proposals for confederation would have to originate in Cape Town, and at present he had no desire to share the Cape's revenue and prosperity with its much poorer neighbours. Nor did he want to share the black burdens of Natal and Transvaal. The Cape Colony's enlightened native policy was working well; he could point to an unprecedented twenty-three years of peace on the Colony's Eastern Frontier.

The clue to Carnarvon's blunder was to be found in the name of a man selected to represent Her Majesty's Government at the proposed conference. He was James Anthony Froude, noted historian and student of imperial affairs. By the time Barkly received the ill-advised despatch, the scholarly delegate was halfway to Cape Town aboard the *Walmer Castle*. Froude was the secret agent Carnarvon had sent to South Africa in August of the previous year.

The simple, austere life of the Boers and their puritanical Calvinism had elicited a sympathetic response in Froude. He had found more to admire in their customs and government than had most contemporary English travellers. The harsh native policies of the Republics had met with his approval, and he had shared their belief that only discipline and labour could civilize the heathen black. In Griqualand West he had scorned Southey's liberal ideas and had spoken openly in support of the combination that had started agitating against the Administration. He had concluded that the biggest obstacle to a South African confederation was Barkly's seizure of the diamond fields. Somehow or other the Republics had to be compensated for the wrong and their goodwill regained: redress this grievance, and the Boers would give favourable consideration to a confederation under the British flag. Such a move, he was convinced, would also receive the enthusiastic support of their many kinsmen in the Western Cape. In Port Elizabeth he had gained the impression that the Eastern Province would back confederation if it were permitted to enter as a separate state. He thought the 'Easterners' would readily come to terms with the stricter native laws of the Republics because of their proximity to the once hostile and still independent Transkei.

Before leaving for home, Froude had had a meeting with Molteno and had concluded that the Prime Minister was sympathetic towards the Free State's claims in Griqualand West and would support any concessions towards them. He had failed to perceive the Premier's isolationist inclinations, his hostility towards any action that might divide the Colony, and the strength of the liberal lobby in the Cape Parliament. Lord Carnarvon had been instrumental in persuading the Canadian provinces to accept a British North American confederation in 1867. It had greatly enhanced his reputation in colonial affairs. In his enthusiasm for a similar settlement in South Africa, he listened too readily to Froude's observations and misconceptions. From them had followed Wolseley's mission to Natal and the 'conference despatch'.

With Carnarvon's missive in his hand, Barkly abandoned his sickroom and summoned Molteno to his presence. The Prime Minister reacted in the expected manner. He would give no consideration whatsoever to proposals that named two representatives for the Cape Colony, and he threatened to resign if Barkly published the despatch, but immediate publication was implicit in Carnarvon's instructions; not to do so would be an act of disobedience on Barkly's part.

Cape Town and the Colony were immediately divided. The 'Old Colonists', remembering Froude's sympathetic attitude towards the Boers, read in the despatch the beginnings of a more just policy towards the Republics; Eastern Province 'Separationists' saw recognition of their cause in the nomination of John Paterson; and railway interests favoured federation because it would remove restrictive frontiers from the northward expanding railroads. Ranged against these factions was the Molteno Ministry which wanted a united colony free of the irksome racial problems that burdened the other states.

Molteno's opponents rallied against the rejection of the despatch. They proposed to honour Froude with a public dinner when he arrived, and show him the Colony's other face. For a while the whole controversy was reduced to a squabble about the dinner. The imperial delegate arrived in Cape Town on 18 June and the dinner committee met him on the gangway with an invitation to speak in public. Barkly advised him not to accept because he would appear to be endorsing the opponents of the Colony's elected government. Froude thought it would provide an 'excellent opportunity of explaining and defending Lord Carnarvon's policy ...' Barkly declined an invitation to the dinner on the grounds that he was expecting a large company at Government House the same night. At the dinner Froude blamed all the difficulties in South Africa on Griqualand West, and followed it with a thinly veiled attack on the man who had spurned the dinner invitation and was responsible for the annexation of the territory.

Genuinely puzzled by Molteno's opposition, and angry at Barkly's apparent reluctance to promote the conference, Froude resolved to leave Cape Town and take the confederation message to the country himself.

Privately he wrote Carnarvon that Barkly would have to go. If necessary the conference could be held in Natal, where Wolseley, he confidently predicted, would have fewer scruples about putting obstinate colonial legislators in their rightful place. On 14 July, Her Majesty's delegate-turned-canvasser set out on a tour of the country districts; and the trouble-burdened Governor of the Cape Colony was given a short respite to attend to the unfinished business in Kimberley. Three days later, he too, left Cape Town.

5

Diamond days

From mining camp to colonial capital in four quick years, then decline. By 1875, life in Barkly had become peaceful and ordered. The restless and the ambitious had long since abandoned the river for the 'dry diggings'. A few old prospectors who had refused to accept the notion of diamonds away from water still panned the Vaal River, but it was a sedate business compared to the frenetic activity in Kimberley. For the officer and men of the Army of the Vaal, camped along a quiet stretch of the river, ugly, brash Kimberley, with its excitement and temptations, was the never-failing attraction.

The road from Barkly entered the great mining camp through a district of crowded, corrugated iron shacks and man-made hills of crushed and sifted rubble that surrounded the gigantic bowl known as the 'New Rush' mine. Ringed by a multitude of tall wooden platforms (the stayings) supporting a giant spider web of cables, it was, from dawn to dusk, the focus of intense activity. Creaking windlasses, clanking waterpumps and humming wires blended with the shout and song of labourers to produce the distinctive clangour that was Kimberley at work.

The neighbourhood near the mine was the 'established' part of town, where the diamond merchants had their corrugated tin offices. The residential area was an even grimmer looking conglomeration of weather-stained canvas houses and tents. Nowhere was a tuft of grass, a bush, or a tree to be seen, and overall hung a heavy cloud of dust. Swarms of flies, that settled indiscriminately on people, animals and food were an ever-present irritation. But the cluttered metropolis of canvas and tin pulsated with an exuberant vitality that caught everyone in its thrall.

Bars, canteens and gambling dens were jammed between the offices of respected merchants. A tin Fox and Hounds next to a canvas Elephant and Castle stood across the street from an identical structure with continental pretensions, the Café Français. Liquor of every description could be readily purchased, but prices were high. A bottle of Bass's beer set back a private soldier the equivalent of five days' pay. 'Cape Smoke', with its rapid assault on the senses and competitive price, was the best seller. The canteens were sociable places. On most nights the soldiers could find a bar where some digger was celebrating his luck with rounds of free drinks. There were canteens where black men scarcely ever set foot, and bars where the patrons were almost exclusively black. The town's team of black prostitutes moved freely between them. But a recent influx of European women had displaced the dusky professionals from the more fashionable venues.

The hotel owned by Benning and Martin was one of the high-class establishments. It had a billiard table, a reputation for good food, and had become a popular social and business centre where diamonds were traded over lunch, and billiards were played for cases of champagne. There and at The Richmond, Her Majesty's officers could find their own social level. Kimberley counted ex-officers, younger sons of titled families, sons of clergymen, and professional men amongst its citizens. These men had established in no time their own exclusive institutions. The Craven, a private club, had become an important meeting place for the future magnates of the diamond fields. A Turf Club had been in existence for some three years, and cricket was played regularly.

On 2 August Henry Barkly's dust-covered travelling wagon pulled up in the market square. Southey welcomed his superior with open arms. He was full of enthusiasm and ready for a fresh start in Griqualand West. But the High Commissioner preferred to retain for himself the role of saviour of the diamond fields. He graciously took full credit for the purchase of Vooruitzicht, the dispatch of the troops, and the restoration of law and order. Southey was quickly placed in a subordinate position. As temporary Head of the Government, Barkly compelled the Legislative Council to establish a Land Court to examine all titles, an innovation which Southey had previously dismissed as impracticable because he feared that the Griquas would be dispossessed of their remaining rights by unscrupulous land-jobbers with money and influence.

Throughout August and September, Barkly laboured in Kimberley. He received deputations, appointed commissions of enquiry, and attended to the numerous problems relating to mining affairs. He was virtually a one-man government, ruling by decree. His activities were directed towards excluding Southey from the administration. He had made up his mind before coming to the diamond fields that the Lieutenant-Governor had been reckless and provocative in his handling of the rebellion, and had communicated his views to Lord Carnarvon. Reducing the size of the Colony's administration and making it more amenable to his wishes, fitted with Carnarvon's plans for the absorption of Griqualand West into a confederation. Before the end of August, Barkly received Colonial Office approval for the dismissal of Southey. It was to be represented as an economic necessity, '... the first step in any complete scheme of retrenchment will be the substitution of a less highly paid officer for the present Lieutenant-Governor'. Southey was to be compensated with a pension secured by the Cape Parliament. On 26 September, the dumbfounded diggers learnt that the man whom Robinson, Tucker, and Aylward had schemed to overthrow by rebellion, had been sacked by the Colonial Office. The new administrator was to be Major Owen Lanyon, a Wolseley nominee. The recall of Southey heralded the end of the era of the small prospector, and the beginning of modern South Africa's black industrial labour policy. Final victory had gone to the men with capital.

Four days later, Barkly announced his imminent departure for Cape Town – Froude had been stirring up a political hornet's nest in the Cape Colony that was threatening to oust the Molteno ministry. Cunynghame, who had earlier returned to Cape Town, was anxious about the welfare of his troops, and had reminded Barkly of their overlong residence in tents. He had wanted them either brought back or given more permanent accommodation. Confident that he had satisfied almost everyone on the diamond fields, Barkly gave orders for the return of the Army of the Vaal to the Cape Colony.

For more than four months the men from the 1st Battalion had lived in the open. They had experienced extremes of weather, marched across a desert and learnt the meaning of fatigue. The notorious 'camp fever', an undulant form of ill-health similar to the disease that had plagued the 1/24th when it was stationed on Malta, left some of the men with a legacy of their diamond days that would recur for years and years.

The cost of sending the troops to Griqualand West was estimated at £20 000. To recover some of it, it was decided to disband the mounted troop and auction off the horses. Left behind too, were four soldiers, listed officially as deserters. When on 10 October, Colonel Glyn's men forsook the diamond fields, few people in Kimberley seemed to remember the original purpose of their visit. It was only the noise from the engines of mining that followed them down the road to Hopetown; their discordant music was the last reminder of an unusual city and its uninterrupted search for wealth.

The shorter route to the sea was selected for the return journey. From Hopetown, the troops were to follow the Orange River to Colesburg, then turn south to Cradock and Port Elizabeth. It was summer, and the days were unbearably hot. The marches were made before sunrise and after sunset. The empty daylight hours were spent hiding from the sun under makeshift awnings. The last part of the journey was made miserable by continuous heavy rain, a time of mud, bogged-down wagons, and constantly wet clothes. On the morning of 17 November, the army entered Port Elizabeth.

'Port Bessie' was undeniably an 'English' colonial town. The streets had familiar sounding names, there was a comfortable club, a granite obelisk in the market square commemorated the marriage of the Prince of Wales to Princess Alexandra, and everyone spoke English. The port had become a jumping-off place for the diamond fields, and wagon-loads of wool, hides and ostrich feathers daily jammed the large market square. Bullion from the Transvaal gold fields was starting to trickle down and regular diamond sales were making the town one of the world's most important diamond markets. A railway terminal, that nineteenth-century monument to progress, had been opened less than two months before. The talk everywhere was of business, separation, Mr Froude, and confederation. The soldiers were not permitted to savour the delights of bustling Port Bessie for long. Within a few days of arrival they were packed into lighters and taken out to the R.M.S. *European*.

On 22 November the 1st Battalion was reunited in Cape Town. Among the passengers joining the *European* after the troops had disembarked, was a solemn looking gentleman: Froude had decided to return to London. The first act in the confederation drama had just been concluded.

Froude's stomp around the country had received wide publicity. His 'unofficial' speeches only pleased those factions that saw fulfilment of their interests in confederation, and he had succeeded in upsetting the delicate political unity between the Eastern and Western Provinces. But in Natal, his alternative venue for a conference, Froude had reaped the unpopularity of carelessly considered past utterances. The settlers had been less than enthusiastic about the man who, on his first visit, had dismissed them as being of little consequence within the South African scheme. Wolseley had proved another disappointment. Froude's idol had refused the role of president of the proposed conference. Sir Garnet had suspected that Froude meant to use him as a figurehead, and he was not the man to play second fiddle to Carnarvon's emissary. Privately Wolseley thought Froude 'a most vindictive and cold-blooded man, incapable of creating any sympathy between himself and others'.

Without Wolseley a conference in Natal would have been a meaningless exercise. President Brand had added to Froude's difficulties by refusing to consider Carnarvon's proposals if Griqualand West was represented. Molteno was the vital link. Should he be willing to attend a conference in Cape Town and support Brand, progress might be possible. Froude next decided to go to Port Elizabeth to enlist Eastern Province backing for the conference. Wolseley, having finished his work in Natal, promised that on his stop in Cape Town he would try and make the Premier see reason. When Wolseley telegraphed from Cape Town that he had been unable to bring about a change of heart in Molteno, Froude came out openly against the Cape Government and succeeded in raising an insistent cry for a special session of Parliament to reconsider the conference issue. At a public dinner in Uitenhage he was made the object of an insulting attack by the new Minister of Lands and Public Works. John Xavier Merriman was loyal to Molteno and could be bitingly vituperative. Feelings ran high, buns were thrown, and the meeting broke up in disorder. The clamour for a special parliamentary session became too strong to ignore, and the date was set for 10 November. For the second time that year the Cape Colony's Prime Minister was faced with a crisis brought about by 'imperial interference', and Barkly again found himself trapped between Molteno's intransigence and the wishes of the Secretary of State for Colonies.

Under the circumstances, Barkly's address to Parliament was non-committal and satisfied no one. Molteno steered the debate into a drawn-out harangue against the 'imperial agitator'. But for all his skill he was unable to postpone the vote that would put his ministry's uncertain popularity to the test. The odds were against him, but at the eleventh hour a despatch arrived in Cape Town from Carnarvon which stated that his conference proposals had received sufficient publicity and that the time was ripe for a confederation conference in London. The special session had lost its purpose – Molteno was reprieved. Froude decided that for the next few months his place was at his chief's side in London. He had had enough of stubborn colonial politicians. But before leaving he made Molteno promise that he would help settle the Griqualand West – Orange Free State dispute. To Froude it still loomed as the biggest obstacle to confederation.

6

A troubled state

To the returned soldiers, the political wrangling over the conference seemed to have little bearing on military affairs. They were much more interested in the vicissitudes within their own establishment. There were many new faces in the garrison. Captain George Vaughan Wardell had arrived in June with a draft of eighty men and Captain William Mostyn had returned to Brecon in July; his place had been taken by Thomas Rainforth, the Battalion's newest company officer. For those members of the 1/24th who had remained in Cape Town, 9 September had been a notable day. Sir Garnet Wolseley and his staff, on their way to England, had been guests at a dinner in the Officers' Mess.

Major Pulleine and his officers had been entertained by a host of anecdotes about Natal's settler society most of whose members, it appeared, were 'weak in their H's'. The amorous escapades of Wolseley's aides with the ingenuous colonial wives and daughters, had been responsible for some of the best laughs of the evening. Wolseley's views on the security of Natal had also been aired. He was convinced that the warlike Zulus were an unsettling influence on Natal's black population, and that sooner or later, they would have to be conquered and their territory annexed. Annexation would create room for the colony's growing native population, secure for Britain the south eastern coastline as far as the Limpopo River, and permanently cut off the Transvaal from the sea. He intimated that had he received the slightest encouragement from the British Government, he would have launched a pre-emptive attack on King Cetshwayo.

But as far as the rank and file were concerned, it was the men returned from Griqualand West who told the most fascinating stories. There were eighteen desertions from the 1/24th after the Army of the Vaal came home.

As a result of Wolseley's recommendation to the War Office, Cunynghame was instructed to reinforce the garrison in Natal. He decided tha the 'left wing' of the 13th Light Infantry, which was stationed in King William's Town, should join its headquarters in Pietermaritzburg, and that its place be taken by two companies of the 24th. Major Henry Degacher commanded the detachment. The other officers were chosen from amongst the men who had missed the Griqualand West expedition. They were Captains Brander and Rainforth and Lieutenants Anstey and Cavaye. Early in January William Degacher and two other 1st Battalion officers also sailed for the Eastern Province – as members of the Cape Town cricket team.

While some of his fellow officers were playing cricket in the Port Elizabeth sunshine, in Southampton, on a bitterly cold afternoon, Nevill Josiah Aylmer Coghill supervised the transfer of his baggage onto the *European*. Fourteen months had passed since he stood on the docks at Gibraltar and watched his battalion sail for South Africa. He had spent a part of that time on a course of instruction at Sandhurst, and had passed the subsequent examination with excellent marks. The result must have atoned for his unimpressive showing in the army entrance examination, for he was promoted shortly afterwards to full lieutenant with seniority backdated to 26 February 1873, the date of his commission as a sublieutenant.

Nevill Coghill was twenty-four years old, and his childhood had coincided with the decade of the Crimean War and the Sepoy Rebellion, military sagas which had contributed substantially to Britain's stock of glorious legends. His uncle Kendal Coghill had been one of the heroes who had stormed the heights in front of Delhi and distinguished himself in the siege. It was therefore not surprising that as soon as he finished his schooling, he asked his father to buy him a commission in the army. But Cardwell had recently become Secretary of State for War and the traditional mode of entry into the army had been suspended. It was only in July 1870, that Coghill was permitted to sit the army entrance examination. He passed with a dismal score. After leaving him to kick his heels about for a year, the army found a place for him in the Dublin Militia as supernumary lieutenant, and it was not until April 1873, that he was placed with a Regiment of the Line.

The Union Line steamer, which the tall, fair-haired officer boarded at Southampton, was six years old and, at 2 272 tons, smaller than the newer ships on the South African run. Smoky oil lamps in the public rooms and solitary candles stuck in recesses between cabins, did little to relieve the gloom of the winter weather and by ten o'clock even these feeble sources of illumination were extinguished. No lights were permitted inside the cabins and for twenty-six days Nevill shared his cabin's darkness with an old man and a boy of eighteen. The boredom of the voyage was aggravated by the ship's dour Captain who frowned on all the lighter forms of entertainment. The only pleasant interlude was the call at St. Helena and the mandatory visit (for a young officer) to the house of Napoleon's incarceration. On 10 February, he thankfully left the *European* to breakfast at the Main Barracks in Cape Town.

Coghill quickly discovered that the 1/24th was divided into three detachments scattered between Cape Town and Simonstown. The arrangement made for frequent turns of duty and it reinforced an ambition he had acquired to become the General's Aide-de-Camp. An ADC had only his chief to obey, 'be affability combined with reticence', and order drinks. He also drew an extra four shillings and sixpence a day and received allowances for a servant and forage for two horses. For a lieutenant, whose monthly salary was less than £8, the additional remuneration was sufficient inducement.

Nevill rated his prospects as reasonably good. He had met Lady Cunynghame at a dinner in London, a family friend had given him a personal letter of introduction to Sir Arthur, and his connection with the peerage (his father was an Irish Peer) could make for preference. Captain Francis Grenfell, one of Cunynghame's ADCs, had been invalided to England after the Griqualand West expedition, and Lieutenant John Dickinson, his temporary replacement, was about to return to Brecon. Within three weeks of landing in Cape Town, Coghill wrote his mother that he had dined twice with the General and had made friends with Colonel Glyn's daughters, achievements which prompted him to add, 'on the whole I have not I think let the grass grow under my feet'. It must have been something of a disappointment when a few weeks later Grenfell returned to South Africa.

The round of duties which Coghill found so irksome was aggravated by a spate of leave-taking. Major Henry Degacher and Captain Sawbridge were departing on a year's leave of absence. William Degacher was expected to be away for four months, Lieutenant Edward Browne, whom Nevill regarded as a close friend, was sent to the Eastern Frontier, and Major Pulleine left to take command of the King William's Town detachment. Most disconcerting, perhaps, was the decision of the battalion's hardworking adjutant, Lieutenant Teignmouth Melvill, to take long leave.

Towards the end of March the *Walmer Castle* steamed into Table Bay with a new addition for the officer complement of the 1/24th. But welcome as Sub-Lieutenant Richard Deane might have been in the officer-depleted garrison, the guard of honour drawn up on the jetty was not for him. Thomas François Burgers, President of the South African Republic, had returned from Europe.

The fashionably dressed man who stepped off the *Walmer Castle* had been president of the northernmost Boer Republic since 1872. Before turning to politics, Burgers had been the Dutch Reformed Church minister of a small Karroo town. But a European education and an inquiring mind had led him to express doubt about the too literal acceptance of the Scriptures. Such free-thinking had resulted in a trial for heresy. It had taken a Cape Supreme Court decision to get him reinstated as a minister. When he became president Burgers threw himself heart and soul into the task of leading his very conservative people into the nineteenth century.

His innovations had been resented by the Boers, and his political opponents had begun to revive his heretical past. Keeping a piano in his house, minting gold coins which carried his image, and the welcome he had extended to foreign prospectors had been held up as examples of his ungodliness. It was with the gold from the valleys of the Eastern Transvaal, however, that he had hoped to finance his programme of modernization. His dream was a railroad to the sea – a line from Pretoria to Delagoa Bay to free him from the greedy stranglehold which the British colonies exerted on the interior.

With a feeling akin to relief, the Transvaalers heard in March 1875, that their restless President intended to convalesce in Europe after an illness. They were much less enthusiastic when they discovered that he was to turn the visit into a loan-raising errand for his railway line. While in Cape Town, Burgers had made some impetuous remarks about a united South Africa independent of the Crown; and it was therefore no coincidence that the ship in which he sailed to Britain carried a secret despatch from Barkly warning Lord Carnarvon that the Transvaal president planned to seek close ties with Germany. Barkly claimed to have had definite information that the Boers were obtaining arms and ammunition through the German Consul in Natal and that German agents were trying to get a hundred-year lease on the port in Delagoa Bay. A month before Carnarvon drafted his controversial 'Conference Despatch', Barkly wrote: 'the intervention of Germany in the affairs of South Africa would create sudden political and commercial complications, and put an end at once and forever to all chance of the formation of the federal union of the difficult states under the British Flag which it is so desirable to see accomplished'.

The Secretary for State had received the Transvaal President with kindness, and Burgers responded with reassuring comments about his country's native policy and a professed interest in confederation. It was from the bankers of Holland, however, that Burgers had chosen to borrow the money for his railroad. A call on Bismarck had further infuriated the Secretary for State; he had begun to fear that the Transvaal might elude the confederation net he was weaving in South Africa. Invigorated by his visit to Europe, and deeply in debt, Burgers returned to South Africa impatient for his republic's leap forward.

A few days after Burgers's departure for the Transvaal, Johannes Hendrikus Brand arrived in Cape Town. Accompanied by his English wife, Brand was on his way to London at Carnarvon's invitation. The President of the Orange Free State was a son of the late Speaker of the Cape Assembly, a member of the Cape Bar, and had held a seat in the Cape Colony's Parliament. Unlike Burgers, Brand understood the character of the people he ruled and knew their limitations. He had been a notable success as President. His colonial upbringing had given him a knowledge and an appreciation of British institutions and he moved comfortably in imperial circles. The esteem in which he was held was amply demonstrated during the week he spent in Cape Town. General Cunynghame, one of his admirers, gave a dinner in his honour and provided Colonel Glyn and his officers with the opportunity to meet the other Boer President.

The coming of the Cape winter heralded the opening of the fox-hunting season, and the Colonel of the 1/24th was an enthusiastic huntsman. ''unting being 'is 'obby', was how Coghill put it. Colonel Glyn was Master of the pack, and his three Irish subalterns, Coghill, Daly and Hodson, were Whips. The men were fond of their commanding officer and made allowances for his obsession, 'as good a little man as ever breathed', in Coghill's opinion. With four daughters and a domineering wife, he probably welcomed the escape afforded him by the hunt. His men knew all about Anne Glyn's cantankerous nature and had a great deal of sympathy for their 'easy-going' colonel.

Outings would sometimes last for ten days. Mornings of hunting the 'fox' (the black-backed Cape jackal) would alternate with shoots for partridge, hare or small buck. The soldier huntsmen were frequently entertained by the farmers from the surrounding districts and welcomed by their daughters as a flirtatious diversion. What with exercising the pack, looking after puppies and frequent hunts, Coghill's military duties took a back seat in that winter of 1876.

Towards the end of June the peace in South Africa was broken by fighting in the Transvaal. The quarrel was between President Burgers and the Bapedi, a people who lived in a mountainous stretch of country near the district of Lydenburg. For many years the Boers had tried with little success to purchase land from them. After repeated attempts at coercion had failed, a treaty had been signed with the Regent Sekwati, which had attempted to define the boundaries of his jurisdiction without actually acknowledging his sovereignty. On Sekwati's death, the chieftainship had been seized by his son Sekhukhune. He had at first maintained friendly relations with his white neighbours and had permitted missionaries into his territory. They had proved too successful for his liking. Convinced that his authority was being undermined, Sekhukhune had turned on the converts and provoked a flight of baptised Bapedi into the Transvaal. One of the fugitives had been his half-brother, Johannes Dinkwahyane.

After a few years of Transvaal sovereignty Johannes had tired of Christian piety and had set himself up as an independent chief. He had taken his followers to the Spekboom River valley and had established a kraal near the Sekhukhuneland border. Sekhukhune had welcomed his lapsed brother back into his fold and had granted him official recognition, a gesture which extended his own influence into the Transvaal. Johannes had prospered and his kraal had grown steadily bigger; but when he began to add fortifications, the Boers in the district became alarmed.

President Burgers had returned to find the Volksraad disenchanted with his dream of a railroad to Delagoa Bay and incensed by the tax increases he needed to pay for it. The Boers considered all forms of taxation an affront to personal liberty, and material progress at the price of mortgaging their republic looked like a very poor bargain to them. Burgers's euphoria of achievement quickly evaporated in Pretoria. His popularity was at a low ebb, and his political opponents, led by Paul Kruger, had grown powerful. His chances of re-election the following year looked dismal. During his absence in Europe, Petrus Joubert, the acting President, had taken a firm line with the Zulus about trespassing into the territory which the Transvaal called its Province of Utrecht. Joubert's handling of the situation had met with general approval, and people were advocating a similar approach towards Sekhukhune. To Burgers, the Bapedi kraals seemed, suddenly, perilously close to the goldfields road and his projected railroad. Moreover, annexation of Sekhukhuneland would make land available that could help pay the interest on the railway loan. All at once the solution to Burgers's problems seemed glaringly obvious – he would lead a popular war against Sekhukhune.

The outcome of his inspiration was a grandiloquent announcement in the Volksraad of his intention to call out a large commando against Sekhukhune. On 12 June he submitted to the Executive Council a detailed plan for the survey, allotment, and sale of Bapedi lands. But the reaction to a military expedition led by Burgers was distinctly luke-warm. The President, whom the Boers regarded, at best, as an eccentric, did not inspire them with martial confidence. Experienced commando leaders like Paul Kruger withheld their services because God's blessing would not rest on an expedition led by so frivolous a man. The political capital that might be derived from Burgers's failure was, in the opinion of some, the more likely explanation for Kruger's behaviour. Despite the mood of mistrust, Burgers raised, by conscription and appeal, a force much larger than his republic could afford to support for any length of time. A large contingent of Swazi warriors, enemies of the Bapedi since Sekwati's days, was a vital addition to his force.

The commando chose Johannes's stronghold for its first onslaught. In the ensuing battle the chief was mortally wounded and his kraal destroyed. The brunt of the fighting was borne by the Swazis, and they accordingly laid claim to all of Johannes's cattle. A rift, which led to the Swazi withdrawal from the campaign, occured when the whites demanded a share of the spoils. Burgers's commando was left on its own.

The news that the weak and impoverished Republic had embarked on a war with a powerful black tribe dismayed the English colonies. Paramount was the dread that Cetshwayo would be unable to resist taking advantage of any Boer reverses; and if the Zulus went on the warpath, they reasoned, would not the black masses in Natal be tempted to rise against the settlers? The Cape Colony feared that trouble in Natal would snowball into another frontier war. The spectre of a black uprising throughout the land began to send shivers down the colonial spines.

The first reports of the Transvaal conflict arrived in Cape Town at a particularly unpropitious time. Parliament was debating the Colony's defensive capabilities, and the population was being subjected daily to gloomy pronouncements from the Eastern Province bloc. One of the most outspoken critics of the Colony's lack of military preparedness was General Cunynghame. He had been instructed by the War Office, at the time of his appointment to the South African command, to urge a sound reorganisation of the Colony's own forces. He had travelled the length and breadth of the Colony, had inspected its defences, and had concluded that the Cape was incapable of defending itself against a black onslaught without substantial aid from British troops. His alarmist views, sometimes tactlessly expressed, had been received with hostility by Molteno's hypersensitive ministry. They regarded him as the interfering type of military buffoon which the War Office was prone to inflict on luckless colonies. Cunynghame's denouncements, backed on this occasion by a vocal parliamentary opposition greatly annoyed Molteno and relations between him and the General became so strained that winter, that Cunynghame offered to resign from the Executive Council in order to avoid open friction between its colonial and imperial members. Molteno, faced with widespread anxiety over Burgers's military adventure, had to agree to the establishment of a parliamentary commission of enquiry into defence. John Gordon Sprigg, the member for East London, was appointed chairman and the committee left immediately for the Eastern Frontier to collect evidence.

The Cape newspapers worked themselves into a frenzy of pessimism long before precise information about the Sekhukhune campaign became available. Rumours of disasters and defeats were printed as fact, the slightest setback was reported as a catastrophe, and Burgers was accused of igniting a conflagration that would consume the whole country. They called for a new government to take over the running of the Transvaal and argued that strong government could only emerge from a confederation under the British flag. The 'Old Colonists' sought a united white front against the common foe and blamed the British Government for thoughtlessly arming blacks against their Transvaal brethren. Barkly wrote to Carnarvon that a full scale war had broken out in the Transvaal and suggested that 'the moment is fast approaching when Her Majesty's Government will be compelled to intervene, and take a very decided line in regard to the proceedings of the South African Republic'.

In July, rumours describing unrest among the tribes on the Eastern Frontier began to arrive in Cape Town. Most of the rumours proved, on investigation, to have originated from vague hints dropped by domestic servants and farm labourers, but Barkly was as susceptible to the prevailing mood of anxiety as the ordinary settler. On very dubious information he detailed to Carnarvon an involved plan about a black uprising scheduled to take place towards the end of the year; a complex strategy which called for Sotho, Thembu and Xhosa impis to rendezvous somewhere in the Amathole mountains. In a letter home, Coghill gave his analysis of the South African situation in the winter of 1876: 'There are three powerful kaffir chiefs, one Chitgao [Cetshwayo] near Natal, one Secononi [Sekhukhune] and another nearest the K.W.T. [King William's Town] frontier, besides other smaller tribes and rumours are abroad that they will rise as soon as the hot weather commences which will be in about two months'.

7

Carnarvon takes action

In June, a draft of eighty men arrived under the charge of Captain Reginald Younghusband. The newcomers found Cape Town in the grip of a dismally wet winter. The rain had turned the streets into bogs, drilling and parades were restricted, and the men were left to idle in the barracks for days on end. Boredom undermined discipline, brawling became commonplace and some of the men fell foul of the civil authorities. Not a sitting of the Magistrate's Court went by that winter without some member of the 1/24th appearing on a charge. The offences varied from drunk and disorderly to assault and robbery, and the sentences from a month's hard labour to release on the recognisances of an officer. Desertion was another consequence of the enforced inactivity and before winter's end, nineteen men had gone missing.

The bad reputation which the 1/24th stood to acquire was assuaged, to some extent, by two Battalion endeavours that gained the approval of the respectable burghers of Cape Town – the Royal Warwick Lodge of Good Templars (founded by soldiers who had taken the pledge) and the Royal Warwick Theatre. The latter drew its members from both rank and file and officers; and Coghill, with his rich Irish brogue, frequently appeared in comic roles. Performances were open to the public and admission was free. In time, the light-hearted productions of the Royal Warwick Theatre came to rival the city's professional companies in popularity.

Coghill also had a modest talent for sketching, and he found employment that winter designing costumes for a 'Calico Ball' that Lady Barkly had decided to give. The evening was to be the entertainment extravaganza of Henry Barkly's socially unexciting governship. And while the military in Cape Town occupied themselves with the preparations for a fancy dress frolic, in distant Transvaal, a very unsoldierly President suffered a humiliating defeat at the hands of a native chief.

It had taken Burgers an exhausting month to bring his commando into a position for an assault on Sekhukhune's citadel, Dsjate. There he discovered that the huge kraal, built on steep rugged hills, could only be approached through narrow passages which had been barricaded with rocks and hedges of tightly packed thorn-trees and needle-sharp aloes. Black men choosing to fight with guns from prepared fortifications had been another nasty surprise for Burgers's experienced 'Kaffir fighters'. The dismounted attack had ground to a halt and no one had known how to deal with the situation. The attackers had stayed pinned down in the hot sun for that whole long day, and only under cover of darkness had the dispirited Transvaalers managed to withdraw and bury their dead. In the morning, Burgers's commando had melted away. Another offensive was out of the question; the Volksraad had neither the enthusiasm nor the money to support one. The war against Sekhukhune was handed over to mercenaries and freebooters. They called themselves the Lydenburg Volunteer Corps and its leaders were those fugitives from Kimberley's failed rebellion, Conrad von Schlickmann and Alfred Aylward.

Burgers's defeat brought forth a chorus of condemnatory outpourings from the colonial newspapers. Fears of a countrywide black uprising started up anew, and stories poured in of assegaais being sharpened in every kraal east of the Kei. Every rumour, speculation and gloomy prophesy found its way into the purple-lined despatch box which travelled between Barkly and Carnarvon, and it reached the Secretary of State for Colonies just as he was about to adjourn a very unproductive conference on southern Africa.

The conference had opened with Carnarvon in the Chair, Garnet Wolseley as Vice-Chairman and Theophilus Shepstone, the delegate from Natal, as the only official representative of a South African state. President Brand had insisted on retaining his unofficial status, Griqualand West had a proxy delegate and Molteno had refused to attend in any capacity, save that of observer. The Transvaal had not been represented. Discussion had centred round a common native policy and the restriction of arms sales to blacks. Confederation as an issue, had been conspicuously avoided. The conference had adjourned halfway through August without having advanced Carnarvon's policy an inch. Carnarvon had been left feeling dissatisfied and cheated. His only consolation had been Barkly's reports of chaos in the Transvaal and alarm throughout the country. They seemed to vindicate his faith in the benefits confederation would bestow on South Africa. Wolseley, impatient with the politicians, urged him to take positive action in the interest of his policy. It was then that the Secretary of State and the Major-General directed their attentions to the conference's only official delegate.

Theophilus Shepstone was three years old when his missionary father came to South Africa with the 1820 wave of British settlers. The family settled amongst the Transkeian tribes and Theophilus exhibited a linguistic talent that very soon allowed him to converse with the tribesmen in their own language. While still a boy, he had the traumatic experience of having to flee his home because of intertribal strife. His familiarity with the Xhosa language soon attracted attention, and in 1835, when the Sixth Frontier War broke out, he found official employment as an interpreter. After the war he was appointed British Resident to the new territory of Kaffraria, and a few years later, when an executive council had to be created for the fledgling colony of Natal, Shepstone found a place on it as diplomatic agent to the tribes living in the Colony. Fear of Natal's large black population had dominated the thoughts of the small settler community from the outset, and Shepstone's office, as a result, grew in importance. He was a member of the Land Commission that evolved a system for separating black from white. In the formulation of Natal's brand of apartheid, Shepstone created eight major reserves where chiefs and headmen were permitted to rule according to tribal custom, but were answerable through the Secretary for Native Affairs to the Natal Executive Council. As the first incumbent of that office Shepstone became the absolute ruler of the 'Natal Kaffirs'.

When Wolseley came to Pietermaritzburg to restrict Natal's autonomy, Shepstone cooperated fully with him and, at the same time, convinced him of the soundness of his native policy. Wolseley came away with the impression that the Secretary for Native Affairs was 'by far the ablest man in the Colony'. Wolsely did have some reservations about Shepstone's personality, but his knowledge of the indigenous languages of South Africa, (the Boer *taal* included) and his successes with Natal's blacks* made him seem well qualified for the scheme that he and Carnarvon hatched after the conference failed: Shepstone was to assume direction over the affairs of the white tribe that ruled the Transvaal.

*Carnarvon had met Shepstone in 1874 when he rushed to London to defend his actions in the Langalibalele affair. He had been impressed with Shepstone's imperial vision of a Natal-type native system extended to the Zambesi and beyond.

On 23 September, the inscrutable Secretary for Native Affairs boarded the *Windsor Castle* at Dartmouth, secure in the knowledge that a Royal Commission and an imperial battalion would shortly follow him to South Africa. Among the one hundred and sixty passengers on board were Lieutenant Teignmouth Melvill and his bride of a few months. In the early hours of 19 October, in a calm sea and under a bright moon, the four-year-old ship struck a reef off Dassen Island. The impact tore a large hole in the iron hull, and within ten minutes all the furnaces were extinguished. The good weather held, and the passengers were landed on Dassen Island.

At daylight, Melvill, and another passenger who had volunteered to take the news of the shipwreck to Cape Town, were rowed to the mainland. They managed to buy a cart and horses in the nearest village and reached Cape Town late the same night after a fifty mile journey plagued by breakdowns and delays. Melvill returned to Dassen Island the following morning aboard the S.S. *Florence*. The passengers were found huddled on the rocks under makeshift awnings to escape the cold wind that had come up in the night. The rescue was effected without loss of life, and Shepstone, whose future actions were destined to alter the course of South African history, was brought safely to Cape Town.

Towards the end of August, Nevill Coghill received the appointment he had set his heart on – ADC to the General. The appointment was meant to be temporary, but the change in duties was welcome. He noted with exaltation that he would no longer be responsible for the 'great and little sins and iniquities' of a quarter of the 1st Battalion, that he could sleep late and have frequent afternoons to himself. He gave up his bug-infested room in the Castle and moved to the General's residence in Rondebosch where he shared quarters with Cunynghame's military secretary, Lieutenant-Colonel Forestier Walker of the Scots Guards.

A few weeks after he took up his new appointment, the General decided to visit the Eastern Frontier to judge for himself the seriousness of the reported unrest. Their journey took them overland from Port Elizabeth to Fort Beaufort and through the western Amatholes to Queenstown. Their route took in the scenes of some of the bitterest fighting of the last frontier war – the ravines and kloofs where the warrior chief Maqoma tied down thousands of soldiers for many months. Coghill met Sandile, the notorious chief whose name in bygone days had spelt terror on the frontier. He thought him an undignified drunk and was disgusted to hear him beg for tobacco. By the middle of October the General's party was back in Cape Town, convinced that the rumours of unrest which had emanated from the Eastern Frontier were largely without foundation. Nevertheless, shortly after his return, Cunynghame decided to reinforce the Frontier Armed and Mounted Police (FAMP) base at Komga on the Transkei border with a squadron of mounted infantry, and sent Lieutenant Fred Carrington to King William's Town to buy horses. He was followed by forty-two men of the 1st Battalion under Lieutenant Ralph Clements who had volunteered for the new mounted infantry squadron.

Coghill had taken an artist's interest in the shades of red and ochre produced by the mixture of clay and fat with which the Xhosas smeared their bodies and blankets. In a letter home he mentioned that he had seen these 'red people' building huts and sowing crops and concluded from this that they would not be going to war. But as an afterthought added, 'the fire once lighted in the Transvaal it is hard to say where it will extend to'.

As spring turned to summer and the feared uprising failed to materialise, the tensions and anxieties of the past few months began to dissipate. The approach of the Christmas holiday season in Cape Town, and the long round of social engagements it afforded (especially to a young unmarried officer), made the continuing unrest in the Transvaal seem very remote. Despite a wound in his leg, from a misdirected assegaai thrown by Daly, Coghill was able to attend two of the mandatory seasonal picnics, as well as a Masonic banquet, a ball in honour of the officers of a visiting German warship, and tennis-parties at Admiralty House. When not dining with the General, he was a guest to dinner in colonial homes, the Officers' Mess, and, on one occasion, aboard a man-of-war in Simonstown. In his free time he shot pool at Mr Cogill's hotel in Wynberg. Boxing Day was given over to a 1st Battalion function, a banquet and dance organised by Burck and the Band for the officers and NCOs: the dancing continued until daylight. Two recent arrivals, Sub-Lieutenants George Palmes and the Hon. Ulick de Rupe Burke Roche, must have found the 1/24th a most convivial battalion and Cape Town a very hospitable city. One disturbing item, however, was the delayed arrival of the summer rains. It was more than a year since the greater part of the country had had any rainfall.

The first weeks of 1877 revealed Carnarvon in active pursuit of confederation. A draft South Africa Bill, permitting states in favour of confederation to unite under one government, arrived in Cape Town shortly after the holidays. When the London Conference failed to reconvene, Carnarvon decided to go ahead and prepare a 'Permissive Act' to encourage confederation. It was to be modelled on the British North America Act of 1867, and was intended to serve as a guide for the incorporation of Griqualand West into the Cape Colony. It was to provide, in addition, the mechanism whereby other South African states could unite with the Cape Colony. To conciliate republican sentiment, the heads of provinces were to be called presidents instead of lieutenant-governors, and the Dutch language was to have the same status as English in any union. The provinces could retain their own franchise arrangements and voting for a federal parliament was to be restricted to whites. A clause safeguarding the rights of the blacks, however, was included – all laws passed by a federal parliament pertaining to non-whites would be subject to approval by Her Majesty's Government.

Publication of the draft 'Permissive Bill' produced immediate argument n Cape Town. Editorial comment ranged along the divisions created by the 'Conference Dispatch', and Molteno would have nothing to do with the bill. Coghill described it as 'a convenient way of expressing no compulsion only you must'. For a while it looked as if the Colony might have to endure a repetition of the schisms that sundered it in 1875. Cape Town, however, was getting accustomed to Carnarvon's federation forays and Molteno's intransigence; the draft bill provoked less popular interest than the preparations for a South African International Exhibition.

At about this time occurred the first death in South Africa of a 24th Regiment officer. On an exceptionally hot January day, Richard Deane and Wilfred Heaton went for a swim in the Liesbeek River. Deane dived in, but failed to surface. He was unconscious when Heaton brought him out. He was carried to the nearby house of Mr John X. Merriman and died there the following day. Deane, 'a nice, quiet gentlemanly fellow', according to Coghill, was twenty years old and he had been in South Africa for ten months.

8

Boers and blesbok

The 31 March in Cape Town started off as a dull, windless day. Dense masses of cloud hovered over Table Mountain and rain was expected. At the dock-side a formal looking knot of civilians and military men waited for the *Balmoral Castle* to lower its gangway. A banner with WELCOME spelled out hung limply from a building on the waterfront. Suddenly, the *Bahiana*, a rusted Brazilian warship, fired its guns in salute. A tall, grey-haired man, resplendent in Windsor uniform, Order of the Bath and Star of India, had appeared on the deck of the mailship. The Guard of Honour drawn up on the jetty came smartly to attention, and the rain began to fall.

Sir Henry Bartle Frere escorted by Cunynghame and Molteno left the docks in the first carriage; Lady Catherine Frere and her daughters followed in the second. A feeble attempt at cheering was drowned out by Drum-Major Doyle doing his best to dispel the gloom of that damp Saturday afternoon. Flags hung from a few windows on the route to Government House, but the wet streets were empty. The following morning, at a simple ceremony in the Council Chamber, the oath of office was quickly administered by the Chief Justice. The Cape Colony had a new Governor and South Africa a new High Commissioner.

The position had been offered to Frere after the inconclusive London conference. Carnarvon had known, and Frere had not hesitated to remind him, that succeeding Barkly as Governor of the Cape Colony could not be construed as promotion for a man of his standing. His real role, Carnarvon had hastened to assure him, would be that of a statesman and architect of confederation. The task, in Carnarvon's estimation, could be accomplished within two years, and success would make him the first Governor-General of the South African Dominion. Both the challenge and the reward were tempting; and Frere had accepted on the condition that he received a substantial allowance over and above a governor's annual salary of £5 000.

Carnarvon's choice had met with wide approval in England. To Froude, Frere was the best alternative to Wolseley; Lord Salisbury, staunch protagonist of the new imperialism, expected him to quickly get the measure of both Boers and blacks; and the Aborigines Protection Society felt it could rely on him to strengthen the hands of those 'who protect the natives from injustice'. The Cape Colony was flattered by the appointment of so distinguished a pro-consul. There was something of the courtier about Frere that contrasted with the more bourgeois style of his predecessor. To Cunynghame he appeared to be a 'first rate statesman ... of very high position', who could help forge a South African army for the defence of the alternate sea-route to India. Molteno regarded him as Carnarvon's agent sent to push his 'Permissive Bill' through the Cape Parliament.

Frere, born in 1815, was almost the same age as the retiring Governor. On finishing his schooling he had joined the East India Company. His first appointment had been that of assistant in the Poona Revenue Department. Alert and intelligent he quickly made himself an authority on local affairs. When Sir George Arthur, the Governor of Bombay, needed a private secretary Frere had been the natural choice: two years later he married the Governor's daughter. In 1864, he was made Resident in the Deccan, and not long after, Commissioner in the Sind. Frere acquired a reputation as a competent administrator who was unafraid of responsibility and his career advanced at a respectable rate by the standards of the time.

It was at the age of forty-two that his career was accelerated dramatically. He had just returned to Karachi from home leave when news reached him of the mutiny in the Punjab. He immediately collected all the loyal forces in the Sind and dispatched them to the Punjab. To do this he had to override the objections of the General Commanding, who feared a local uprising. But Frere was prepared to shoulder all the blame if the move was the wrong one. As it turned out, his decision was greatly appreciated by his superiors, and such troubles as occurred in the Sind were easily dealt with. After the mutiny Frere received a KCB and an appointment to the Viceroy's Council. In 1862, he was made Governor of Bombay. Boldness and the ability to take decisions had been well rewarded.

His administration was characterised by the belief that discretionary power must rest with the man on the spot. He would not wait for instruction from some civil servant in London who was totally unfamiliar with conditions in Bombay. The seemingly gentle Governor had a will of iron; a trait Wolseley recognised, when he wrote, 'underneath the mild

Top: Cape Town 1875 ... the beginning *(Album of Bandmaster Burck).*
Bottom: Laying the foundation-stone of the Cape Colony's Houses of Parliament: Guard of Honour supplied by the 1/24th.

Top left: Sir Henry Barkly *(from: M. MacMillan, Sir Henry Barkly [Balkema, 1970])*
Top right: Lord Carnarvon *(South African Library, Cape Town). Bottom left:* James Anthony Froude *(from W. H. Dunn: James Anthony Froude 1857-1894 [Clarendon Press, 1963]). Bottom right:* Major-General Sir Garnet Wolseley with 'powdered French Imperial'.

Top: Kimberley in the mid 1870s: 'Mount Ararat' on the left. *Bottom:* The 'New Rush' Mine in 1875.

Top left: Sir Richard Southey. *Top right:* J. B. Robinson – a contemporary photograph *(South African Library, Cape Town)*. *Bottom left:* Henry Tucker. *Bottom right:* Conrad von Schlickmann *(Cape Archives)*.

Top: The Grand Parade and the Commercial Exchange from the Castle ramparts 1876.
Bottom: Rathfelder's Hotel, Diep River: the Headquarters of the Cape Hunt.
(Both photographs: Album of Bandmaster Burck).

Colonel Richard Glyn: the pipe and beard are souvenirs of the Transkeian campaign. A water-colour drawing by Major J. N. Crealock *(from R. A. Brown, ed.,* The Road to Ulundi [*University of Natal Press, 1969*]*)*.

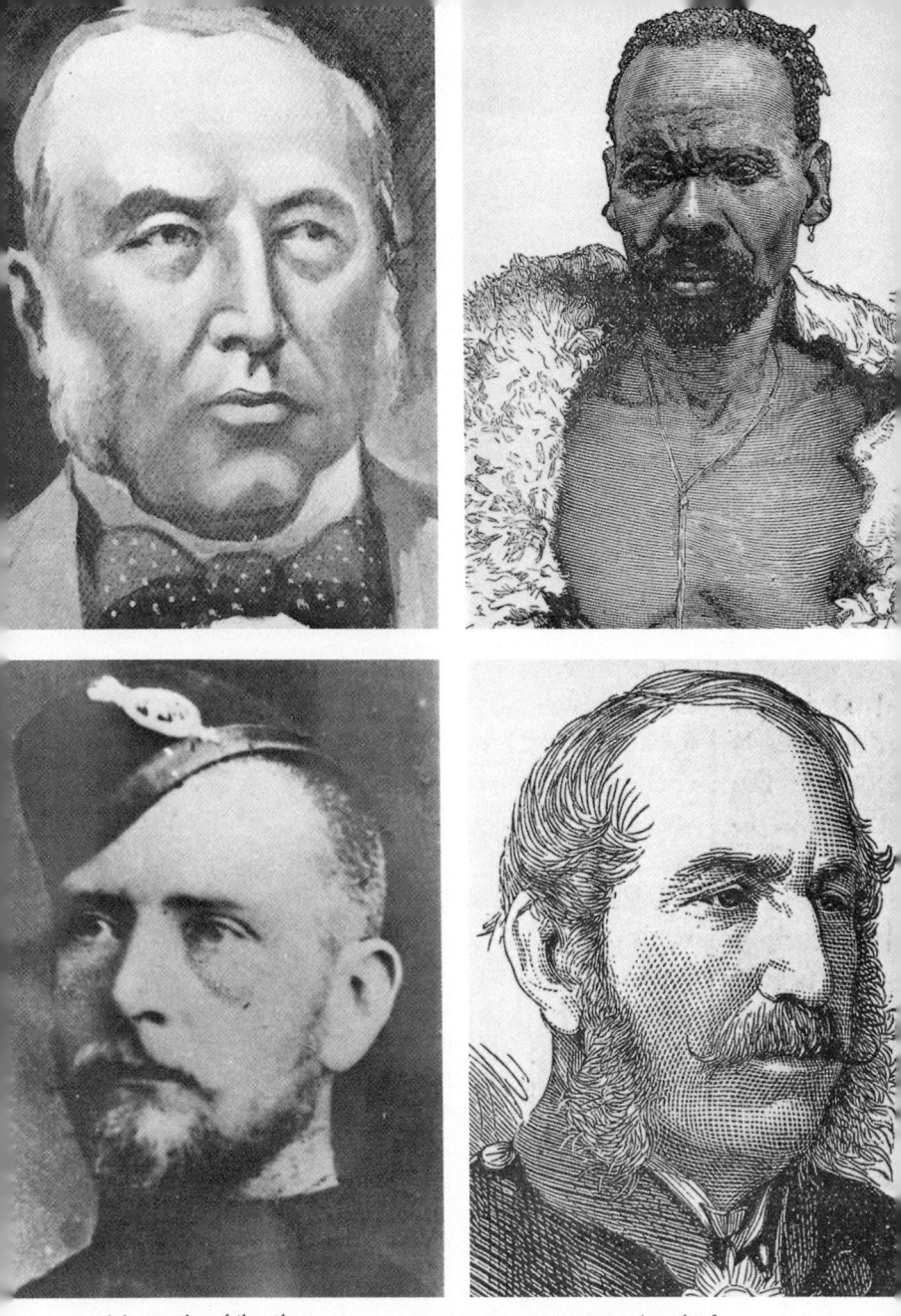

Top left: Sir Theophilus Shepstone: a contemporary portrait. *Top right:* Chief Sekhukhune *(Illustrated London News)*. *Bottom left:* Lieutenant Nevill Coghill: a photograph taken shortly before the Anglo-Zulu War *(Killie Campbell Africana Library, Durban)*. *Bottom right:* Lieutenant-General Sir Arthur Cunynghame G.C.B. *(Illustrated London News)*.

Top: A view of the Military Reserve (King William's Town) across the Buffalo River.
Bottom: A street in King William's Town, 1877 *(Both photographs: Album of Bandmaster Burck).*

aspect of gold-spectacled respectability and Exeter Hall humanity there was, however, a man's heart full of that determination which makes heros [sic] and great men'. At the end of his term as Governor Frere was recognised as Britain's foremost authority on India and the East and elected member of the India Council. In 1872, he undertook a mission to persuade the Sultan of Zanzibar to abandon the slave trade. At first, the Sultan either obstructed or evaded his every proposal; but when Frere saw that he was getting nowhere with diplomatic appeals, he instructed the commander of the British naval force in East African waters to blockade the island. He had exceeded his instructions, but the strategy worked, and the Sultan gave in. Frere was acclaimed for his success against the notorious bastion of slavery. He was made a Fellow of the Royal Society, a Freeman of the City of London, and a Privy Councillor. When in 1875 the Prince of Wales undertook a six months' tour of India, Frere was the natural choice for adviser and attendant. At sixty-one, Frere was a national figure, within his chosen field he could go no further, but fame had made him neither a rich man nor a peer: then came Carnarvon's offer.

Two days after Frere took the oath of office, Barkly was guest of honour at a banquet in the Commercial Exchange. The undemonstrative ex-Governor, who had never sought personal popularity, had earned, by the end of his term, a considerable measure of respect and affection. Even the 'Old Colonists', who had resented his high-handed dealings with the Boer Republics, had to admit that his deepest concern, at all times, had been the welfare of the Cape Colony. His tenure of office had coincided with a period of unprecedented prosperity, and responsible government, to which he had been mid-wife, looked firmly established. Barkly's send-off was a tumultuous affair. A huge crowd gathered on the dockside to cheer the departing family. As the R.M.S. *African* drew away from the quay, the 1st Battalion band began to play 'Auld Lang Syne'. The crowd joined in and continued singing until the ship was well out to sea.

Less than three weeks after Frere's arrival, the news was made public that on 12 April Theophilus Shepstone had annexed the Transvaal. It was the audacious climax to a saga which had begun more than three months before.

When Shepstone was brought off Dassen Island, the Transvaal was still making news. To his satisfaction most of it was bad. The war waged by Burgers's mercenaries had degenerated into skirmishes and raids more noteworthy for their brutality than for their tactical decisiveness. Reports of atrocities committed against the Bapedi had become the daily newspaper fare. Real, exaggerated or imagined, they added a 'humanitarian' ustification for interfering in the affairs of the Republic.

In Shepstone's judgement, however, conditions in the Transvaal had not yet reached the stage of desperation that Carnarvon imagined. He preferred the slow approach. Years of dealing with blacks had taught him the value of patience. Towards the end of December, in a letter which was a masterpiece of generalisation, he informed Burgers that he proposed visiting Pretoria. The President was given to understand that Shepstone's object was to investigate and remedy, if possible, the Republic's difficulties. About the same time, a certain Mr Joseph Henderson, who had a reputation in Natal for being an astute business man, and was also the father-in-law of Shepstone's son, George, left Pietermaritzburg.

Reports that the more implacable Paul Kruger was likely to oust Burgers in the forthcoming presidential elections, finally persuaded Shepstone to start out for the Transvaal. His party consisted of seven civilians escorted by fifteen Natal Mounted Police. The journey to Pretoria was a leisurely progression, and in the Transvaal it took on the appearances of a public relations exercise. Burgers, undecided about what attitude he should adopt towards the Special Commissioner, played it safe and sent the presidential carriage to bring him into the capital. A hundred horsemen, most of them English-speaking, rode out to cheer the party in. The first week was a continuous round of banquets and parties, Pretoria's market square resounded with cries of 'God save the Queen' and the English community, in general, carried on as if the Transvaal was already part of the Empire.

On 26 January, three days after his arrival, Shepstone appeared before the Transvaal Executive Council. To enquiries about the purpose of his visit, he hinted, in broad terms, that Transvaal independence constituted a threat to its neighbours and itself. The members of the council remained strangely unresponsive to their republic's perilous situation as outlined by Shepstone. In order to give his visit an air of purpose, Shepstone induced Burgers to agree to a mission to Sekhukhune and to a special session of the Volksraad to debate the reforms he sought. Paul Kruger dominated the session with questions that demanded unequivocal answers. Accustomed to the circumlocutions of the *indaba*, a perplexed Shepstone fell back on the threat of a Zulu invasion – a tactic Wolseley had recommended. It was only the British Government, Shepstone argued, that prevented the impis of the 'evil-inclined' King Cetshwayo from taking revenge on the people responsible for the destruction of his uncle, King Dingane. Burgers, deluded into believing he would retain the presidency if the Volksraad adopted the reforms, leapt to Shepstone's support; he seemed to relish the spectacle of his obstructive and disobedient Volksraad being admonished by Britain's emissary. The elected representatives of the Boers approved a few minor changes, appointed Kruger to the vice-presidency, and adjourned.

It had taken Shepstone two frustrating months to wring out a few insignificant concessions from the Boers. His mission had lost its impetus, and it began to look as if the ex-Secretary for Native Affairs, who had swayed many a meeting of tribal elders with his commanding silence, had met his match in the Boers. A British officer, who was in Pretoria at the time, later recalled that the Special Commissioner was discouraged to the point of abandoning the mission when Henderson, who had invested heavily in the Transvaal, 'persuaded Shepstone against his own better judgement to go beyond his instructions and issue the annexation proclamation he did'.

On 12 April, by virtue of a Royal Commission signed at Balmoral Castle on the 5th day of October 1876, Shepstone annexed the Transvaal. In his proclamation the Boers were blamed for disclosing 'for the first time to the native tribes outside the Republic, from the Zambesi to the Cape, the great change that had taken place in the relative strength of the White and Black races. That this disclosure at once shook the prestige of the white man in South Africa, and placed every European Community in peril. That this common danger had caused universal anxiety, had given to all concerned the right to investigate its causes, and protect themselves from its consequences, and had imposed the duty upon those who had the power to shield enfeebled civilisation from the encroachment of barbarism and inhumanity'. What the proclamation failed to reveal, was Carnarvon's concern that if Britain did not intervene, 'Germany would be induced to undertake the protection of the Transvaal'.

Shepstone had added the Transvaal to the list of states amenable to Carnarvon's directives. Frere had only to bring the Cape Colony into line, and the Orange Free State, isolated within a united British South Africa, was bound to submit. He began by tackling Molteno about the draft South Africa Bill, and quickly discovered what Barkly and Froude had been up against. Molteno's standing in the Western Province, moreover, had been strengthened immeasurably by events in the Transvaal. The 'Old Colonists', once Froude's most enthusiastic allies, came out strongly in support of their premier and his dogged opposition to the perfidious Secretary of State. An alliance between the 'Old Colonists' and the Cape liberals dashed all Frere's hopes of getting the Western Province to agree to a South African confederation. He decided to be courteous and correct while in Cape Town and, at the earliest opportunity, exert pressure where Molteno was vulnerable, in the Eastern Province.

The changed boundaries of British South Africa and the uncertain temper of the Queen's new subjects, forced Cunynghame to redeploy the troops under his command. Colonel Montgomery was instructed to take the 1/13th across the Transvaal border to Pretoria and the mounted infantry detachment at Komga was ordered to proceed to northern Natal. Within days of the annexation, Frederick Carrington and Edward Browne left Cape Town to take charge of the mounted infrantrymen. The Eastern Frontier, for the moment, appeared to be tranquil, and Pulleine's detachment was brought back from King William's Town. The General, however, wanted to see for himself where new military bases should be established and prepared for a lengthy tour of Britain's newest possession. Coghill, who had known since January that he might soon get an opportunity to hunt game on the Transvaal highveld, was eager for a trip to that remote corner of South Africa. On 3 May, General Cunynghame and his ADC sailed in the S.S. *Teuton* for Durban.

Durban was sub-tropical plants and clean, wide streets; strong spicy smells and abominable odours; handsome villas on the hill behind the town and forlorn hotels; Indian girls in colourful saris and tablecloths black with flies. And the garrison, as Cunynghame discovered, was under-strength. Before starting for Pietermaritzburg Coghill had to send a message to Colonel Glyn requesting the transfer to Durban of half a company from the 1/24th. On the road to Pietermaritzburg Cunynghame and Coghill met Anthony William Durnford, the controversial hero of the Bushman's River Pass fracas. The engineering officer was now a lieutenant-colonel and in receipt of a disability pension. He had been back in Natal less than two months. Half a year in Europe and a fruitless attempt to cure his paralysed arm, had made him long for Natal's warm climate and the company of Frances Colenso, the Bishop's second daughter. With the cooperation of his replacement Durnford had managed to wangle back his old job. He had returned to Natal while Shepstone was in Pretoria lecturing to the Volksraad, and had conceived the notion that the Special Commissioner was in a perilous position. Without further ado he had galloped to the rescue. Durnford's unsought-for presence in Pretoria had proved an embarrassment to Shepstone, and he asked him to return to Natal. Convinced that the Commissioner had underestimated the danger, Durnford, on his own initiative, had hastened the three hundred men of the recently landed 80th Regiment to Newcastle. As soon as he met Cunynghame the restless knight-errant tried to convince him of the advantage of raising a detachment of mounted Basothos to augment the Colony's forces.

A three day journey from Pietermaritzburg by mule cart brought the General and his ADC to Newcastle, Natal's northernmost settlement. The small town, with many streets and a handful of buildings, was the jumping-off point for both the Transvaal and northern Zululand. A clean hotel with bathing facilities was a welcome, if unexpected, find. Major Amiels's detachment from the 80th Regiment had established an encampment with defensive earthworks on the outskirts of the town; but Cunynghame, impressed by the strategic importance of Newcastle, instructed him to erect barracks and a permanent fort on the heights overlooking the town.

Twenty miles from Newcastle, the wagon-road to the north began its steep and tortuous ascent over Laing's Nek Pass to the Transvaal highveld. The first Boer settlement which Cunynghame and Coghill came across was at Stander's Drift on the Vaal River. The village straddled the road to Pretoria and was equally well situated for the dispatch of forces to the Province of Utrecht. Moreover, the horse-sickness so prevalent in the eastern parts of the country, was almost unknown in Standerton. Instructions were sent to Carrington in Newcastle to ride up and choose a site for a cavalry station. Coghill was so taken with Standerton's economic prospects that he bought a plot of ground there.

Their path lay across a vast, empty grassland turned brown and brittle-dry by summer drought and winter frost, a featureless savanna stretching towards an unblemished horizon. At great intervals a clump of leafless willows standing near the grey, dried-out banks of a muddy stream gave notice to the travellers that they were approaching the simple dwelling of a man who believed that six thousand acres was the minimum respectable size for a farm.

Two generations of Boers had grown up on the Transvaal highveld since the first pioneer families ascended the great plateau with their lumbering ox-wagons. Having forsaken the Cape Colony they turned their backs to the sea which disseminated the thought and passion of nineteenth century Europe. The zeal for reform, which had burnt 'like fire beneath the hard surface of the age of iron and steam', never penetrated to the people of the interior of southern Africa. Industrialism and intellectual exploration, as the miners on the goldfields and Burgers's imported school teachers discovered respectively, were treated with suspicion and hostility.

The admiration which the British settlers in the Cape Colony had felt for the men and women who forsook their homes to make a new life in the barbaric interior, had been replaced by scorn when their descendants showed little inclination to better the crude conditions of the early years on the highveld. The praiseworthy pioneers had turned out to be sorry civilisers, and their failure to support Burgers against Sekhukhune had added cowardice to the list of detractions. The proximity of colonies governed by the most self-assured nation in a supremely optimistic age seemed to accentuate the backwardness of the Boer Republics: and none denigrated the Boer more than the representatives of Her Majesty's Army. They looked upon him as a person sliding towards the abyss from which Africa was beginning to emerge, a degenerate offshoot of Europe with no justifiable claim to a dominant destiny on the sub-continent.

Yet Cunynghame found much that he approved of in the highveld Boer society. He was impressed by the sturdy young men, their natural equestrian skill and their familiarity with fire-arms. In his opinion, 'men more fit for the Grenadier Guards, could not be found'. He had visited Russia before coming to South Africa, and thought that the Boers of the veld and the Cossacks of the steppes had much in common. He hoped to raise a mounted squadron of young Boers officered by professional British soldiers. Such a unit, he was sure, would make a valuable adjunct to the imperial forces in South Africa. The full implication of Shepstone's subreption seemed not to have been fully comprehended by the Boers on their isolated farms when the General and his ADC began their tour of the Transvaal. But the notion was beginning to take root in the minds of the Boers that annexation had been accomplished by a threat to unleash King Cetshwayo's impis on the land. For one white nation to intimidate another with the menace of a savage black horde was, to the Boers, a heinous concept.

The temper of the Boers, however, did not interest the two British officers quite as much as the condition of the game in the Transvaal. When the 1/24th first heard about its imminent move to the Cape Colony, a rush had followed on books about travel and sport in southern Africa. One of the most popular books had been *Five Years of a Hunter's*

Life in the Far Interior of South Africa, written by an Indian Army officer who had made his reputation by destroying wild life in South Africa on a gargantuan scale. But the hunting enthusiasts in the 1/24th had been greatly disappointed when they discovered that the compensation which South Africa was expected to offer them for their exertions had to be sought hundreds of miles away from the established garrisons. Most of the larger animals in the Cape Colony had been almost exterminated and the survivors had been driven deep into the hinterland. Lion, elephant and the larger antelope species had disappeared even from the highveld; what Cunynghame and Coghill found in quantity were black wildebees and blesbok. Two years of drought had dried up most of the waterholes, but by seeking out the pans with a few inches of water they could still encounter large herds of blesbok and Coghill recorded the slaughter of thirty-two head of game in four days. Cunynghame discovered the African wart-hog, and found it a fast, wiry adversary with vicious tusks. He would have preferred to have hunted it with spears, but shooting from horseback was almost as enjoyable. It pleased him that an 'Indian' sport was available to the British officers stationed in the Transvaal.

In this fashion the General and his ADC reached Pretoria all too soon. The twenty-year-old capital of the Transvaal was little more than a village, but numerous willow trees and neat rose gardens gave it an established air. The Union Jack fluttered overhead, red-coated soldiers lounged on the street corners and everyone spoke English. Pretoria had been transformed into a thorough little outpost of Empire. Speculators, merchants and fortune-seekers were arriving daily from Griqualand West and Natal and a 'general prosperity seemed to have set in'.

The camp of the 1/13th was situated on a slope overlooking the town. A commanding position from a defensive point of view, but a health threat to the townspeople as the rivulets and streams which ran down the hills supplied water to the town. Few doubted that the occupation would be a permanent one and Cunynghame gave instructions for the establishment of a military cantonment consisting of barracks, a hospital, bathing-houses and a fort. On 21 June, after a continuous round of parties and balls, Cunynghame and Coghill took the road to the recently troubled Lydenburg district and the goldfields.

In Lydenburg the General and his ADC found some unemployed members of the disbanded Lydenburg Volunteer Corps hanging around the canteens, and Coghill spoke to one who claimed to have been with Conrad von Schlickmann on that November day when he met his end leading a charge against a Bapedi strongpoint. British intervention, they griped, had ruined their fun. The people of Lydenburg gave a dinner in Cunynghame's honour, and vice-chairman of the entertainment committee was that notorious 'Fenian' from the diamond fields, Alfred Aylward. Despite a dusty banquet hall, an underdone turkey, and soup that was too sweet, the General was in great humour. He took the presence of the ex-rebel in his stride and his speech was carefully calculated to offend no one. Aylward attributed Cunynghame's good fellowship to his hunting successes.

From the Eastern Transvaal the tireless, sixty-five-year-old General and his ADC went south again to Standerton for a meeting with Lieutenant Carrington and to choose a site for a cavalry cantonment. Coghill sold the plot of ground he had purchased on his first visit for a profit sufficient to convince him of the Transvaal's great future. 'This is an immensely rich country', he wrote his father, 'as soon as peace and order are established and the natives begin to trust Europeans, the possessor of 6 000 acres in certain portions of the Transvaal will be able to build a palace on Lake Como'. Having established permanent military posts in Newcastle, Standerton and Pretoria, Cunynghame turned westwards for his second visit to the diamond fields.

Coghill could at least see for himself the wonders of the famous mining town about which his friends from the Army of the Vaal never tired of talking. The 'Big Hole' was by then more than two hundred feet deep and three hundred feet in diameter: 'the most extraordinary sight I think I have ever witnessed'. He went down into the very depths of the mine and was given a small diamond as a keepsake. After about a week in Kimberley, reports of trouble on the Cape Colony's frontier reached the General. The Gcalekas and the Mfengu, it appeared, were at each other's throats, there was a risk of settler involvement and Frere wanted him back in the Cape Colony.

Cunynghame and Coghill were camped on the Kabousie River, a day's journey from King William's Town, when Charles Griffith, the Cape Colony's magistrate to the Basothos, rode in. He was on his way to take command of the Frontier Armed and Mounted Police (FAMP) at Sir Bartle's request. A passing post-cart also drew up at the camp site and the driver yelled, 'General, the war cry has gone forth in Kreli's [Sarhili's] country; the kaffirs have risen'. The following day Coghill was reunited with his fellow officers of the 1/24th. The battalion, by then, had been in King William's Town for seven weeks.

Part Two

September 1877 to August 1878

9

A wedding-feast in the Transkei

A number of changes had taken place within the battalion hierarchy since Coghill left on his tour of the Transvaal. Most important had been the promotion of Henry Degacher to the lieutenant-colonelcy of the 2/24th. Henry Pulleine, with almost the same length of service (twenty-two years), had become the Regiment's senior field-officer and was next in line for a battalion command. Quartermaster William Charters, the Battalion's last link with Chillianwala, had retired at the end of June, and James Pullen, after twenty-six years in the ranks, had succeeded him as Quartermaster and honorary officer. There had also been a change in the band: Drum-Major Doyle had been discharged and his place had been taken by Lance-Corporal Robert Taylor. Captain Upcher, who had been brought back from the supernumerary list, arrived in Cape Town on 24 July aboard the troopship *Orontes* with a draft of sixty-eight men for the 1/24th. The *Orontes* also brought the 88th Regiment (Connaught Rangers) to Cape Town. Its arrival had freed the 1st Battalion for duty on the Eastern Frontier. On Friday 3 August, the 1/24th sailed for East London.

The town of East London was an untidy sprawl of unkempt buildings on the mouth of the Buffalo River. Thirty years after its founding it it still looked like a misconceived afterthought. But there was a railway-station, and the forty miles of track to King William's Town had been open for two months. Four days from the Castle in Cape Town to the Military Reserve in 'King' was a new record, and, according to military commentators, border defence had been transformed by the miracle of steam transportation.

The capital town of British Kaffraria had a business-like air, and though a trifle bare, was a much pleasanter place than East London. There was even a public park where Burck and his musicians could earn their keep by giving Sunday afternoon concerts. The townspeople, who usually went to bed after sunset, kept a stern eye on the behaviour of the troops in the

Military Reserve. Colonel Glyn was warned that his biggest problem on the frontier would be the management of his bored soldiers and that he must under no circumstances permit them to molest coloured girls in the streets.

King William's Town was spawned in a trouble era. It started off as a fortified post on the Buffalo river during the frontier war of 1835. It was abandoned shortly after the war on a Colonial Office directive, and re-occupied ten years later when the next frontier war broke out. Within three years the fledgeling town became a place of refuge in yet another frontier war. The importance of its situation was dramatically emphasised, and building continued at an accelerated pace throughout the war and into the years of the uneasy peace that followed. In 1866, when British Kaffraria was incorporated into the Cape Colony, King William's Town became the third largest town in the Eastern Province. When the 1/24th took over garrison duty the frontier had known peace for twenty-five years; but the Military Reserve, which occupied a large tract of land on the east bank of the Buffalo River, bore testimony to the importance that had been attached to King William's Town in border defence. The buildings in the Reserve were of white-washed brick or stone, had thatched roofs and were solidly built. The whole establishment with its neat, no-nonsense appearance, had the air of a sturdy, frontier outpost.

The men of the 1st Battalion expected their stay in 'King' to last about six months. It was known that the General had suggested to the War Office that the next battalion in South Africa to be relieved should be either the 1/24th or the 1/13th. Major Pulleine, who had spent the previous year in King William's Town, felt very much at home there. He was popular with the settler community and had been missed for his affable manner and skilful whist playing. The local newspapers had welcomed his return to the frontier. Like the rest of the battalion he too looked forward to a relaxed interlude in pleasant rural surroundings before returning home. But less than two weeks after the arrival of the 1/24th, 'King' was again restless with rumours of war.

The trouble began when the Gcaleka Xhosas in the Transkei turned their aggressive attention on their Mfengu neighbours. It surprised no one that a people like the Gcalekas, who had always rejected the benefits of white guidance, should become envious of the more industrious Mfengu who, for forty years, had cooperated with the Colony. Some of the settlers conceded that the Mfengu were inclined to taunt their former masters (the Gcalekas) with their more affluent way of life, and would have preferred it if Mfengu arrogance had not been displayed under an expectation of colonial protection. They feared that if the Colony became involved on the side of the Mfengu the Gcalekas would appeal for help to their Ngqika relatives who were settled uncomfortably close to King William's Town in uneasy subservience.

In the Transkei the coastline was held by independent tribes. The Gcaleka division of the Xhosa nation occupied a narrow strip between the Kei and the Bashee rivers; the Mpondo nation held sway between the Mtata and Mtamvuna rivers and the Bomvanas, wedged between Mpondoland and Gcalekaland, owed allegiance to the latter. On the inland borders of the independent coastal nations were a number of tribes linked to the Cape Colony by treaties, and consequently more amenable to the will of the colonial Parliament. Tribal quarrels, however, were frequent, and the danger of colonial military involvement was ever present. It was an unsatisfactory arrangement that largely owed its existence to the arrested development of Sir George Grey's policy.

In 1852, at the conclusion of the hard-fought Eighth Frontier War General George Cathcart resolved to punish the vanquished tribes by dispossessing them of their traditional lands. To eliminate future strife he wanted the Ngqika Xhosas out of their mountain fastnesses in the Amatholes. The highland where the Ngqika chief, Sandile, had grown up, was proclaimed a reserve and parcelled out to loyal Mfengu clans. The Ngqikas were relocated on a poorly defensible plain between the Amatholes and the Kei River. The Thembus, who had allied themselves with Sandile in the war, were forced across the Kei and their territory was given over to white settlement. It became the District of Queenstown. Cathcart's arrangement crowded the banks of the Kei River with resentful tribes and produced territorial pressure in the Transkei. At this point he was succeeded as governor of the Cape Colony by Sir George Grey.

Grey's solution to the perennial border wars was integration of the races. The blacks, he was confident, would emancipate themselves by working for the Europeans and living amongst them. His first task, as he saw it, was to destroy the tribal system by breaking the power of the chiefs and witchdoctors. To compete with the tribal physicians he built a modern hospital for blacks in King William's Town. To ruin the chiefs and disrupt the tribal strongholds in the Transkei he would bring in settlers. But he could not change the *status quo* in independent Transkei without risking another war. Grey, however, was not a military governor, and conquest was not his way. The solution to his dilemma was supplied by the witchdoctors he despised.

After eight futile wars that had yielded nothing more than a progressive loss of territory and an erosion of their national pride, a great spiritual depression overcame the Xhosa people. Born of this despondency was a longing for metaphysical intervention. Sarhili, the Xhosa Paramount Chief, who had been denounced by some of his people as ineffectual, longed to lift the curse that had fallen upon his nation. He turned to Mhlakaza, the chief prophet of the Gcalekas, for guidance.

Mhlakaza employed Nongqawuse, his young niece, as a medium, and from her visions he made a series of revelations. The details varied but the theme remained unchanged. Help from the spirit world would be forthcoming, but only after great sacrifice had been made by the living. On a certain day in March 1856, Nongqawuse saw a vision in a pool of water that startled Mhlakaza with its importance and Gcalekaland with his interpretation of it. The great leaders of the past would return from the spirit world, assume the bodies of living men and lead the nation to victory over the white invaders. A golden age would dawn and Kaffraria would once more become an unspoilt haven of sweet grass and fat cattle. The game herds would return and the amaXhosa would hold dominion over all. But before the Xhosa messiahs returned to proclaim the millenium, the people would have to rid themselves of their wealth. They were to slaughter all their livestock (dogs and horses were exempt) and destroy their grain stores. The ripening crops were to be buried and the fields left untilled. The commitment to victory was to be total and irrevocable. Sarhili glimpsed in Nongqawuse's prophecy the inspiration for a great crusade, one that would unite his people in suffering and generate resolution out of desperation. He ordered the killing of all Xhosa cattle. The hesitant were intimidated and the scoffers were 'eaten-up'.*

Where Europeans' influence was weakest, obedience to the directives of the prophecy was strongest. The time taken by the Xhosa people to discharge the conditions prescribed by Mhlakaza was prolonged by their natural reluctance to comply with the irrational; and when the great day finally dawned there were no celestial omens, no heroic armies of inspired warriors – all there was, was a cachectic nation struggling to find, with

*A witch-hunt in which the possessions and sometimes the life of the victim were forfeited to the chief.

THE EASTERN FRONTIER

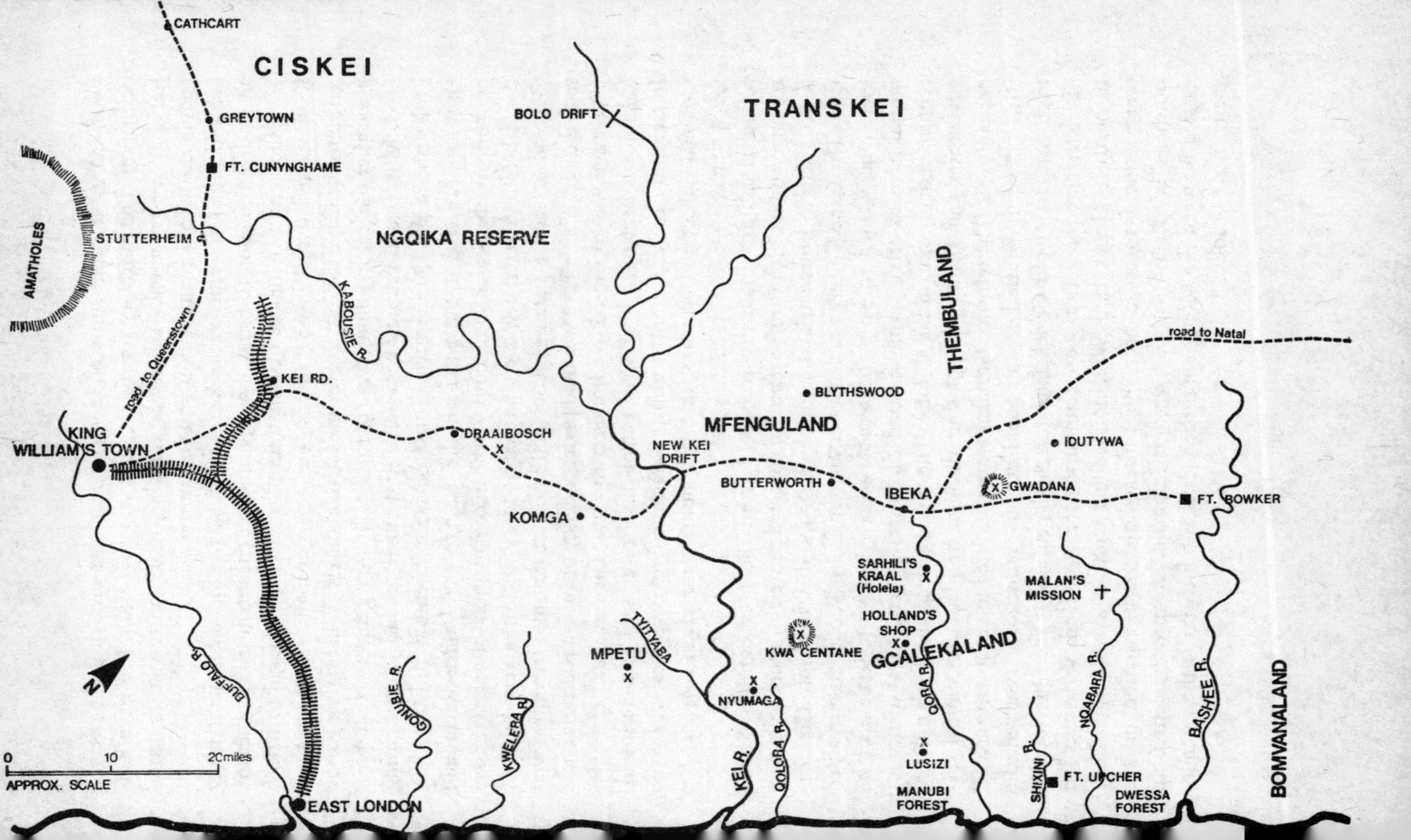

what energy it could summon, something to eat in a drought-ravaged desolation. The mortality from starvation was staggering. In British Kaffraria, where emergency relief was available, nearly forty-two thousand people died from malnutrition and its complications.

Sir George Grey entered the Xhosa wasteland with aid for the starving and a determination to bring about permanent change in tribal structure. Two thousand five hundred German immigrants were brought to British Kaffraria and settled in new towns. Ten times as many tribesmen were sent into the Cape Colony to become farm labourers. What fighting took place after the 'cattle-killing' was confined to hungry gangs over scraps of food. Murder and robbery became daily occurrences and when fighting broke out in the Queenstown district between Thembus and Gcalekas, Grey's police chased the latter all the way to the Bashee River and beyond. With Gcalekaland empty, the reorganisation of the Transkei could begin. A reserve was established at Idutywa, in the very heart of Gcalekaland, and a heterogeneous collection of destitute tribesmen was settled there. The reserve was made a dependency of British Kaffraria and a magistrate was appointed to administer the law. The remainder of Gcalekaland was kept open by FAMP patrols until more settlers were found. In the midst of his reconstruction programme Grey was recalled by the Colonial Office; and his plans for the Transkei were left in abeyance for seven years.

The amaXhosa gradually recovered from the great famine. Sarhili regained some of his former prestige, attracted more and more followers to his kraals in Bomvanaland, and they began to drift back into Gcalekaland. The Cape Colony's new Governor, Sir Philip Wodehouse, realised that if he wanted to keep the territory open for white settlement he would have to drive Sarhili beyond the Mtata River. It was a time of economic depression in the Colony. The mood was against fresh military adventures and Britain was passing through its phase of colonial disenchantment. The returned Gcalekas were permitted to occupy the coastal strip between the Bashee and the Kei, but Wodehouse reserved the northern part of old Gcalekaland for the Thembus of the Queenstown district where the settlers were clamouring for more land. What was left of northern Gcalekaland Wodehouse filled with 40 000 Mfengu. They were induced to settle near the Butterworth mission station on the northern border of Sarhili's vestigial domain. A special relationship existed between the Mfengu and the Gcalekas which made the arrangement an act of folly.

At the time of the *Mfecane* – the holocaust triggered off in Natal by the wars that established King Shaka's supremacy – many refugees found their way into the Transkei. Common misery brought them together in a new tribal grouping that came to be called Mfengu (the wanderers). The Gcaleka chief, Hintsa, Sarhili's father, offered them a home; but in exchange for his protection the Mfengu were expected to serve the ama-Xhosa. When the colonial forces invaded the Transkei in the war o 1835, the Mfengu appealed to the whites to rescue them from their 'protectors'. Some 16 000 were escorted out of the Transkei and settled in the Fort Peddie district. They brought out 30 000 cattle which their Xhosa masters had left in their charge – an act the Gcalekas found impossible to forgive. The Mfengu were an industrious people. Delivered from bondage they worked hard and prospered. In two subsequent frontier wars they remained loyal to the Colony and gained recognition as useful auxiliaries. In temperament the Mfengu differed greatly from the Gcalekas. They were described as calculating, acquisitive and cold-blooded, while the Gcalekas were considered careless, quick-tempered and proud. These two tribes had little in common except old scores. When Wodehouse moved the Mfengu into the Transkei, Sarhili warned him that placing Hintsa's former servants on his border and allocating to them traditional Gcaleka land, could have consequences he might not be able to control. The Mfengu understood the realities of their situation only too well, and demanded colonial protection as a condition for their relocation – Wodehouse acceded to the condition.

Many tribes occupying a territory with ill-defined borders and a scarcity of grazing, particularly in years of drought, made the Transkei unstable and a threat to the peace on the Colony's eastern frontier. Old grudges and rivalries between chiefs added to the Transkeian ferment. No matter how much the Cape Colony wanted to disassociate itself from 'Kaffirland' politics, it was repeatedly called upon to keep the peace, and within the past decade it had been compelled to extend its protection to half the tribes in the territory. Under pressure from Frere, Molteno had announced, in the parliamentary session just ended, that he was willing to annex Mfenguland, the Idutywa Reserve, Thembuland and Griqualand East. The independent Gcalekas, Bomvanas and Mpondos would soon be the only obstacles to a common border between the Cape Colony and Natal. But even before Parliament rose there were indications that the

Gcalekas might themselves soon provide the excuses necessary for relieving them of their independence. Maki, Sarhili's chief counsellor and a man of peace, had fled to Idutywa after being denounced as a sorcerer. His place had been taken by Ngubo, the commander of the Gcaleka army, a man known for his hostility to whites. Reports from Colonel Eustace, the Gcaleka Resident, had stressed that Gcalekaland was becoming too small for its people. The Gcaleka army had grown to 12 000 warriors, and Sigcau, Sarhili's son, was reported to be attracting an expansionist party to him.

A brawl at a marriage feast in the kraal of a Mfengu headman named Ngcayichibi provided the spark that was to kindle the Ninth Frontier War. The kraal was situated near the Gcina River which formed part of the boundary between Mfenguland and Gcalekaland. Two minor chieftains belonging to the clan of Mapasa, a cousin of Sarhili, crossed the river to join the festivities at Ngcayichibi's kraal. The visitors, having come a long way, were reluctant to depart at the end of the day, and demanded more beer. A misunderstanding, in which the proprieties due to a Gcaleka headman were ignored, resulted in a fight. The numerically superior Mfengu drove their Gcaleka guests back across the river. Both notables sustained injuries from which one of them later died. The following morning kinsmen of the aggrieved Gcalekas gathered on the river bank to shout threats and fire a few shots in the direction of Ngcayichibi's kraal. Honour, however, was not satisfied by the demonstration. A few days later some of Mapasa's young men attacked the offending kraal and burnt it to the ground. A neighbouring kraal was put to the torch for emphasis, and compensation was exacted by driving off Mfengu cattle. James Ayliff, the resident magistrate in Mfenguland, asked Colonel Eustace to persuade Sarhili to use his influence in getting the stolen Mfengu cattle returned. But Sarhili denied all knowledge of the raids and claimed not to have any influence over Mapasa or his followers. Bad feelings had existed between Sarhili and his cousin Mapasa since the last Gcaleka-Thembu disturbance. Mapasa, at that time, had urged him to fight the Thembus, but had backed out of the war when hostilities began.

By the end of August, the wedding fracas and its aftermath was beginning to attract the attentions of the frontier settlers. Some blamed the Mfengu, but most thought the Gcalekas at fault. All wanted justice to be administered vigorously. The most popular refrain advocated punishment for those who had taken up arms against the 'Children of the Queen' (Mfengu). Some suggested that the disturbances be used as a lever to move

Sarhili into the Queen's 'kindergarten'. The *Mercury* found affairs in the Transkei ominous, and commented, 'rain is badly wanted all over Kaffraria. Food is scarce and dear . . .' Drought had accentuated the country's problems once again.

The raids and counter-raids continued even while Colonel Eustace and Mr Ayliff held their inquiry into the Ngcayichibi affair. Traders and outlying farmers began sending their families into the Colony and a detachment of the FAMP was ordered to set up camp near Butterworth. Colonel Glyn, in command of the largest and best-organised force on the frontier, was fettered by instructions from Molteno which prohibited the Commandant of Police, the Civil Commissioner, or any other colonial officer from communicating directly with the Imperial Command on the frontier. All exchange between the two authorities had to be done through the Ministry in Cape Town. Deprived of official information, and forced to make assessments from newspaper articles, rumours and gossip, Glyn decided to send his own observer to the Transkei. On 28 August, Teignmouth Melvill left King William's Town for the trouble-zone.

He found Komga filled with refugees from the Transkei and in a state of tension. At New Kei Drift, all work had been suspended on the first bridge over the river. The labourers had deserted and the overseers were mounting guard over the uncompleted span. In Butterworth he met up with Inspector Chalmers of the FAMP and accompanied him to Ibeka, a small trading post near the source of the Qora River. There he had his first sight of a Xhosa fighting force. On the slope of a nearby hill, their clay-smeared bodies and blankets red against the bleached grass of the hillside, stood a Gcaleka force of over two thousand men. Never before, he learnt, had so many Xhosa warriors carried firearms. The warriors had entered Mfenguland to sack the kraal of Veldman Bikitsha, a senior Mfengu chief who lived in a European-styled house near Butterworth. But Chalmers had persuaded them to retire to their own territory. Their withdrawal was finally effected by the personal intervention of Sarhili.

On his return journey, Melvill thought he detected unusual activity amongst the tribesmen near New Kei Drift. At about the same time in the Idutywa Reserve, young Mrs Prichard, the recently arrived wife of a supervisor in the company that was erecting the telegraph line in the Transkei, noticed a new attitude in the blacks: 'all was changed; the men swaggered past me with a most insolent air; after brushing my dress carelessly with their assegaais, for all were armed to the teeth, and displayed their weapons as much as possible. From what he had seen and heard, Melvill concluded that affairs in the Transkei were highly critical, that Sarhili was still master of his people, and that not the slightest attempt had been made to organise defences for the protection of the whites in the territory. The day after his return to King William's Town Melvill was asked to present his report to Sir Bartle Frere in person.

10

Frontier War

The parliamentary session that had kept Frere in Cape Town until the end of August had brought him little satisfaction. The only interesting development had been the emergence of John Gordon Sprigg as leader of what could be termed an opposition party. The Defence Commission, of which he was chairman, had produced a report that was startling in its urgency. The recommendations had included an enlarged mounted police force, a trained burgher reserve and a greatly increased expenditure on defence. Molteno had dismissed the Commissioner's report about the situation on the frontier as a gross exaggeration and had made it known that he would not hold himself bound by its findings. It was the extent of the support Sprigg received in Parliament that had surprised the Ministry. One Western Province editor had suggested that Sprigg 'would make a very efficient Prime Minister'. The emergence of a possible alternative to Molteno had been for Frere the only cheerful item in a thoroughly disappointing session.

As soon as he was free to leave Cape Town, Frere set off on his planned visit to the Eastern Province. His spirits were elevated the moment he set foot in Port Elizabeth and found himself among 'loyal colonists' who displayed an interest in confederation. It made a welcome contrast to the suspicion and obstruction he had experienced in the Colony's capital city. His guide and adviser was John Xavier Merriman who, as Minister for Crown Lands and Public Works, was about to undertake a tour of inspection of railroad and telegraph progress in the Eastern Province.

Merriman was the eldest son of the Bishop of Grahamstown, and the product of an unconventional and intellectual household. At the age of twenty-eight, almost for lack of anything better to do, he entered Parliament as the representative for the farming constituency of Aliwal North. Molteno recognised his intellectual qualities and great energy, and in 1875, at the age of thirty-four, Merriman became the youngest member in the Government. His talents as a politician, however, were marred by an undisguised intolerance of people who disagreed with him and impatience with those who could not keep up with his agile brain: defects that sometimes led to outbursts of temper, and what Frere was later to call a 'loss of discipline'.

The arrival of the gubernatorial party in King William's Town coincided with a public meeting called to protest the Government's dilatory attitude towards border defence. The meeting made it known that the settlers looked to the Governor to rectify their grievances. If Sir Bartle had any doubt that his presence was needed on the very confused frontier, the *Cape Mercury* spelt it out for him, '... if the Governor were to fly from one of the Eastern Province towns, or give the impression that unpublished information warned him of danger ... all the farmers in the country would *trek* into laager and the townspeople arm for war'. Publicly Frere stated that the difficulties with the blacks were overrated and not insuperable; but privately, he sent a message to the General asking him to cut short his visit to Griqualand West, and one to Charles Griffith requesting him to come and replace the ailing commandant of the FAMP. His own task, as he saw it, was to go to the Transkei and confer with the disputatious chieftains.

On 13 September, Frere left for the Transkei accompanied by Merriman, Charles Brownlee (the Colony's Secretary for Native Affairs), and Colonel Glyn. At Butterworth the party pitched tents and settled down to await the arrival of the Transkeian notables. The Thembu chief, Ngangelizwe, and the Mfengu headman, Veldman Bikitsha, answered his summons, but Sarhili merely sent a message saying that he was too weak to make the ten-mile journey. Colonel Eustace attributed Sarhili's reluctance to a fear of being taken hostage – a fate which had befallen his father in 1835.

To try and allay Sarhili's fears, Frere sent Brownlee to arrange a meeting, but the chief refused to see him. Sarhili was determined to avoid a meeting at which promises and guarantees he might not be able to enforce would be extracted from him. Since the last frontier war a generation had grown to manhood that had never known defeat at the hands of the *abelungu*. The young men of his tribe, whose war experience was confined to successful forays against Ngangelizwe's Thembus, were spoiling for a fight, and Sarhili felt that in their present mood, war with the Mfengu was unavoidable. He hoped that after one or two battles colonial officials would step in, and as happened during the fighting with the Thembu, arrange a truce. Sarhili's reckoning, however, failed to take into account the will and the purpose of the new High Commissioner.

Frere felt insulted that a native chief should be so suspicious of the good faith of a British High Commissioner as not to trust himself in his camp. He attributed Sarhili's behaviour to an arrogance fostered by the Ministry's ambivalent attitude towards the Transkei. Colonel Eustace was told to issue a general warning to Sarhili and to declare him responsible for all transgressions into Mfengu territory. The High Commissioner had made up his mind; Gcaleka independence was an anachronism that had no place in his future plans for the Transkei. As soon as he reached King William's Town, he appointed Griffith Commandant of the FAMP and told him to hasten to the Transkei. Colonel Glyn was freed from his position of impotence and placed in command of the Colony's eastern districts. On 25 September, a special notice was published which listed the FAMP posts where refuge could be taken. An 'Indian style' authority was starting to operate on the frontier.

The first clash between the Gcalekas and colonial forces occurred on the following day. Chief Sitshaka, while on the way to Sarhili's kraal, where the clans had been summoned to discuss the fast developing crisis, passed a small Mfengu kraal in a valley to the west of Gwadana Hill. His followers could not resist the temptation to sack it. Inspector Chalmers, who had been informed earlier that morning that a large Gcaleka force had moved into the Idutywa Reserve, was attracted to the scene by the smoke from the burning huts. James Ayliff with about a thousand Mfengu levies was also in the vicinity. Chalmers told him that Griffith had given instructions to the police to fire on any Xhosas who were found threatening loyal tribesmen; after a brief consultation, they decided to take up a position on Gwadana in preparation for an attack on Sitshaka's men. But when they reached the summit they found the Gcalekas waiting for them on the opposite slope of the hill. A quick glance told Chalmers that his force was greatly outnumbered. The poorly-armed levies were of doubtful value in what might turn out to be a defensive action, but he hoped that superior fire-power of the police would tilt the balance in his favour. Without further consideration he ordered Sub-Inspector Cochrane to commence firing into the concentration below with the 7-pounder his men had dragged up the hill. The first few shells caused consternation in the Gcaleka ranks, but after ten rounds had been fired, the gun-carriage, a locally made substitute for the one that lay under the sea in the *Windsor Castle*, collapsed. As soon as the shelling stopped the Gcalekas began a rapid advance in three tight formations. The police carbines kept them in check for a while, but the mood on top of Gwadana changed when Cochrane and his escort began to retire the disabled gun. The Mfengut who had enjoyed the havoc caused by the exploding shells, were completely disheartened by the withdrawal of the artillery piece, and when he, Gcalekas made a determined effort to occupy a thicket on their left, brok- and fled. The police, with barely enough men to hold the right and centre of the line on top of the hill, could do nothing about the exposed flank. The confusion created by Ayliff's levies rushing in all directions, stampeded the horses. Panic overcame the inexperienced troopers and most of them abandoned their positions to chase after their mounts. A sub-inspector and six police troopers were killed by Gcalekas in the chaotic retreat.

The inglorious outcome of the first battle of the Ninth Frontier War sent waves of panic through the border districts. The disastrous beginnings of past frontier wars were recalled. 'Blunder at the outset, – and this conflagration will be fanned, and sweep over hill and dale. Let the long delay in 1834, – the innocent walk into ambush which cost the whole baggage train of the Dragoon Guards in 1847, and the Boma Pass business in 1851, tell the consequences of failing in the first blow'. But Sarhili, who remembered the outcome of those wars, sent his son under a flag of truce to FAMP headquarters at Ibeka to apologise for the death of the troopers, offer oxen in compensation and reiterate that the Gcaleka quarrel was only with the Mfengu. Captain Robinson, a 'peppery man' in command of the police artillery, rebuffed the emissaries and threatened them with dire consequences for Gwadana.

After Chalmers's setback, Griffith decided to concentrate his forces at Ibeka and abandon the Idutywa Reserve. The tiny community of traders and government officials was advised to move to the fortified mission station at Blythswood. Among the refugees was the inimitable Mrs Prichard. She described the flight from Idutywa with dramatic gusto: '... we were driving for our lives: – it was a race with the Foe, and the prize was life'. The only white family at Ibeka was also evacuated. Their brick trading-store was made the nucleus of a fortification. A three-foot-deep ditch was dug around the property and earthworks were thrown up. Three bastions, reinforced by sandbags, were constructed to house Griffith's artillery. Inside the fort he placed one hundred and twenty police troopers and two thousand Mfengu under Veldman Bikitsha. The Ibeka trading station was situated near the junction of several ridges from which the Qora River took origin. It commanded open country which afforded little natural cover for an attacking army. The only ground that overlooked the fortifications was a low eminence eight hundred yards to the left. On Saturday 29 September, at about eight o'clock in the morning, a rider from an outlying vedette galloped in with the news that a large army was approaching from the south.

Their success on Gwadana had filled the Gcaleka war-party with a determination to drive the Mfengu and their white protectors out of their lost lands. The mood was contagious and the ministrations of their war-doctor promised invulnerability. Even the cautious Sarhili caught the fever. A woman diviner had promised victory if they fought the white man with his weapons in traditional Xhosa formation. A densely packed central body with flying columns on the wings and a strong reserve of veterans was the formation they had employed successfully against other tribes, but had abandoned as too costly against the white man with his cannons and muskets. Now, in possession of more guns than ever before, they prepared to fight as in days of old.

The Gcaleka army halted less than two miles from Ibeka. The time had arrived for the Paramount Chief to give the *ukuyolela*, the official command to fight the enemy. The confidence that had brought Sarhili this far, suddenly deserted him. He could not bring himself to give the signal that he must have felt would lead to the downfall of the Gcaleka people. It was his general, Ngubo, who gave the shout. His son Sigcau, took command of the royal clans, and one of the largest Gcaleka armies ever mustered began to advance on the earthworks at Ibeka.

Within the fortifications Griffith was ready and waiting. The horses, bridled and saddled, stood tethered to a rope strung between two blue-gum trees; barrels filled with water and open ammunition-boxes had been placed in convenient positions. The FAMP and a contingent of Mfengu under Veldman covered the centre and the more vulnerable left side of the defences; Inspector Allan Maclean with the remainder of the Mfengu protected the right.

The attack began with the Gcaleka horsemen attempting a charge up the stony ridge to the left of the fort. Captain Robinson's artillery opened on them with an accuracy that quickly forced them to dismount and seek whatever protection they could find. The concentrated fire of his three 7-pounders and two rocket-tubes was then directed at the advancing infantry columns. The carnage on the open southern slope was frightful. Under the exhortations of a wildly prancing female diviner the warriors tried to close the large gaps that appeared in their ranks. They managed a short advance, then broke into skirmishing lines. A desperate charge to get ahead of the bursting shells brought them within range of the Sniders. The Gcalekas encountered a rate of fire that even the veteran *amatwala ndwe* (wearers of blue crane feathers) had never experienced. The concentrated volleys from rifles that could be loaded at the breech and fired from the prone position were to be decisive in the last of the frontier wars. Whatever advantage the Xhosas thought they had secured by building up an arsenal of Kimberley muzzle-loaders, had been nullified by the breech-loader.

The Gcalekas attacked again and again, but the defences held. Each wave was thrown back with heavy losses. Gradually they began to resort to sniping from behind bushes and stones, but their markmanship was woefully inaccurate. At about five o'clock, Ngubo regrouped his army for the final charge. Led by their amazon witch-doctor they threw themselves once more at the fortifications. The attack brought them right on to the muzzles of the guns: 'We poured shells, case rockets and Snider bullets into them', and they fell back, leaving their prophetess dead in the grass. It was the turn of the Mfengu. The smell of victory was in their nostrils and they fell upon the retreating Gcalekas with a fury, killing stragglers and wounded alike. The field in front of Ibeka was covered with hundreds of bodies, and where the Mfengu passed, none rose again.

With the coming of darkness it began to rain. The defenders, exhausted and hungry, settled down to a sleepness night under arms. The wet evening turned into a bitterly cold night, but the order to stand down was not given. Daylight revealed Gcaleka skirmishing parties once more on the ridge to the left of the fort; but this time there was no reckless charge, only a cautious darting from rock to rock. Griffith let Veldman take his men out under a covering fire. Suddenly, a heavy mist came up and hid the ridge from view. When it cleared under the warm mid-morning sun, not a single live Gcaleka was to be seen. The battle of Ibeka was over. It had cost the defenders six Mfengu killed and a like number wounded. The grisly trophy that went to the victors, was the white-painted head of the prophetess. A British officer who had been attached to Griffith as an observer, wrote that the defence of Ibeka had 'arrested the tide of invasion, and afforded the Colony time to collect its forces for the struggle'. The Gcalekas, in reality, had shot their bolt and were ready to make peace. But the High Commissioner's thoughts were on a Gcalekaland cleared for white settlement in preparation for inclusion in a greater South Africa.

Frere lost no time setting up a war council. It consisted of himself, Cunynghame and the two Cabinet Ministers at hand. Merriman assumed the unofficial title of 'Minister of War', but the driving force in council was the Governor. He used his prestige, and when necessary, his authority, to make the two colonial members of the Council look to him rather than Cape Town for guidance. Daily meetings were held, and decisions were taken in consultation with the Military. Frere, nevertheless, had to exert considerable pressure on Merriman before he agreed to Cunynghame's appointment to the command of all the forces. Tacit in Merriman's consent was an understanding that Cunynghame would confine his authority to military matters in the Ciskei and leave Griffith in unfettered control of operations in the Transkei. Frere wrote to Carnarvon that the Ministers were 'aghast at such innovations as a daily council at which the General would sit as Commandant of the Forces'.

Frere's experiences during the Indian Mutiny had left him with a mistrust for civilian volunteer organisations. Motivated by revenge, they had committed enough atrocities to have made him wonder on whose side the barbarians were fighting. His preference was for the disciplined, professional soldier with few vested interests beyond his own welfare and promotion. Molteno's feelings about the Queen's soldiers were based on his personal experiences in the frontier war of 1846. He considered them too costly for the Colony to support, and too slow for the fast-moving Xhosa. Burgher volunteers preferred to thrash the Kaffir as quickly as possible, carry off as many of his cattle as they could in compensation for their tribulation and return to their farms with the booty. There was a great deal of truth in Molteno's strongly-held opinions. Burgher commandos were much more mobile, required little in the way of supplies and had seldom been caught unawares by their wily foe. Thirty years had passed since Molteno did his stint of active service, and the Military, however slow to learn, had accumulated a considerable amount of bush-fighting experience in the two subsequent frontier wars. Colonial forces excelled in quick, offensive actions, but the tedious wearing down of the enemy, that ultimately ended the wars, invariably fell to Her Majesty's plodding battalions. What Molteno, as Premier, disliked most about the prospect of employing regulars, was the financial contribution the Colony had to make to their upkeep. The annual, average cost of maintaining an imperial infantryman in South Africa, wages, rations, uniforms and barrack accommodation included, was about £80.

The War Council went ahead with the appointment of regional commandants without reference to governmental preference. Griffith was given the temporary rank of a colonel in Her Majesty's Army to exercise in the Transkei; but Colonel Glyn was made commander of all the forces in the Ciskei. It was agreed that the 1st Battalion would supply instructors, train volunteers, and leave the fighting in the Transkei to the colonists. Supervision of volunteer training was entrusted to Henry Pulleine, the most popular army officer with the civilian population. Next, the War Council took a hard look at the forces available for the defence of the Colony.

The only permanent unit the Colony possessed was the para-military Frontier Armed and Mounted Police. It had come into existence after the last frontier war as the successor to the Imperial Cape Mounted Rifles – a mixed force of whites and coloureds, which had been disbanded after some of its coloured members defected to the Xhosas. The FAMP, as a result, accepted only white recruits. In its early years, the ranks had been filled with men drawn from among the settlers' sons. They could ride hard, shoot straight, and what they lacked in discipline was compensated for by their knowledge of bush-craft. The force did useful work in maintaining the peace during the unsettled months of the great 'cattle-killing'. In the more ordered years that followed, many of the experienced men left the force to become farmers, and colonial recruitment almost dried up. To maintain the all-white composition of the FAMP the Cape Government had resorted to recruiting in Britain. It attracted inexperienced youngsters in search of adventure, boys who found the three-year contract and the four shillings and sixpence a day more attractive than twelve years and a shilling a day in the regular army. Disillusionment came early to the young trooper. After deductions for his rations and fodder for his horse, he was, financially, little better off than the regular soldier. The Western Province-dominated government regarded him as an irksome expenditure, and economised on his accommodation and equipment. Very few of the better men stayed longer than the contracted time; discipline, as a result, fell into the hands of incompetent bullies who had neither the ambition nor the ability to make a life for themselves outside the force. The FAMP lacked discipline, officers of calibre, and training. Its morale, low before the start of hostilities, had suffered a serious blow on Gwadana.

Both Frere and Cunynghame thought the troopers fine young men whose capabilities had been squandered by a disinterested government. They found the equipment of the men in poor condition and commissariat arrangements non-existent. Even Merriman had to agree that the force was untrained and unreliable. When fighting broke out, its 1 100 men were scattered in small detachments, throughout British Kaffraria and the Transkei.

The volunteer detachments were an unknown quantity. A great deal of patriotic fervour had been roused by the defeat on Gwadana, but the numbers that came forward to volunteer were disappointingly small. The law for the enrolment of burghers was obsolete and cumbersome in emergencies. It allowed men serving away from their own district to return home whenever it suited them. The colonial mode of life encouraged the giving of orders rather than obeying them, and the independent outlook of the colonists did not allow them to act readily in conjunction with others. It was thanks to Cunynghame's foresight and obstinancy that there were three thousand Snider-Enfields available for the arming of the volunteers. When the imperial troops in South Africa were issued with the Martini-Henry, Cunynghame had advised the Ministry to buy the superseded Sniders. His offer had been turned down; but he had kept the rifles in the Colony instead of sending them back to Britain as the War Office required.

The best trained, most dependable force on the frontier was the 1/24th. But a battalion of eight hundred men fell far short of the fifteen-thousand soldiers that had had to be called out before the previous Xhosa war was won. Cunynghame was unwilling to withdraw troops from either Natal or the Transvaal. Sekhukhune, Cetshwayo and the Boers were sufficient reasons for not depleting those distant garrisons. Reinforcements would have to come from Cape Town. On 28 September, two hundred men of the 88th were embarked on H.M.S. *Active*. The General was disturbed by his lack of cavalry, and with Carrington and Browne escorting Shepstone around his new domain, the 1st Battalion was asked to supply yet another mounted detachment for special duties. Lieutenant Ralph Clements was made responsible for its organisation.

The immediate decision that faced the War Council was how best to utilise the available forces. The General would have preferred to send his regulars into the Transkei, but the Government insisted that the war was a colonial matter which it intended to conclude as quickly as possible with minimal interference from the Queen's representatives. Accordingly, all FAMP and volunteer detachments in British Kaffraria were ordered to join Griffith at Ibeka. Cunynghame was prevailed upon to guard the supply route to the Transkei. He was against using 'red coats' in small, isolated detachments, but was persuaded that the sight of their uniforms would act as a deterrent to the uncommitted tribes within the Colony's borders.

The troops in King William's Town were placed under the command of Henry Pulleine, whose duties included the creation of a 'Home Guard' of clerks and salesmen for the defence of the capital. The sounds of sleepy 'King' were becoming increasingly martial. The noise of marching feet, cantering horses and yelled commands constantly filled the air; Burck and his band played stirring music at daily concerts; and a regular stream of messengers moved between the Military Reserve and the new telegraph office which was kept open day and night. The crowded bars kept similar hours. The patriotic pastime was to 'liquor up' before disappearing into the wilds of 'Kaffirland'; and the volunteers, in uniforms of every description and colour, were doing their patriotic best. The merchants of 'King' found a ready market for revolvers, blankets and saddles, and prices rose to meet the demand. The town acquired a suburb of tents and wagons on its outskirts because the farmers near the Ngqika location feared an irruption of Sandile's warriors and brought their families there for safety.

The War Council could not ignore the widely held belief that the Gcaleka uprising was part of a Xhosa plan to reconquer the border districts. Sarhili, it was popularly believed, intended drawing the Colony's forces across the Kei so that Sandile could fall upon the unprotected settlements in British Kaffraria. The tall, once-handsome chief with the withered left leg, was more feared and more distrusted than all the other Xhosa leaders. But it was circumstances, rather than blood-thirsty ambition, that had made this unusual leader of the Ngqikas the *bête noire* of the border.

Sandile was eight years old when his father, Ngqika, died. Too young to rule, he was made the ward of a regency council consisting of his mother and his half-brothers. His eldest brother, Maqoma, was already a warrior of repute, and in his heroic shadow the young heir had to prepare for his future role as a head of the House of Rarabe. Sandile's insecurity was aggravated by an illness that had left him with a wasted leg. In 1835, the crippled boy had to watch Maqoma gain fame as a general in one of the most bitter wars against the white man. But even while Maqoma was enhancing his reputation, Sutu, Sandile's percipient mother, impressed upon her son the importance of retaining some of the enemy's goodwill in case of deafeat – a lesson that was to make Sandile a survivor when more dazzling leaders perished.

At nineteen, Sandile became the Chief of the Rarabes. On horseback he looked an impressive leader but walking and running turned him into a caricature of a warrior chief. Chance, more than military ambition decided that the tribes under his authority should become the principal antagonists of the settlers in the next two border wars. The Seventh and Eighth Frontier Wars outstripped all the previous ones in ferocity, and Sandile's name became synonymous with border strife. In both wars Sandile had found himself torn between counsellors who advocated peace with the white man at all costs and warriors who sought to make him the rallying figure for war. His inclination had been to imitate Maqoma, but instinct had told him that survival depended on good relations with the white man. This conflict had made him indecisive and unpredictable, and he acquired a reputation as a cunning and treacherous opponent.

After the Eighth Frontier War, Sandile had to suffer the humiliation of seeing his people moved from their Amathole home to a reservation. The Ngqikas were made British subjects and a white supervisor was attached to his kraal. In the ensuing years mission stations were established in the Ngqika reservation and traders moved in. With the traders came canteens, '... we poured brandy into Gaikaland and succeeded in making Sandile a drunkard', wrote Charles Brownlee's wife. Humiliation and despair helped him succumb to the weakness that had ruined his father and his half-brother, Maqoma. The year before, a member of the Cape Parliament had remarked, 'Sandile when sober always expressed himself for peace', to which someone replied, 'as the gentleman in question is nearly always drunk, I do not think this particularly good news'. Such was the man Frere sought out once war in the Transkei became inevitable.

Sandile received the Governor sitting down with a large kaross draped around his waist to hide his crippled limb. He was deliberately vague and evasive in his replies. The obtuse display might have been mistaken for inebriation, but Brownlee, who accompanied Frere, had seen it practised on other Governors and their emissaries, and warned him not to underestimate the Chief. Sandile countered Frere's questions about his commitment to Sarhili with complaints about his poor health. He admitted to some dissatisfaction amongst his people but attributed it to the poor wages they received from the railway contractors. His feelings about the Gcaleka war he kept to himself. In the end, Frere had to be content with an oblique warning that the soldiers in Fort Cunynghame and Komga were there to take care of 'all people who behaved themselves'. He left with the impression that the Ngqikas had lost less of their independent spirit than their neighbours, that they were united and self assured, and that civilising influences in the Colony had not made much impact on them. Frere felt that the 'old fox' would have to be watched, but was confident that the war could be confined to the Transkei.

After his meeting with Sandile, Frere had to hurry back to King William's Town to intercede in a developing confrontation between Merriman and Cunynghame. No two men could have differed more in temperament and outlook than the impetuous, young 'Minister of War' and the cautious, tradition-moulded General, and they were incapable of cooperating without his moderating authority. They had come into collision over who should have control of the commissariat supplying Griffith's forces in the Transkei. Cunynghame believed that the colonists were too inexperienced to undertake so specialized a job and had offered the services of Major Strickland, his senior commissary officer. But Merriman had told him that regular army expertise was a luxury the Colony could ill afford. As it subsequently turned out, the inexperienced 'Minister of War' grossly underestimated the problems involved in supplying an army in the field with ammunition, food, clothing and fodder, and himself became the target of complaints and accusations. Added to the problems created by their incompatible personalities was the continuous stream of telegrams from Molteno warning Merriman against the General; in particular, warning him not to permit Cunynghame to build up large forces for a 'Kaffir War of the old type', nor sanction appeals to the War Office for reinforcements. Frere had to assure the suspicious Premier that all the General had asked for was the transfer of one artillery battery from St. Helena to South Africa.

John Gordon Sprigg was also in King William's Town, and conscious of his new-found status as an opposition leader, was contributing to the discord between colonial and imperial officialdom by pointing out at public meetings the incongruity of a policy which sent civilians to the front while professional soldiers were kept in safe posts. Sprigg was not very popular with the General and his officers, but in this matter they were in full agreement with him. His denouncements on the Ministry's unpreparedness were gaining him a strong following on the frontier, and people were saying that a general uprising of the tribes would vindicate his stand against the Government. His opponents accused him of wanting a war to fulfil his prophecies and bring down Molteno. As early as the first week in October, the *Eastern Star*, which supported Sprigg, urged Frere to rid himself of his ministerial advisers and pointed out that the

Colony's constitution gave him that power.

On 10 October, Merriman announced, on Frere's instructions, that Sarhili was deposed as chief, and that Griffith was empowered to arrange for the future administration of Gcalekaland as part of Her Majesty's possessions in South Africa. He also hinted at a future colonial commitment to settle whites in that territory. Molteno was furious that so important a proclamation had been issued without his approval and threatened to come to the frontier and deal with the imperial clique that was trying to usurp the role of his Government. The 1st Battalion had become a pawn in a disagreeable controversy that was beginning to divide the Colony and was putting the Government against the Military and the Governor. But despite all the bickering, the war had to be pursued. For the time being it would be conducted according to Molteno's specifications. The regulars were to stay in their 'safe' posts in the Ciskei while Griffith took the offensive with his army of civilians.

The fortified trading-post at Ibeka had become an assembly place for white volunteers and black levies. Ngangelizwe, who realised sooner than the colonists that Sarhili had lost his big gamble after the attack on Ibeka, brought his tribe into the war on the side of the Colony. Major Henry Elliot, a Crimean War veteran and recently appointed Chief Magistrate of Thembuland, took command of the Thembu forces. He promptly crossed the Bashee River and re-occupied Idutywa. Molteno had inundated Griffith with telegrams urging an immediate offensive to finish the war. To satisfy the Prime Minister he decided to make a quick punitive raid on Sarhili's kraal, Holela, some seven miles to the south of Ibeka. The attack took place on 9 October, and a fair measure of surprise was achieved.

The grass and wattle huts at Holela were put to the torch and the grain stores destroyed. The nearby kraal of Sigcau suffered the same fate. There were grumblings of disappointment when Griffith refused a general pursuit and ordered a return to Ibeka. Bertram Bowker, a fiery veteran of the last frontier war and leader of a privately raised force that included some twenty relatives, was blunt in his condemnation of the Commandant and the excessive caution displayed during the raid.

Having made his gesture, Griffith spent another nine days building up his forces and supplies before undertaking a systematic sweep through Gcalekaland. During that time Sarhili made a veiled bid for peace. He sent messengers to Ibeka with a request for Colonel Eustace to return to him. But colonial temper was high and peace before conquest was unacceptable to the authorities in King William's Town. It was decided to treat Sarhili's overtures as delaying tactics. Preparations for the laying waste of Gcalekaland continued uninterrupted; and on 18 October, eight thousand men, two-thirds of them black, invaded his homeland.

The lightly equipped, rapidly moving colonial forces encountered no opposition in their drive to the sea. The tribesmen they chanced upon melted into the bush before the first shots were fired. The villages and kraals had either been abandoned or left in the care of old men and women. The invaders cleared out the grain pits in every kraal and what they could not feed to the levies and the horses, they burnt. Ploughshares, clay pots and anything of functional value were smashed, and the huts set alight. So many cattle were rounded up that their management began to pose a problem, but neither colonists nor Mfengu were prepared to relinquish this all-important prize. Griffith was later to complain that the confiscated cattle eventually paralysed his every move.

It was at Lusizi that the only organised Gcaleka attempt to obstruct the invaders was made. While waiting for the arrival of Griffith's column, Inspector Hook's men were surprised in the late afternoon by a large warrior force. The engagement was noteworthy for the spirited resistance put up by the Mfengu contingent. The manner in which they repulsed the attackers earned them the respect of the colonial bystanders. In following up the Gcaleka retreat, two brothers recklessly tried to dislodge a group of warriors holed up in a narrow defile, and became the first white casualties in Griffith's offensive.

The Gcalekas, with Elliot's Thembus on their flank and Griffith's army behind them, managed to ford the Bashee with their herds and families. Griffith had sent messengers to the Bomvana chief, Moni, ordering him to guard the drifts and prevent the Gcalekas from crossing. But despite his protestations of neutrality, Moni remained loyal to Sarhili. Once inside Bomvanaland the Gcalekas and their cattle vanished. Moni claimed that they had passed through his country and crossed the Mtata River into Pondoland. Griffith entered Bomvanaland, rounded up any stray cattle he thought belonged to the Gcalekas and called a halt on the Mtata River. It was in Moni's territory that Colonel Glyn and Colonel William Bellairs, Cunynghame's Deputy Adjutant General, caught up with Griffith. They had been on a tour of inspection of the Idutywa Reserve, and carried a message from Frere cautioning against antagonising, at this stage, the tribes that had remained neutral. The Commandant was quite happy to call off the pursuit. Some of his officers remonstrated with him, arguing that the Gcalekas would reassemble as quickly as they had dispersed, but

Griffith maintained that they were thoroughly beaten and demoralised. He knew that his own supply lines were disintegrating and that most of the volunteers were eager to return home with their booty. Bowker thought the campaign a 'wretched affair', and felt that the Commandant had 'neither push, tact, drive thought or forethought in his composition'.

By 19 November, the Gcaleka war was described, officially, as over. A few small colonial detachments were retained to guard strategic outposts in the empty Gcalekaland while the remainder headed for home as quickly as their mounts would carry them. Her Majesty's soldiers in their 'safe' posts in the Ciskei had to watch the victorious colonists stream home and listen to the exaggerated praise that was heaped on 'the sons of the soil'. The regulars had worked hard in irksome, organisational jobs, but they received scant recognition. Coghill described the time as 'work day and night combining the duties of ADC, Deputy Assistant Adjutant General, Assistant Quartermaster-General and private secretary'. The glory had gone to the amateurs – it had not been the 1st Battalion's finest hour.

11

The Ngqika Rebellion

On 14 November Frere published a notice inviting application for five hundred farms in Gcalekaland. He was prepared to let the Gcalekas return as colonial subjects after the offer had been taken up. A week later, Merriman announced that the Government was willing to forgive all Gcalekas who had not been leaders in the 'rebellion' and who surrendered their arms. Molteno was furious when he heard about the Governor's scheme. Protecting settlers in the Transkei could be a costly burden on the Colony; his preference was to fill Gcalekaland with Mfengu. There was, however, one group about whom there could be no argument, and who could be located immediately in the territory – the Gcalekas who had taken refuge in the Colony. Chief Mapasa's Ntsonyana clan, from whose numbers the instigators of the quarrel with the Mfengu had come, had deserted the Gcaleka cause when hostilities began. It was a repetition of his behaviour in the Gcaleka war with the Thembus. His action had divided the clan, and many of the younger men had broken away to join Sigcau; one of them, called Khiva, was a warrior of considerable repute. Brownlee had settled Mapasa's clan on empty land between Mpetu and Kei Mouth. The settlers had seen Mapasa's action as a cunning ruse that would allow Sarhili's cattle to graze in British Kaffraria while he waged war in the Transkei, but Captain Brabant, under whose supervision they had been placed, found that they were very cooperative and gave no trouble. The farmers in the district, however, disliked their presence and accused them of stealing every ox that went astray.

Colonel Glyn, after visiting the 1/24th's post at Mpetu, had strongly represented against allowing these Xhosas to remain armed. His recommendation was in line with Frere's plans for a disarmamemt of all the tribes, and a directive was issued for Brownlee to disarm Mapasa's followers before sending them back to Gcalekaland. Captain Brabant disagreed with Colonel Glyn's proposal, calling it an unnecessary and dangerous act and Molteno sent a telegram warning about the danger of a 'too high-handed and unnecessarily harsh policy being adopted'. He thought the order to disarm Mapasa's 'terror-stricken men', an act of harassment that might drive them to desperation. But by then Charles Brownlee was at Mpetu. He informed Makinana, a minor chief who had followed Mapasa into the Colony, that disarmament would commence with his followers on the following Monday. The message was transmitted on the Friday. By Sunday Makinana had worked himself up into a rage composed of part resentment and part panic, and with his followers, made a sudden dash for the Ngqika location. Brownlee and his escort made an attempt to head them off, but failed.

A few days before, the *Eastern Star* had predicted trouble with the Ngqikas; and Sprigg, whose credibility had suffered from the easy victory in Gcalekaland, had been issuing gloomy warnings about a general rising in the Ciskei. Makinana's escape precipitated a new attack of jitters on the frontier. A general alarm was sounded and Lieutenant Cavaye's company was ordered out of Komga in pursuit. Makinana eluded his pursuers and reached Ndimba's kraal safely. Brownlee called off the chase at the Ngqika border and found himself berated by all and sundry. Merriman, who was particularly irate, wanted to know by what stretch of the imagination were the Ngqikas, as colonial subjects, accorded independent borders. Cunynghame was influenced by the prevailing mood of anxiety and without reference to the colonial authorities, attempted to surround the Ngqika location with a thinly stretched 'red line'.

The delicate relationship between Merriman and the General collapsed under the strain of the Makinana escapade. Cunynghame's hasty dispatch of troops to the Ngqika border, his agitation for fresh burger forces followed by a request to the War Office for cavalry and artillery reinforcements, resulted in a rift with the 'Minister of War' which became unbridgeable. Merriman, made sensitive by criticism of his unprofessional commissariat, disappointed by Brownlee's bungling of the disarmament mission and at the receiving end of Molteno's wrath, lashed out at the man whose image was most vulnerable in the Colony. Cunynghame was made the scapegoat for the 'instant panic which pervaded the whole of this town . . .' To Molteno he wrote that 'nothing can save the Colony from a tremendous disaster if the outbreak of a war should find the General in his present place . . . there is a time when twaddle and red tape become a crime and we are not far off that now. I would rather resign than have to listen to his silly prate every morning . . . When I spoke of the General before he was merely an ornamental puppet leaving the work to be done for him. Now he is an active source of Danger...' At about this time the news was made public that Cunynghame had been promoted Lieutenant-General and would complete his normal term in South Africa. The unfortunate coincidence was more than Molteno could stand; he wrote to the Colonial Office demanding Cunynghame's recall.

In the Ngqika location Brownlee was having a difficult time with Sandile. The Chief, burdened with guilt for not having gone to Sarhili's aid was being urged by his young men to enter the war. His respected elder counsellor, Tyhala, on the other hand, was pushing him in the direction of peace. And now the white rulers wanted him to surrender a Xhosa who had fled to him for sanctuary. His indecisiveness made him churlish. He threatened Brownlee, backed down, then threatened again: 'if you tread on a snake it will turn and bite you'. He admitted to recalling his followers who had been working on the railway line and to making defensive preparations, but blamed it on the presence of 'red-coats' on his borders. Brownlee promised him that Makinana would be allowed to stay with Ndimba for the time being, provided he paid a fine and made a token surrender of arms. Sandile's natural caution prevailed. Everyone breathed easily again. The Makinana affair had been settled and Sandile, the drunken coward, was going to keep the peace. The welcome news had barely reached 'King', when the community was shaken by a disaster in the Transkei.

At Ibeka, Griffith's volunteer units had been disappearing at a faster rate than they had assembled. But, even while the dismemberment of the colonial forces was taking place, reports had started to come in of Gcaleka infiltrators returning to their homeland. On 1 December, a column made up of one hundred and twenty-seven men of the Prince Alfred Guard (Port Elizabeth Regiment), two guns manned by colonial artillerymen and No. 9 troop FAMP under Inspector Bourne, had left Ibeka on a routine patrol. They had followed the well-trodden path to Sarhili's kraal and had camped there for the night. In the morning, the mounted detachment, which had ridden ahead, had blundered into hundreds of well-armed warriors near the burnt-out remains of what had once been known as Holland's Shop. Fighting had broken out immediately and a trooper had been killed in the first exchange. The Gcalekas had proved amazingly tenacious, and had made repeated attacks in an effort to outflank the column. The police, in attempting to stop the movement, had been vigorously repulsed, and Inspector Bourne had great difficulty regrouping them. The following afternoon, before dusk, the warriors made a series of determined attempts to surround the column. When they finally broke off the engagement, they took most of the column's horses and oxen away with them.

Griffith was completely unsettled by the encounter on the Msintsana stream, and sent an urgent telegram to Cunynghame asking for reinforcements. But the Colony was without a reserve, and the Gcalekaland campaign had glaringly revealed the gross deficiencies of the FAMP. Merriman recommended the immediate raising of a colonial militia. Molteno refused to sanction such a step on the grounds that he needed parliamentary approval. He feared that a militia which could be called out at every whim, would end up protecting Frere's settlers in Gcalekaland. His answer to Griffith's urgent plea was an instruction to send in the Mfengu in large numbers. Frere was against raising to pre-eminence one black nation over another, or differentiating too greatly between loyal and hostile tribes. The blacks were to be incorporated as a detribalised mass in the confederation he visualized. He supported Merriman's suggestion for a colonial militia and urged the Premier to give his 'Minister of War' a freer hand. But Molteno dismissed the scheme as going 'beyond the exigencies of the moment', and cautioned against the employment of imperial troops in the Transkei, unless the entire cost was borne by the British Government.

This was precisely what Frere had in mind. Communications between King William's Town and London took many weeks, the question of who was to pay could be resolved at a later date. In a devious note to Merriman he admitted wanting to get rid of Griffith, and to do it without discrediting the Commandant, he proposed that the Ministry announce the end of active war, so that Colonel Glyn could take charge of the military headquarters at Ibeka and free Griffith for police duties. On Friday 7 December, Colonel Glyn was appointed Commander in the Transkei with the rank of Colonel on the Staff and a brevet of Brigadier-General.

Richard Thomas Glyn, the only son of a member of the Honourable East India Company, was forty-six years old. He had joined the army in 1850 and had served in the Crimea with the 82nd Regiment. He had come out of the war with some campaign medals and the rank of captain. An opportunity had arisen shortly afterwards, to exchange into the 24th Regiment which had been stationed in India since 1846. He had arrived in time to participate in the arduous work of policing the Pubjab and chasing mutineers. When the 1st Battalion returned home, Glyn purchased his majority. In 1867 he purchased the Lieutenant-Colonelcy of the 1/24th and four years later was promoted full colonel. It was almost twenty years since he and his battalion had seen military action.

General Order No. 142 announced the imminent departure of Her Majesty's forces for the Transkei. An air of excitement filled the Military Reserve; everybody, rank and file included, were eager to show the colonials how professionals conducted a military campaign. Two senior 1st Battalion officers had arrived in King William's Town in November. One of them, Walter Bernardino Logan, was the field-officer who had replaced Henry Degacher. He was to accompany the troops to the Transkei as commander of the 1/24th. The other one was Captain George Paton, who for a number of years had been ADC to the Governor of the Straits Settlement. His service in Perak had coincided with a period of military and political upheaval, experiences that were to be repeated when he became military secretary to Colonel William Bellairs, the new commander of the Colony's eastern districts. Two 1st Battalion officers, however, missed the move to the Transkei by a few days. Reginald Younghusband and Teignmouth Melvill had sailed for England on 4 December. The former, with marriage in mind, was taking long leave, and Melvill, who had passed the Staff College entrance examination, hoped to find a place on the two-year course conducted by the College. Lieutenant Archer Morshead, the Battalion's only Staff College graduate and Melvill's junior by one year, was made District Adjutant for the Transkei. Lieutenant George Hodson became Colonel Glyn's orderly officer and Commandant Gray of the Gonubie Volunteers joined his staff as interpreter. Within ten days of taking command the Colonel and his staff were at Ibeka. 'A', 'B', 'G', and 'F' Companies were to follow as soon as they handed over their posts in the Ciskei to reinforcements from the 88th.

The first few weeks in December were a hectic period in the Military Reserve, and Coghill had time for only one brief entry in his diary, 'Immense excitement, Column to cross Kei; Opposition of Ministry'. Henry Pulleine, however, was to remain in 'King'. He was to raise and organise a unit of volunteer infantry. His personal popularity, it was hoped, would be the drawcard; the unit was to be called Pulleine's Rangers. The intention was to keep the volunteers under military control. The men who answered the call to serve under Her Majesty's rules and regulations were the unemployed dropouts and drunkards from the diggings and the railway gangs, and the unit soon acquired the cynical nickname of 'Pulleine's Lambs'. To remedy his want of cavalry, Cunynghame proposed raising a mounted squadron along similar lines. In this instance the draw was to be Fred Carrington who had been recalled from the Transvaal. The volunteer horsemen were to be called the Frontier Light Horse, but while Carrington led them, they would be known to all as 'Carrington's Horse'.

The General had ordered the remainder of the 88th Regiment to the Eastern Frontier, and on 10 December they embarked on the H.M.S. *Active* and the S.S. *Florence*. A plan had been formulated for the landing of a force at Mazeppa Bay and was the only proposal for which Molteno had any enthusiasm. When they reached East London fifty Connaught Rangers were kept on board the *Active* to supplement the two hundred sailors and marines who had been organised into a Naval Brigade for the possible landing on the shores of Gcalekaland. The remainder were packed into lighters for transfer across the treacherous East London bar. The lighters had not gone far when a sudden fierce wind made further progress impossible. They had to drop anchor in the rapidly roughening sea to try and ride out the gale. The hatches were battened down and the wretched soldiers were incarcerated in the dark tightly packed holds without water or sanitary facilities. It took twenty-four hours before the lighters, foul with sea-sickness, could be brought to shore. Most of the men were on the verge of collapse when the holds were opened.

The hazards of bringing the men ashore at East London decided Frere and Cunynghame against attempting a landing on the wild Transkeian coast. The Naval Brigade was disembarked, instead, at East London. Half the newly arrived troops were sent to Ibeka and the remainder were divided between Komga and Fort Cunynghame. In a communication to Commodore Sullivan, the Commander of the Naval Station at Simonstown, Frere warned that the Naval Brigade might be used in other theatres of war; there was 'every chance of hostilities in the debatable land between the Transvaal, Zululand and Natal'. With men drawn off to guard the supply route to the Transkei and fill strategic posts on the borders of the Ngqika location, the Military Reserve became dangerously depleted. Efforts were made to arm and drill the non-combatants in the 1/24th. The band was allocated a 7-pounder and instructed in artillery drill. After ten days the musicians were able to bring the gun into action within fifteen seconds.

The General kept control of the commissariat in his own hands, using

Merriman's earlier argument that 'supply and command control must go together'. The base at Ibeka, which had been reduced to about one week's supply of food, ammunition and fodder, began to receive supplies in quantities undreamed of by the colonial forces. Weighing heavily on Cunynghame's mind was the memory of the heavy rains, which in the summer of 1874 had made the Kei River unfordable for three months, and he refused to undertake a campaign in the Transkei until he had built up a large reserve of food and ammunition in the territory.

In reality, very little had happened in the Transkei since the engagement near Holland's Shop; all the brawling was taking place in the offices of the War Council. When Molteno realised that Merriman had become little more than a rubber stamp for the Governor, he began to invent reasons for inducing Frere to return to Cape Town. But Frere insisted that it would be foolhardy for the two Ministers and himself to leave 'in the present excited state of the frontier', and certainly not before the Government made worthwhile arrangements 'for ensuring the peace of the frontier districts'. They were the only ones, he argued who could prevent a civil war from breaking out in British Kaffraria. The war with the Xhosas had taken second place to the conflict between the Government and the Governor.

On 21 December, two weeks after taking charge of the war in the Transkei, Cunynghame departed for Ibeka. The following morning, as he was preparing to leave Komga, a message was received which stated that Khiva, Mapasa's nephew, had crossed the Kei with some of his warriors and was heading for the Kabousie River. He was expected to pass close to Komga, and Major Hans Moore of the 88th was asked to take out a small detachment of FAMP and search the hilly terrain between Komga and the Kei River. Coghill, who was in Komga with the General, offered to accompany him.

Moore caught up with Khiva's rearguard near a distinctive flat-topped hill known as Moordenaar's Kop (murderer's head). The hill had acquired its sinister name in the war of 1846, when five British officers were ambushed on its slopes and hacked to pieces. Moore's men followed the disappearing trail of Khiva's band for some miles. The terrain at the foot of the hill became progressively more broken and forced them, eventually, to dismount and lead their horses. Khiva led his pursuers into a narrow valley, then turned about and waited. The police were outnumbered and the ground totally unsuited for a mounted action. For a while the two groups gazed at each other without making a move; but when it became apparent that Moore would not risk an engagement, the Gcalekas stood up and continued their journey to the Kabousie River. Neither Moore nor Coghill could have realised that they had contributed to the prolongation of the war by allowing Khiva to reach the Ngqika location.

Since coming to the Transkei Colonel Glyn had been fully occupied finding the levies he needed for his offensive. He had met with Major Elliott and discussed the practicability of again using Ngangelizwe's Thembu to guard the Bashee against a Gcaleka flight into Bomvanaland. The river was tortuous and its banks were intersected by bush-filled valleys and ravines large enough to afford concealment for the whole Gcaleka nation. Elliott thought it a near impossible task with the numbers at his disposal. He would have preferred to patrol the Bashee from the Bomvana side, but Frere refused permission for a Thembu invasion of Moni's country. Later events would compel him to agree to this strategy.

On 19 December, Sarhili had sent emissaries to Colonel Glyn asking him to spell out terms for a conclusion of hostilities. They had been sent back with what amounted to a demand for unconditional surrender. The only guarantee Colonel Glyn had been prepared to give, was an assurance that the Chief's life would be spared. He had allowed Sarhili six days in which to make up his mind, and had promised that no offensive action would be undertaken during that time. When the emissaries failed to return by Christmas Day the sigh of relief was almost audible in the military camp that had grown up around Mr Barnett's trading-store. Glyn's command looked a mixed lot. His regular force was made up of four hundred 'red-coats', one hundred 'blue-jackets' from the Naval Brigade, a handful of Marines and a few hundred police troopers in black corduroy jackets. The most bizarre groups were Her Majesty's Mfengu levies. Their uniform ranged from near naked to blankets and ancient coats. Old military tunics were the clear favourites, but clerical fashions also had their adherents. Trousers were conspicuously infrequent and footwear almost unknown, but all sported some form of headgear decorated with colourful feathers. Each man carried a bundle of assegaais and a knobkerrie, most had a firearm of some description, and a small élite had Sniders. Uniformity was ensured by a piece of red cloth tied around an arm or the forehead. Its purpose was to prevent the soldiers from mistaking their allies for the enemy.

On 27 December, the plan formulated by Colonel Glyn was put into operation. It was largely a repetition of Griffith's sweep through Gcalekaland. Three columns were to push towards the coast, turn east and drive the Gcaleka remnants towards the Thembus in the Bashee valley. The Right Column, commanded by Major Edward Hopton (88th Regiment), included 'A' Company, 1/24th, under Lieutenant Charles Cavaye. It was to start out from Butterworth and clear the country between the Kei and Qora rivers. The Central Column was made up of 'G' Company under Captain Thomas Rainforth, the Naval Brigade, one hundred and twenty-five FAMP troopers and Lieutenant Clement's mounted contingent. This column was to scour the kloofs and ravines along the Qora River and rendezvous with the Right Column near Qora mouth. Captain Russel Upcher, the 1st Battalion's senior company officer, was given command of the Left Column. His force consisted of 'F' Company, enlarged to one hundred and thirty men, the Royal Marines with their rocket-tube and a detachment of police. He, too, was to start out from Ibeka, but his objective was the country between the Qora and Nqabora rivers. Each column was supported by either one or two 7-pounders mounted on ox-drawn Cape carts, and had attached to it between five hundred and one thousand Mfengu. Such were the 'well-organised columns' assembled for the second Gcaleka campaign, and for which, according to Merriman, Cunynghame had let precious weeks slip by before striking a blow. Colonel Glyn and his staff (Lieutenant Morshead and George Hodson), attached themselves to the Central Column. Major Walter Logan, new to South Africa, overweight and out of condition, was left behind in command of 'Fort Glyn' (the new name for the earthworks at Ibeka).

The Gcalekaland countryside looked like the English Downs; but roads were almost non-existent and near the river valleys the topography changed dramatically. Bush-filled ravines radiated from the rivers in directions that always seemed to run at right-angles to the lines of march, the very places that had to be carefully searched for hidden warriors. Inside the ravines the midsummer heat lay heavy and still. It made oven-walls out of the rocky cliffs and baked the red-coated columns as they struggled through the undergrowth. The hot, windless days soon began to take their toll and heat stroke became the dreaded companion that marched one step behind the infantry.

At each halt another torment would begin. The swarm of flies that hovered over the columns on the move, descended to search out the hot sticky faces when they stopped. The flies covered the food while it was being prepared and every spoonful was followed into the mouth by a buzzing cloud. A listlessness developed in the ranks that could have made the soldiers easy victims in an ambush; but it was then that the Mfengu displayed their real worth. They seemed unaffected by the heat or flies and were tireless in their scouring of the bush. The soldiers gradually developed an admiration for their black allies, and after a while ceased to make derogatory remarks about the undisciplined savages who were paid twice as much as a private in the Queen's Army.

The procedure adopted for scouring the bush was to keep the soldiers back and let the Mfengu flush out any Gcalekas that might be hidden there. Their method was to fire a few blind volleys into the thickets before rushing in in loose skirmishing order; and the staccato hissing noise they made when they killed a Gcaleka was not easily forgotten by those who heard it. Meat was their reward. The soldiers, themselves accustomed to crude eating habits, were astounded by the manner in which the black levies devoured their rations. No part of the slaughtered beast was considered unfit for eating. The abdominal contents, intestines, organs and fatty omentum, barely cooked and sometimes unwashed, were stuffed into the mouth and chewed with relish. In General Cunynghame's columns no one went hungry. A police trooper, who had taken part in Griffith's drive through Gcalekaland was lavish in his praise of the Imperial Commissariat, 'we had plenty to eat, with sufficient time for meals, and we went over the ground quite as rapidly, if not more so than before, and one always continued to camp in daylight instead of dark'.

Progress was rapid. The enemy had vanished and the land was almost deserted. In the space of five days the column passed the ruins of Holela, scoured the Manubi Forest and reached the mouth of the Qora River. They crossed the Qora on barrel-rafts only to be held up again by the wide mouth of another river. It was there that Captain Upcher's men, driving a huge herd of captured cattle, caught up with the Colonel's column. Colonel Glyn was exasperated by the many rivers that barred his way to Bomvanaland and the elusive foe that was always five jumps ahead of him. He decided to lead a force of mounted men and Mfengu in a dash for the Dwessa Forest where rumour had it that Sarhili was hiding. Glyn's rush took him all the way to the Bashee River, but his effort was unrewarded; the only Gcalekas he found were herding cattle on Moni's side of the river.

The infantry and the wagons had been sent inland to the mission founded by Major Malan, a Crimean War veteran who had decided to bring the Word to the heathens. A bell hanging from a pole was all that was left of the Major's well intentioned enterprise. It was there, on the upper reaches of the Shixini and Nqabora rivers, that Glyn decided to build a fortification, the first of a seies of earthworks designed to prevent a Gcaleka incursion from Bomvanaland. Captain Rainforth's company was selected to garrison Malan's Mission. It was renamed 'Fort Nixon' after the engineering officer in charge of its construction.

Colonel Glyn's columns had swept the greater part of Gcalekaland in under a fortnight. The campaign had resulted in the capture of two thousand head of cattle and the death of about one hundred and twenty Xhosas. The apparently deserted territory, guarded by scattered detachments in fortified posts, seemed safe enough for white settlement to commence. One of Frere's objectives had been achieved. The only thing that puzzled the Colonel as he hurried back to Ibeka at Cunynghame's bidding, was the whereabouts of Sarhili and the Gcaleka army. At 'Fort Glyn' he got his answer and learnt how the complexity of the war had changed.

The man responsible for the change was the one whom Coghill and Major Moore on that December morning near Moordenaar's Kop, had watched disappear in the direction of the Kabousie River. Khiva had arrived in the Ngqika location three weeks after Sandile had capitulated on the Makinana issue. This visitor was not a minor chief who had gone over to the colonists when fighting began, but a warrior hero from the Gcaleka army who might inspire the Ngqikas to rise in rebellion. That he would bring colonial authorities in his wake was a foregone conclusion, but the irresolute Sandile could no longer struggle against a fate that pushed him inexorably into the conflict with the white man. The Chief of the fighting House of Rarabe had made up his mind.

When the inevitable emissary arrived to demand the surrender of Khiva, he found Sandile strangely different from the man he remembered. There were no more evasions, only a sober directive – the Government must remain quiet until the tribe gave its answer. The Ngqika decision became apparent when old Tyhala, the voice for peace, left the reservation to seek asylum in the Colony. The rebellion had begun. The first act was a combined Ngqika-Gcaleka raid on a Mfengu kraal some six miles from Blythswood. For the Ngqikas, the habits of twenty-five years as a subject people vanished in the flames that consumed the Mfengu kraal. Their next objective was the road that carried supplies to the

Transkei. On Boxing Day the store and the hotel at Draaibosch were burnt to the ground. Several farmhouses in the vicinity were destroyed and a post-cart carrying mail from Ibeka was seized. The supply line from King William's Town to Ibeka was cut.

Despite attempts by Major Moore in Komga – attempts which gained him the first Victoria Cross won in South Africa – to break the blockade, the road between King William's Town and Komga stayed closed for three weeks. But the Xhosas denied themselves the full advantage afforded by the situation when they failed to cut the new telegraph line that linked King William's Town with the Transkei.

On the last day of the year, three colonial officials, who had been tracking stolen cattle, were overtaken by Ngqika rebels and killed. The incident occurred on the upper reaches of the Nahoon River, well within the boundaries of British Kaffraria and not far from 'King'; it horrifyingly emphasised the extent of the insurrection.

When Glyn's columns started their drive through Gcalekaland, Sarhili's men quietly slipped westwards towards the Kei. They eluded Major Hopton's column, crossed the Kei and joined forces with Khiva and the Ngqikas in the densely wooded Tyityaba valley, which roughly paralleled the west bank of the Kei for about thirteen miles. Access to the valley was by precipitous paths through rugged ravines. In there the Xhosas were able to conceal themselves with their herds and defy pursuers. Occupation of the Tyityaba posed an immediate threat to two colonial manned forts in the vicinity: Fort Buffalo near the Kei mouth, and Fort Linsingen at the junction of the Tyityaba and the Kei, had a combined complement of fifty-seven men. The nearest large garrison was the one at Mpetu which overlooked the western approaches to the valley. Substantial earthworks had been built there by 'D' Company of the 1/24th and named Fort Warwick in honour of the Regiment. It was, in the opinion of one man, 'a snug little place, very well built, with huts and tents inside'. When Colonel Lambert made Komga his headquarters, Captain George Wardell of the 1/24th took command of Fort Warwick.

The volunteers in Fort Buffalo abandoned their post as soon as they realised that the enemy was concentrating in the Kei and Tyityaba valleys. They fell back on Fort Warwick, as did the farmers who lived in the district. There were far too many people seeking refuge to be accommodated inside the fort, and tents sprang up outside the walls. Wagons were drawn up in a laager and livestock was herded into kraals made of aloe bushes. After a while Wardell's command came to resemble a village market on a Saturday morning. The men in Fort Linsingen, however, were besieged before they could make their escape. The recently built blockhouse could be defended by a small garrison, but it could not withstand a prolonged siege.

Wardell felt obliged to come to their aid, but a fierce night attack on Fort Warwick followed by an audacious daylight theft of the commissariat oxen, convinced him that the Xhosas would welcome his venturing into the open. On 6 January, a messenger got through to Komga with a letter from Wardell; it stated, 'the enemy being so strong between us and the Chichaba [Tyityaba], it will be as much as we can do to hold our own here'. He thought he had enough food for ten days, but requested ammunition, artillery and rockets. Instead of sending supplies, Colonel Lambert organised a relief column of eight hundred men. The column reached Mpetu three days after Wardell sent the message. The defenders of Fort Linsingen had broken out by then, and were safe in Fort Warwick. Their miraculous escape had been achieved through an unexpected diversion created by the Gcaleka defector, Mapasa. Colonel Lambert thought Fort Warwick too vulnerable, and was unwilling to reinforce the garrison. 'D' Company was ordered to return to Komga. Everything that could be carried away was removed from the Fort, and the huts set alight.

The inglorious abandonment of Fort Warwick was regarded by the colonists as a dangerous error. The lower reaches of the Kei had been left undefended and the coastal district as far as East London was open to the enemy. Harsh comments were made about the ineptitude of the Imperial Command, and Frere was compelled to have hard words with Cunynghame. It was obvious to all that the Gcaleka army had secreted itself in the valleys and ravines of the lower Kei and that the Ngqikas, having opened up the route between the Kabousie and Kei Mouth, had reinforced Sarhili's men. Guarding the Bashee had become a meaningless exercise and in consequence of the changed situation, the message had gone out from Ibeka urging Colonel Glyn to return with all speed.

12

Nyumaga and Centane

The changed situation decided Cunynghame on an immediate offensive in the lower Kei valley. In an attempt to contain the Ngqikas, every soldier in King William's Town who could be spared from non-combat duties was sent to reinforce the posts guarding the approaches into the Amatholes. Major Hopton, who had commanded Colonel Glyn's Right Column, was ordered to Cathcart to organise the defences on the Ngqika border, and an appeal was made to the burghers of Stutterheim and Queenstown to patrol the line between these posts. To the still untrained Frontier Light Horse (FLH), and Pulleine's Rangers, fell the task of opening up the road to the Transkei. For his Kei offensive Cunynghame proposed a two-pronged drive on the river valley. A force under Colonel Glyn, based on Ibeka, was to clear the Transkei side of the valley; and one, under Colonel Lambert, based on Komga, was to drive the Ciskei side. Cunynghame's biggest headache was to find enough Mfengu levies to spearhead the drive. Most of them had deserted the Army of the Transkei when they heard that Sandile's sons were raiding in Mfenguland. Raising new contingents and finding the right men to lead them received top priority.

The offensive was scheduled to start on 14 January. Colonel Glyn recalled all the men he could spare from the Bashee, and with a hastily assembled force set out from Ibeka to link up with the Right Column which had been directed to remain on the west bank of the Qolora River and guard the approaches to the Kei valley. After Hopton was recalled to Cathcart, Major Owen of the 88th had taken command. His force, including Cavaye's 'A' Company, totalled one hundred and eighty-eight men. Colonel Glyn's command was about three hundred strong and had as its hardcore Captain Upcher's 'F' Company. On the morning of the 13th, Glyn led his troops out of Ibeka. His staff included Archer Morshead, George Hodson and Nevill Coghill on loan from the

General. They reached Kwa Centane at one o'clock, and were about to start the midday meal when Cunynghame's Naval ADC galloped in with forty police troopers. Information had reached the General that a large Xhosa force, thought to be commanded by Khiva, was collecting between Major Owen and the Kei. Lunch was abandoned and the troops directed to proceed with all speed to Owen's camp some nine miles away near a stream called the Nyumaga.

The Nyumaga, for part of its length, ran through undulating countryside, but as it neared the Kei River the terrain changed to deep ravines filled with thick bush. Owen's force was camped on an open stretch of ground near the stream: on his right stretched the Tala Ridge, a series of low hills reaching towards the Kei valley. Throughout the morning warriors had been gathering on the ridge and by mid-afternoon the concentration had become sufficiently large to pose a threat to Owen's flank. The Xhosa build-up, however, had been conducted at a leisurely pace; and by four o'clock, when Colonel Glyn galloped into the camp with his Mounted Infantry and a detachment of FAMP, no attempt had been made to attack the camp. Glyn immediately ordered Owen to form his men into one long line facing the ridge. The company of Connaught Rangers was placed on the left, Cavaye's men on the right, and in the centre he positioned the Column's two 7-pounders. As his own troops came up, Glyn formed a second line under the command of Russell Upcher, but the Royal Marines with their rocket-launcher were sent forward to reinforce the artillery. A troop of FAMP was posted on each flank to guard against a surprise attack from the watercourses which ran from the ridge towards the camp. As soon as the lines were ready Glyn ordered the advance to begin. The second line was to remain a few hundred paces behind the front line and act as a reserve. Captain Robinson of the FAMP, with his two artillery pieces and seventy police troopers, was left to guard the camp site and protect the rear of the advancing lines.

While Colonel Glyn was preparing his battle line, the Xhosas disappeared from view. The lines had to advance almost a mile before they reached the brow of the nearest hill and found the Xhosas drawn up and waiting on the opposite hill. The rocket party immediately opened fire. After the second burst the warriors began moving down the hill towards Owen's line. Glyn at last had a chance to bring the Xhosas to battle and was determined not to waste it. The line was opened up into skirmishing order, and with two hundred Mfengu running ahead, he ordered a general movement in the direction of the enemy. The left of the line was the first to make contact, and the men of the 88th were soon hotly engaged. The Xhosas stood their ground and put up a discouraging barrage with their muzzle-loaders. All kinds of missiles whizzed over the soldiers' heads, from pebbles to pot-legs. The latter made a flesh-creeping whistling noise and could be seen, sometimes, whirling through the air. The left suffered a few casulaties and Glyn directed Lieutenant Clements to take the Mounted Infantry to their support. Leaving their horses on their brow of the hill, the horse soldiers of the 1/24th reinforced the 88th on foot. The additional rifles were sufficient to dislodge the Xhosas from their position. They backed off, but for a short distance only. More and more of them continued to emerge from the watercourses running down the hill, and in no time the line was facing a force estimated at nearly two thousand men. The Xhosa fire, inaccurate though it was, made further advance down the hill too hazardous. Glyn decided to throw in his reserve. Upcher's line which had stayed out of sight, moved up at the double and filled in the gaps in the front line. The sudden increase of fire-power started to take a toll in the Xhosa ranks; but firing down the slope from a kneeling position did not make for accurate shooting, and the Xhosas were able to hold their positions. At times they came to within thirty yards of the 'redcoats', but the rifles never let up, and slowly the warriors began to fall back. The retreat continued in reasonable order for about a mile, then panic seized the Xhosas and everyone made a rush for the nearest watercourse. Chief Veldman had anticipated such a move, and his Mfengu had concealed themselves in the dry watercourses. Much killing took place that late afternoon in the shallow, bush-filled ravines. The Mfengu missed few and spared none; and whenever a group tried to make a stand the police rode in and finished the work of the Mfengu.

At six o'clock, as light was beginning to fail, Colonel Glyn called off the pursuit. The infantrymen, too exhausted to do more than stand around after the fever of battle left them, watched with horrified fascination as the Mfengu flushed the last Xhosa stragglers from their hiding places and butchered the wounded and the prisoners.

The battle at Nyumaga took place on the twenty-ninth anniversary of Chillianwala, and at almost the same time of day. The much happier outcome did not pass without comment; it was regarded by Coghill, who had been present throughout the engagement, as a good portent for the future. But when the enemy dead had been counted only about fifty bodies were found. A disappointingly small number when equated with the amount of ammunition expended by a reputedly 'crack regiment like the 24th', was the colonial comment.

The first open encounter between the Xhosas and the regular soldiers had led to a Xhosa defeat, and for a while all organised resistance ceased. A few desultory skirmishes took place as Colonel Glyn's troops probed the ravines and valleys near Kei mouth, but the soldiers' real enemy, immediately after Nyumaga, was heat and thirst. Drought, four months of war, and the scorched-earth policy of the invaders had turned Gcalekaland into a famine-stricken wasteland. Starving women and children surrendered in such droves that their very numbers began to immobilise the troops. Colonel Glyn's force had exhausted its field-supplies and even Major Strickland's usually reliable commissariat was having trouble supplying his scattered detachments. The Army of the Transkei, by then, had been continuously in the field for nearly a month, and it was decided to bring most of the troops back to Ibeka for re-equipping.

Cunynghame hoped that the fight had gone out of the Gcalekas. He intended to proceed against the Ngqikas as soon as reinforcements arrived from England, but as a safeguard, he decided to establish a forward base near Kwa Centane, a prominent hill with a solitary tree on its summit, to guard against a Gcaleka movement away from the lower Kei. The chosen site overlooked the dense Mnyameni bush which concealed the Transkei exits from the Tyityaba and Kei valleys. The wagon-trail from Ibeka passed nearby, and concentrating supplies there would facilitate operations on the lower Kei and reduce the journey to the base at Ibeka by twenty difficult miles. The camp was to be located on some flat ground below the southern slope of Kwa Centane. The road from Ibeka approached the camp site from the east; on the other three sides the ground sloped gently down for about three hundred yards to a shallow ravine in which water flowed. The terrain beyond the ravine was flat and bare for about half a mile to the Mnyameni bush. The bush was densest below the hilly Tala ridge that stretched from Kwa Centane to the Kei valley.

Two 1st Battalion Companies, 'F' and 'G', were sent from Ibeka to begin the construction of the camp at Centane. The company officers were Russell Upcher and Thomas Rainforth. Rainforth had joined the 24th six months before Upcher, but the latter had managed to purchase his captaincy just before the practice was banned, and was, as a result, Rainforth's senior by five years. The subalterns with the troops were Charles Atkinson, Edgar Anstey and George Palmes. In addition to the two enlarged infantry companies, Upcher's command included eighty-five police troopers, twenty-five sailors from the Naval Brigade and three hundred

Mfengu under Veldman Bikitsha. The troops had no sooner arrived, when scouts brought reports of enemy concentrations in the Mnyameni bush. Upcher immediately sent out parties to probe the area. It was soon obvious that the Xhosas had not been driven from the bush after Nyumaga. A full scale search of the area was considered too dangerous and the men were put to work fortifying the camp.

Upcher's first precaution was to draw up his wagons into a cattle-laager. Next, a rectangle, measuring thirty by forty yards was marked out and a trench dug with earthworks on the inner perimeter. On the slope below the entrenchment he had his men excavate a series of rifle-pits. In the meantime Veldman's scouts kept coming back with reports of an enemy build-up in the Mnyameni bush. Upcher intensified the work on the fortifications and sent a messenger to Ibeka with the information.

The news from Centane reinforced the rumours which had been filtering through to Colonel Glyn that the Xhosas planned a new offensive in the Transkei. Their objective, he believed, might be either Ibeka or the camp at Centane. Fearing that Upcher's defences were not as well prepared as those at Ibeka, Glyn decided to reinforce him. Lieutenant Carrington, who had ridden in with a detachment of Frontier Light Horse the day Glyn received Upcher's message, was told to hasten to Centane with fifty men. As an additional precaution he decided to station a reserve midway between Ibeka and Centane. Two hundred men under Captain Robinson of the police artillery were directed to a burnt-out mission station on the Tutura River. They arrived there in pouring rain on the evening of the sixth, and Robinson immediately dispatched two horsemen to inform Upcher that help, if needed, was ten miles away.

Sandile, from the outset of the rebellion, had favoured a move into the Amathole mountains where he could make common cause with other Rarabe clans. The forceful Khiva, however, had persuaded him to join forces with Sarhili in the Transkei. The meeting of the two venerable Xhosa chiefs had taken place near the mouth of the Qolora River. Both men had known forty years of intermittent strife against the white man and neither expected to win this newest war; they realised that the warriors took inspiration from their link with the nation's heroic past, and hoped that the Ngqika and Gcaleka tribes in combination might be capable of delivering a devastating blow in the Transkei. Sandile suggested a massive raid on Mfengu villages followed by a withdrawal into the Amatholes;

but the physical condition of the two armies differed greatly. The Gcalekas were half-starved and desperately short of arms and ammunition. The well-stocked bases at Centane and Ibeka seemed tempting prizes, and of the two, Centane seemed the more vulnerable. Sigcau, Khiva and Dalasile, the nation's greatest warriors would lead the attack, the renowned Xhosa war-doctor, Ngxitho would perform all the rituals necessary for success, and the *ukuyolela* would be given by the two senior chiefs. Sarhili and Sandile could not resist the honour bestowed on them.

Messengers, carrying the official ox-tail insignia, went out to all the clans with orders to assemble in the Mnyameni bush. When all had gathered Ngxitho began the *ukukhafula*, the ceremony of making 'invulnerable'. With much incantation he prepared a magical concoction from powdered roots and ox-gall; and while the warriors sang of the nation's great deeds, the potion was passed around for each man to swallow. This was followed by a ritual cleansing in the 'doctored' waters of a nearby stream. The black 'war-mark' was painted on every warrior's forehead, and each man was given a wooden block to hang around the neck, as an amulet against the enemy's bullets.

On 7 February, the army gathered around Sarhili to hear the *ukuyolela*. Wrapped in his kaross, looking gaunt and tired, the Xhosa Paramount Chief spoke words that contrasted incongruously with his appearance – 'I, Sarhili, the old tree, who has shadowed you for so long, stand before you this day. I am the tree your fathers have lain under, safe and sheltered, and for whom your fathers had often fought the white man. To-day you can show if you are the white man's dogs, or if you are your fathers' sons'. The authority to do battle had been given, but at the last moment Sandile's old caution reasserted itself, he excused himself from the frontal attack on the camp by saying that the Ngqika left was threatened by Mapasa's people, and that before attacking the soldiers he would have to deal with the Ntsonyanas. The next morning, long before sunrise, the Gcaleka army assembled in three columns of about a thousand men each, the main body that was to attack Upcher's camp from the south and west. A flying column would try and attain surprise by occupying the ravine to the north of the camp and the Ngqikas were to sweep down the ridge from the north-west after the attack began. As the first light brightened the sky behind Centane, on the wet, misty morning of 7 February, the Gcaleka army came out of the bush.

In the camp, the Mfengu leader woke Upcher shortly after 5 : 00 a.m. with the news that a great army was advancing towards them. The soldiers were quickly roused and the tents were struck. The infantry were issued seventy rounds apiece and ordered into the rifle-pits with strict instructions not to show themselves. It had been a wet night, and as they took up their positions in the muddy dug-outs, a light rain started to fall. The two artillery-pieces Upcher had in this command were faced south and west. The naval contingent had brought its rocket-tube and he sited it in the southwest corner. Captain Francis Grenfell, who had ridden in the night before, was the ranking officer in the camp. But a quick inspection had convinced him that Upcher's dispositions could not be faulted, and he decided to place himself under his orders.

Carrington was impatient for the Xhosas to show themselves. His greatest fear was that they might shun battle at the last minute. All the officers knew about the hit-and-run tactics which the Xhosas had employed in past wars, and were just as anxious as Carrington to bring the black army to battle. Rainforth offered to advance 'G' Company as a bait. It was agreed that his men and the FLH should move out of the camp and entice the Xhosas on to the waiting guns. Their orders were to fire on the enemy and immediately retire. Moving along the edge of the ravine in the direction of the Mnyameni bush, the FLH chanced upon the Gcaleka flying-column creeping through the thicket-filled depths. In Carrington's words, 'we played in front of them and their scouts dropped a few bullets among my troops'. The horsemen fired a few volleys in return, before starting the planned retirement on the camp. The sight of the retreating soldiers had the hoped-for effect; the warriors swarmed out of the ravine in eager pursuit.

The main body, by then, had reached the flat ground to the left front of the camp. Dalasile saw the flying-column chasing the 'red-coats' and hurried the advance. In the early morning light the densely packed warrior columns looked formidable. Their pace quickened and the south-eastern horizon became an ochre tide rushing to envelop the camp. When they were about 1 200 yards from the camp, the FAMP 7-pounder opened fire. The effect was disappointing, and in between its thunderous discharges the soldiers could hear the shouted challenges hurled by the Gcalekas. The Mfengu had been positioned well down the slope, ahead of the rifle-pits; one detachment faced south, the other west, and between them Carrington dismounted his detachment. At nine hundred yards the Mfengu and the FLH opened fire. The range was too great for the muzzle-loaders and carbines to do much damage. A few figures fell, but there was no detectable hesitation in the Gcaleka ranks. As the columns drew nearer, the

Mfengu started to fall back on the camp. Seeing their old foes retreating, the Gcalekas broke into a triumphant run. They reached the watercourses at the foot of the hill, when suddenly, out of the ground, popped a long row of white helmets. Seconds later a disciplined volley crashed out and warriors were falling on top of one another. A Gcaleka survivor remembered it as 'a sudden blaze' and 'our men fell like grass'. Five aimed rounds a minute meant a thousand lead-bullets pouring into the Gcaleka front ranks before they could stop the momentum of their charge. Such a wall of fire, so accurate at that distance, was unknown to tribal memory. For twenty minutes the columns stood their ground. Isolated attempts were made to rush the trenches but the fire was too sustained and cover was nowhere to be had. Hundreds of fallen figures dotted the grass like lumps of red clay, and every bush, every rock, no matter how insubstantial, became a desirable refuge. The proud columns began to disintegrate. Suddenly, a mist started to come in. It mingled with the drifting smoke from the guns and threw a temporary veil over the battlefield.

Fears that the troops might be robbed of a great victory were dispelled when twenty minutes later the mist cleared to show that the Xhosas were still in front of the camp; some had even crept to within a hundred yards of the trenches. For 'F' and 'G' Companies it was like a rifle-practice, with their old musketry-instructor, Lieutenant Carrington, shouting encouragement. The artillery pieces joined in and showered the Gcalekas with case shot. The renewed barrage was more than the exposed warriors could face; abandoning everything except their wooden amulets, they broke and ran. The Mfengu saw the chance and went after them. So began a chase that did not stop until they reached the Qolora River. Carrington too, could not wait. He led his horsemen out of the camp in a charge that 'scattered them like dirt'. With a revolver in one hand and a stick in the other, he seemed to have no need for reins. Galloping a hundred yards ahead of his men he pursued the fleeing enemy into the kloofs of the Mnyameni bush. Those he overlooked were sought out by the FAMP, who for the greater part of the engagement had guarded the eastern approach to the camp and the road to Ibeka. When Carrington returned to the camp, breakfast was about to be served.

But before the soldiers could start their meal, a Xhosa force was spotted on the ridge to the north-west of the camp. Captain Grenfell, who had played a passive role during the battle, thought he would like to repeat Rainforth's manoeuvre. To bait the trap he took out a troop of police and fifty infantrymen under Lieutenant Atkinson. The police, who were the first to reach the high ground beyond the ravine, blundered into a concealed body of warriors – the Ngqika advance guard. In a rapid move round their right flank the warriors cut off their path of retreat.

Upcher saw that their position was serious and sent another FAMP troop in support, while the FLH galloped towards their left in an attempt to prolong the line. Carrington quickly discovered that what had looked like an empty space was filled with warriors hidden in the long grass. Carrington's men were forced to dismount and cautiously lead their horses towards the embattled police; but twenty yards from the police they were compelled to turn and defend their own left against a stealthy Ngqika attempt to outflank them. Carrington, who had remounted, found himself the target of four determined snipers who kept shooting at him until his horse was hit.

Further to the left, Atkinson's men had engaged another Ngqika force and were slowly pushing them back along the ridge. But Grenfell, worried about the plight of the mounted men, requested him to turn his detachment about and join the line on Carrington's left. The infantry executed the manoeuvre under fire and succeeded in closing the gap between themselves and the Frontier Light Horse, who by then, were fighting virtually hand to hand. Those who tried to mount had their horses shot under them, and one man was dragged from his horse. But Atkinson's right-about-turn put an end to further Ngqika attempts at outflanking and lessened the pressure on the mounted troops.

Grenfell had sent a message to Captain Robinson on the Tutura before the battle started. It had reached him at 6 : 40 a.m., and within half an hour his force was on the road to Centane. The overnight rain had made the ground heavy with mud and the going was hard, but the troops covered seven miles in one and a half hours. They were still three miles from Upcher's camp when they learnt that the Gcaleka attack had been beaten off. Robinson's own scouts, however, had reported that Xhosa warriors, hidden from the camp, were collecting behind the ridge that stretched from Kwa Centane to the Kei valley. Instead of pushing on to the camp, Robinson directed his small mounted contingent to ride behind the ridge and engage, at a safe distance, any Xhosas who might be concealed there. His two artillery-pieces followed at a gallop, and behind them, at the double, came Lieutenant Morshead with fifty men of the 1st Battalion and a like number of Pulleine's Rangers.

Sandile's men had observed the failure of the Gcaleka assault, and had joined battle in the stealthy manner which bitter experience had taught

THE BATTLE OF CENTANE
ADAPTED FROM A MAP DRAWN BY
CAPT. FRANCIS GRENFELL

them was best suited for fighting white men. Grenfell, by taking out a small force, had played right into their hands. Their strategy was to isolate an outnumbered detachment, inflict the maximum number of casualties, and withdraw. Robinson's arrival was as unexpected as it was unwelcome. To persist in attacking in the open after the element of surprise had been lost was contrary to the dictates of Ngqika experience, and they began to withdraw. That was the signal for Carrington to send all the troops on the ridge in pursuit. The Ngqikas made no attempt to fight back, but ran until they reached a conical hill well out of range of the white man's guns. They left sixteen dead warriors behind, but Sandile's army had survived to fight again on its chosen terrain.

The battle was not quite over. A group of warriors had been spotted trying to creep through the watercourse near the camp. Upcher assembled 'F' Company, his naval contingent and whatever Mfengu he could find, and went in after them. It took almost an hour to flush out this remnant of the Xhosa army, but by 10 : 30 a.m. the fight for Centane was over.

Casualties amongst the defenders had been extremely light, three Mfengu killed and three mounted men wounded. Over two hundred and sixty Xhosa dead were found near the camp, and a like number, it was believed, died in the bush from wounds. By the time the count was completed all the fallen had had their bellies opened by Mfengu knives.

Centane was the decisive battle of the Transkeian campaign. Even though none of the Xhosa leaders had been killed or captured, it marked the end of organised Gcaleka resistance. Khiva collected a modest force to attack his traitorous uncle, Mapasa, who had become the focus of all his hatred; but he was killed in a skirmish with some Mfengu less than a month after Centane. Mapasa escaped retribution, but the Ntsonyana clan was never forgiven by the Gcaleka nation. Fifty years after the war their defection to the white man was still recalled in tribal councils. The hunt for Sarhili was to go on for many months, but the elusive old chief stayed one step ahead of his pursuers. Sandile left the Gcalekas to fend for themselves and took the war into the Ciskei.

Frere and Cunynghame desperately needed a triumph of imperial arms, and made much of the victory in which four hundred and fifty soldiers, aided by five hundred Mfengu had defeated four thousand warriors. Captain Upcher came in for a great deal of praise, Carrington's reckless charges earned him an heroic reputation, and Charles Atkinson was mentioned in despatches. The 1/24th shared in the eulogies. Cunynghame wrote about the 'high state of drill and discipline and the admirable instruction', which had made the victory possible. Frere sang their praises to Carnarvon: 'The 24th are old, steady shots whose every bullet told', and to the Duke of Cambridge he wrote, 'What good reason we have had to be thoroughly satisfied in every way with Colonel Glyn and his regiment the 1st 24th . . .'

The conduct of the battle was made the subject of frequent discussions in the Military Reserve; two aspects were considered important enough to bring to the notice of the Secretary for War: the deployment of a company of infantry to draw the warriors onto the guns of the camp – 'the best mode of warfare with Kaffirs is to allow them to appear to gain at first some advantage in the attack, merely to lure them on to their destruction', and the efficacy of the Martini-Henry as a defensive weapon in the hands of disciplined infantry. Nyumaga and Centane had been the rifle's first trial in battle, and the verdict was unqualified confidence. Frere commented that Centane might have had a different outcome in the days of 'Brown Bess'; and on 17 February he echoed the thoughts of the military when he wrote to Carnarvon, 'It has been in many respects a very instructive action; not only as regards the vastly increased power in our improved weapons and organisation, but as showing the Kaffir persistance in the new tactics of attacking us in the open in masses. At present this is their fatal error . . .' But within a few weeks, Sandile was to show the Governor that by reverting to guerrilla tactics, he could prolong the war by five months; and within a year, the Zulus would show him, with terrible consequence, what a massed attack in the open could achieve against infantrymen armed with the dependable Martini-Henry.

13

The old order changes

While the greater part of the 1st Battalion was scouring the humid valleys and bush-filled ravines on the lower Kei, those whose duties had kept them in the Military Reserve, found themselves observers at a very different kind of contest – a struggle for supremacy between the Governor and the Cape Premier.

When the Ngqikas went into rebellion, Molteno's first reaction was to make Frere the scapegoat. The irruption was seen as the consequence of a speech in which he had stated that permanent peace would entail a complete disarmament of all the tribes, loyal as well as hostile. Molteno had described it as an unrealistic threat which revealed the Governor's profound ignorance of the black man's values, a blunder akin to the issuing of cartridges greased with pig fat to the Sepoys. Frere in turn, demanded that Molteno sanction a request to the War Office for the immediate dispatch of the two battalions which had been detailed to relieve the 1/13th and the 1/24th, and the right to retain the 'relieved' battalions in the Colony. He painted a gloomy picture of conditions on the frontier and denigrated Griffith's arrangements in the Transkei. The prospect of having to pay for a few thousand additional 'red-coats' whose capabilities he held in contempt, brought a flat refusal. But Frere was accustomed to taking unilateral decisions, and a letter*, requesting reinforcements, was dispatched despite Molteno's opposition. The Premier needed no further urging, and on 9 January he arrived in 'King'.

His first act was to create a mini-cabinet consisting of himself, Brownlee and Merriman. Frere was advised that in their dealings with him they would adopt the formal constitutional procedures which the Cabinet followed in Cape Town. A few days later he learnt that preparations were

---

*The wording of the letter left little doubt that 'the threatening aspect of affairs on the Zulu border' might require a military solution in the not too distant future.

well advanced for a colonial operation against the Ngqikas. From the moment Cunynghame took control of military operations in the Transkei Merriman became a 'Minister of War' without an army. He was temperamentally unsuited for a passive role, and when the Ngqikas broke out, made up his mind to treat the rebellion as an exclusively colonial affair. He had prepared plans for a colonial attack on the Ngqika location but had remained in a state of ineffectual restlessness until Molteno's arrival. The plan was for Commandant Frost to direct three colonial columns in a sweep from Greytown to Bolo Drift on the Kei, cut off the insurgents from the Amatholes and force them down the Kei valley to the coast. The operation was to be conducted without reference to Cunynghame and the Military.

Frere showed the plan to Colonel Bellairs, who had favoured a similar action but had dismissed it for lack of cavalry, artillery and levies. He was convinced that an 'imperfectly organised column' in the rough country near the junction of the Kabousie and Kei rivers could only succeed at the risk of high casualties. Furthermore, the Mfengu levies whom Frost planned to employ would, in his opinion, be better utilised in Cunynghame's proposed offensive on the Tyityaba valley. At a four-hour meeting with Molteno, Frere stressed Colonel Bellairs's criticisms and made it clear that he, personally, would take no responsibility for the consequences of the operation.

Molteno decided that the time had come for plain speaking. He told Frere that the Colony did not want its affairs managed by British Officers, that their interference had prevented the colonists from coming forward to defend the border and that the Government, which was competent to restore peace, needed neither his approval nor reinforcements from Britain. He also told him that he would be much happier if the Military confined its activities to the Transkei and left the management of operations in the Ciskei to colonial forces; and that it was high time that Griffith was returned from his subordinate duties at Ibeka to take command in the Ciskei; and as for the Governor himself, the Ministery would prefer it if he returned to Cape Town and stopped meddling in military affairs. Muttering that reinforcements would have been unnecessary if the colonists had done their duty, Frere retired to brood over the Prime Minister's challenge to his authority.

While battle lines were being drawn in the council rooms in King William's Town, Commandant Frost rode through the Ngqika location like an avenging fury. His visitation lasted a week, and at the end of that time he was forced to admit that the country through which he had passed was 'almost destitute of male Kafirs', then added, consolingly, that 'few, if any, of those who came within rifle shot escaped'. The reports that filtered through to the Governor made Frost's raid sound more like an act of vengeance than a tactical operation. Memories of atrocities committed by irregulars who had failed to distinguish between innocent and mutineers in the Sepoy Rebellion returned to Frere, and reinforced his resolve to keep the control of the war in his own hands.

The next clash between the Governor and the Prime Minister occurred when the latter proposed removing the colonial forces from the command of General Cunynghame. He wanted to place them under a Commandant-General responsible solely to the Government. This time Frere dropped his correct official manner, and told Molteno that as far as he was concerned the office of Commandant-General was unknown and, without the sanction of Parliament, illegal. Unless Griffith remained under Cunynghame's orders, his actions would be beyond the law.

Molteno took no notice of the Governor's remonstrances and went ahead with his scheme. The appointment was gazetted. Frere lodged a strong protest, but was told that as Commander-in-Chief he had no special power over Griffith. He was reminded that he could only exercise authority as Governor on the advice of the Cabinet, advice, which in the normal course of events, required neither his opinion nor his agreement. Frere deliberated for four days then sent Molteno a detailed, legalistic analysis of a governor's authority, which emphasised that his role as Commander-in-Chief was embodied in the governorship, and that the two were not divisible.

Merriman, in the meantime, exhilarated by the success of the colonial foray into the Ngqika location, was planning a punitive action into northern Thembuland. Volunteers from the Colony's northern districts were pouring into Queenstown and he thought it a good opportunity to levy a fine on the Tshatshu clan, believed to be responsible for a spate of stockthefts in the Queenstown district. The Resident Magistrate of Queenstown was told to take out a warrant against their chief, Gungubele, with instructions to depose him if the fine was not paid. The 'police action' was undertaken by a substantial volunteer force. Gungubele refused to accept the warrant. A skirmish took place, and the Magistrate's escort had to beat a hurried retreat. The slight to the Magistrate was treated as a major uprising, and Merriman launched the whole Queenstown volunteer division and the combined forces of Frost, Rorke and

Ayliff against the Tshatshu and their allies.

The fury and savagery of the attack on the northern Thembu surprised everyone. The *Cape Argus* called it 'one of the most wicked and atrocious acts ever perpetrated in Her Majesty's dominions, veiled under the pretence of serving a civil warrant'. Another paper suggested that it 'should lead to the summary fall of some person or persons whom an inquiry can alone disclose as being responsible for what appears to be an unjustifiable wrong'. Frere was outraged both by the brutality of the attack and the fact that it had been undertaken without the knowledge of the General. Ayliff's Mfengu, in fact, had been summarily withdrawn from Cunynghame's command without his permission. Frere accused Merriman of becoming a 'military dictator', whose 'insane attempts to ape Gambetta had caused a serious aggravation of warfever'. And behind the impetuous young minister's actions he thought he could detect the inciting bulk of Molteno.

Matters came to a head on the last day of January, when Frere requested Molteno to sign treasury warrants to provide for the landing of five companies of the 90th Light Infantry which were expected at any day. Molteno expressed indignant surprise, and denied having any previous knowledge of an official request for more troops. As far as he was concerned the 90th Regiment could carry on sailing to where 'the necessities of Empire' might find better employment for them. The treasury warrants remained unsigned. The next day, Molteno, Merriman and Brownlee were summoned to a meeting of the Executive Council in the Officers' Quarters. Molteno realised there was trouble afoot, and arrived with a prepared minute objecting to a meeting called at such short notice about which he had had no prior briefing. Frere then threatened to summon the Executive Council every day until the Ministers were prepared to discuss his complaints. The meeting was reconvened the next afternoon. In the presence of General Cunynghame, he accused the Ministers of creating a dual command before its legality had been established. This left him no choice but to accept the resignation of the Prime Minister and those who agreed with him. Molteno knew he was battling for his political life. He scorned Frere's suggestion of a resignation then, foolishly, suggested that the Governor could of course *dismiss* his Ministers. Frere, at this stage, was more than willing to take the step. Four days later, on 6 February, Molteno, Merriman and Brownlee were served with their dismissals by the Magistrate of King William's Town.

The reaction in the Colony was surprise rather than outrage. There

The 'War Council', staff and officers of the 1/24th in the Military Reserve, 1877. *Standing left to right:* Capt. W. T. Much, Capt. T. Rainforth, Paymaster F. F. White, Capt. Hillier (staff), Capt. H. H. Parr (staff), Q. M. J. Pullen, Lt. F. P. Porteous, Maj. H. B. Pulleine, Lt. G. F. J. Hodson, Lt.-Col. F. W. E. Walker (staff), Mr. J. Sivewright (Manager of the Telegraph Company), Lt. C. J. Atkinson, Capt. G. V. Wardell. *Sitting left to right:* Lt. J. P. Daly, Hon. C. P. Brownlee, Sir Bartle Frere, Lt.-Gen. Sir Arthur Cunynghame, Col. R. T. Glyn, Hon. J. X. Merriman. *Sitting on ground:* Lt. N. J. A. Coghill (staff), Hon. W. Littleton (Secretary to Frere) (*Album of Bandmaster Burck*).

Top left: Sir Bartle Frere: a contemporary portrait revealing something of the iron will behind the façade of 'Exeter Hall humanity' *(Africana Museum, Johannesburg). Top right:* Hon. J. C. Molteno. *Bottom left:* Hon. J. X. Merriman: a contemporary portrait *(Africana Museum, Johannesburg). Bottom right:* Paramount Chief Sarhili *(Parliament Library, Cape Town).*

Top left: Captain Veldman Bikitsha *(Parliament Library, Cape Town). Top right:*
Captain Russel Upcher: the hero of Centane *(24th Regiment Museum, Brecon).*
Bottom left: Captain G. V. Wardell *(Courtesy J. B. Hayward & Son, Piccadilly).*
Bottom right: Chief Sandile.

Top: The Relief of Fort Warwick *(Illustrated London News). Bottom:* The Battle of Centane *(Illustrated London News).*

Top: A detachment of Mfengu levies and their commandant *(Illustrated London News)*. *Bottom:* Mfengu viewing the body of Sandile *(The Graphic)*.

Left: A trooper of the Frontier Armed and Mounted Police in black corduroy uniform (*Africana Museum, Johannesburg*). *Right*: Soldiers of the 1/24th (with Martini-Henry rifle) after the Transkeian campaign (*A sketch by Lt. W. W. Lloyd*

Top left: Lieutenant-General Frederick Thesiger (Lord Chelmsford). *Top right:* Lieutenant-Colonel Henry Degacher: commander of the 2/24th *(24th Regiment Museum, Brecon).* Bottom left: Major Henry Pulleine *(Courtesy J. B. Hayward & Son, Piccadilly).* Bottom right: Lieutenant and Adjutant Teignmouth Melvill *(Courtesy J. B. Hayward & Son, Piccadilly).*

Top left: Captain Frederick Carrington *(24th Regiment Museum, Brecon)*.
Top right: Lieutenant Edward Browne (a later photograph) *(24th Regiment Museum, Brecon)*. *Bottom:* A Mounted Infantryman (Carrington's Horse) 1877.

was much comment, but the general concensus held that the Governor had done what was in the best interests of the Colony. The task of forming a new ministry was offered to the conveniently at hand 'opposition leader' – John Gordon Sprigg. The Eastern Province was delighted to have a Prime Minister who represented their interests, and Frere was pleased to have a man at the head of Government who promised to reconsider the confederation proposals. But he little knew, when he sat down to write an account of his actions for Lord Carnarvon, that the Secretary of State was no longer in office. Carnarvon had left Disraeli's Cabinet on 25 January, in protest over a decision to send the British Fleet through the Dardanelles, because it might provoke a war with Russia. His management of colonial affairs had not been at issue. His successor, Sir Michael Hicks Beach, had little knowledge of South African affairs and no special interest in confederation. In future, all decisions relating to that policy would betaken by Carnarvon's Proconsul in South Africa.

The officers in the Military Reserve had known that a confrontation was looming between the Governor and the Ministry, and Nevill Coghill, who had returned to King William's Town when the General was recalled from Ibeka to attend the Executive Council meeting, expressed the feelings of most of the officers when he wrote, 'the potter of crayfish [Merriman] and the sheep-farmer [Molteno] have a deal to answer for the Colony'. All of them had been pleased by the Governor's stand, but few had been more delighted about the fall of Molteno and Merriman than Cunynghame. The triumph of imperial arms at Centane came in time to crown the political victory with a dazzling military success. His forces had been augmented by one hundred and fifty very useful mounted volunteers from the diamond fields, and the 90th Light Infantry had landed in East London. He at last felt that he was in a position to wind up the war in a fitting manner before his term of command came to an end.

The General's exultation was short lived. Five days before the Ministry was dismissed the Duke of Cambridge had drafted a letter to Cunynghame which stated, 'because of the want of cordiality existing between you and the Ministry ... the Secretary of State for War has deemed it advisable ... that another General Officer should at once be appointed to the Command of the Troops in the Colony, and I have therefore to request that you will be prepared to hand over your duties on the arrival of your successor, Lieutenant-General (Local Rank) The Hon. F. A. Thesiger, C.B. who will leave this country immediately'. Cunynghame's retirement was represented as a promotion; he was given the unemployed rank of full General. By the time the Duke's letter reached him, Thesiger was nearing Cape Town.

Despite his recent successes in the Transkei, Cunynghame had not won the hearts of the colonists. His criticisms of the Colony's defensive arrangements and his occasional tactless utterances had not been forgotten. The press reacted to his recall with a condemnatory silence. Coghill was genuinely distressed. He guessed that the retirement was the result of political pressure, and thought that Henry Barkly had been Molteno's agent in London. The General, Coghill, wrote, '*had not made a single mistake* and all his operations have been *thoroughly successful*'. His assessment of the General may have been too generous, but it was largely due to Cunynghame's agitation that the Colony had not found itself completely defenceless when war came. His preparations for the second Transkei offensive had been thorough and effective. Glyn's troops had cleared Gcalekaland in a shorter time than the colonial forces; and unlike the latter, had not dispersed with the booty, but had stayed on to harass the enemy and win a major battle against one of the largest Xhosa forces ever to have challenged white troops.

Colonel Forestier Walker and Captain Francis Grenfell, Cunynghame's senior aides, felt that their interests would be best served by remaining in South Africa, and it fell to the General's youngest aide to accompany him on his voyage into retirement. His compensations were to be a few months home leave and a mention in despatches.

Frederic Augustus Thesiger arrived in King William's Town on 4 March, three days before Cunynghame and Coghill sailed for England. The new General-Commanding in South Africa was fifty-one years old. He had been promoted Major-General the year before with seniority back-dated to 1868, the year he was chosen by Sir Robert Napier to serve as Deputy Adjutant-General to the Abyssinian Expeditionary Force. Half his military life had been spent in India, and he was DAG to British troops in Bombay when Frere became Governor. He returned to England in 1874, and for the past two years had commanded the First Infantry Brigade at Aldershot.

Thesiger was a tall, spare-looking man with a bushy, square-cut beard. In civilian garb he might have been mistaken for a university don or a clergyman. He was a teetotaller and always kept a tight rein on his emotions. Diplomacy rather than argument was his style. Aware of the circumstances that surrounded Cunynghame's recall, he beseeched his staff to take the utmost care not to offend either the retiring general or the men who had served under him. It was in his dealings with the colonial troops that the change in imperial command was to have the greatest impact. He seconded men from his personal staff to act as liaison officers with the senior colonial commandants and brought colonial officers on to his staff. A minor innovation that proved particularly popular with the colonial volunteers, was the right to use the military post for their letters home – a privilege denied them by Cunynghame.

Thesiger's staff had been selected from amongst the men who had served him at Aldershot. Major John North Crealock, Deputy Assistant Adjutant-General at Aldershot, became his Military Secretary. His ADCs were Captain Matthew Gosset, the Brigade-Major of the First Infantry Brigade, and Lieutenant William Molyneux, his ADC at Aldershot. In addition, five senior officers had been seconded to him for special service. One of them was Colonel Henry Evelyn Wood, the Assistant Quartermaster-General at Aldershot. Wood was a mournful-looking man who had seen a great deal of action in the course of an unusually varied career. His appearance belied his skill as a field-commander and his inclination for the daring deed: he had received the Victoria Cross before he was twenty and had accumulated an inordinate number of war wounds in the pursuit of his profession. Wood's regiment was the 90th Light Infantry, and he expected to take command of it when Colonel Palmer, the present Commanding Officer, retired in April. Major Redvers Buller, another of Thesiger's special service officers, was physically the more impressive specimen. He looked what he was, a courageous soldier, an accomplished horseman and a fearless leader in battle. As an officer he had much in common with Fred Carrington and was to succeed him as commander of the Frontier Light Horse.

When Thesiger and his staff arrived in King William's Town they were told that the war was practically over, and that 'they should probably be back in Cape Town in a month'. But some recent developments in the Ciskei should have cast doubt on so optimistic a prediction. Unrest among the tribes in the Fort Beaufort district, the heartland of frontier strife in past wars, had become manifest early in February. The kloofs, kranses and valleys of the western Amatholes had been the chosen fighting ground of Sandile's half-brother, Maqoma. It was there, during the Eighth Frontier War, that he tied up thousands of soldiers in an exhausting and costly campaign. After the war Maqoma's people had been driven from the district;

but with the passing of time many had returned surreptitiously, to their former haunts, and Maqoma's son, Tini, had come to rule over a substantial following near Fort Beaufort. His father's notoriety was sufficient to endow him with the status of a serious potential adversary and an apprehensive vigil had been kept on his kraal since the flare-up in the Ngqika location.

Tini, at first, had shown little of his father's bellicosity; but in February reports began arriving of armed gatherings in his kraal and of cattle thefts in the district. One of Cunynghame's last acts in the Cape Colony had been the dispatch of the newly arrived 90th Light Infantry to Fort Beaufort. The appearances of Colonel Palmer's 'short-service' soldiers had done little to instill confidence in the local farmers. A military commentator, who had watched the 90th embark at Southampton, had written, 'a more miserable, limp, half-grown shambling batch of boys never left England inside Her Majesty's uniform, even in the worst crisis of the Crimean War', Colonel Wood ascribed their youthfulness to an economy measure whereby men who would complete their 'long-service' that year, had been deliberately left in the regimental depot to save passage money. The settlers, however, chose to believe that the experienced soldiers had been kept back for a war against Russia, and that raw recruits were considered good enough for a colonial war. Cunynghame, too, had been unimpressed with the new troops, and had added the 1st Battalion's 'C' Company to Colonel Palmer's command. Captain William Mostyn, recently returned from Brecon, had taken charge of the company. At Fort Beaufort, Colonel Palmer discovered that Tini had abandoned his kraal and had moved with over a thousand warriors into the Waterkloof, Maqoma's old stronghold. It began to look as if the Colony might have to prepare for what Merriman called another 'real old-fashioned Kaffir War'.

At about the same time a number of disturbing incidents occurred in the East London district. The offensive in the Kei and Tyityaba valleys had scattered the Xhosa army, but small groups of marauders had begun to operate as far west as the Gonubie River. Captain William Much, in command at Fort Glamorgan was being inundated with complaints about stock-thefts and raids on isolated farms. His undermanned infantry garrison was helpless against raiders who struck swiftly and melted away into the bush, and he was forced to rely on hesitant volunteers to patrol the district.

An event of some significance occurred on 23 February. A detachment of Queenstown volunteers, while patrolling the Thomas River valley (the northern gateway into the Amatholes), stopped for breakfast at an attractive spot on the banks of the river. Not having seen any Xhosas for some days, the officer in charge neglected to post any vedettes. Suddenly, a large warrior party under Sandile's son, Matanzima, attacked them. The volunteers managed to extricate themselves after a fight lasting almost two hours, but only because their attackers were poorly armed. The size of Matanzima's force implied that the Ngqikas were making a determined effort to reach the Amathole sanctuary and a commando was hastily organised under the Commandant-General to block their way. Griffith denuded the garrisons at Stutterheim, Greytown and Cathcart and concentrated his men along the Thomas River, leaving only a handful to patrol the eastern approaches into the Amatholes. Such was the state of affairs in the Ciskei when Thesiger inherited the all but finished war.

On 9 March, while at dinner in the Military Reserve, the General was handed an urgent telegram. It informed him that a huge body of Xhosas had slipped past Stutterheim and was heading for the Sidenge Range in the Amatholes. He had to act quickly if Sandile was to be isolated in the eastern Amatholes and prevented from linking up with Tini's warriors in the Waterkloof. The five companies of the 90th were committed in the Fort Beaufort district, and the troops at hand amounted to one under-strength company of the 1/24th. More men were urgently needed: the very next morning, a train, carrying two companies of the 24th Regiment's 2nd Battalion, pulled into the King William's Town station.

The Sepoy Rebellion had convinced the British Government that its standing army was too small to police an Empire that had almost doubled in size since Victoria came to the throne. As a result twenty-five new battalions were raised in 1858. One of them became the 2/24th. Pulleine, Sawbridge and Wardell were numbered amongst the 2nd Battalion's founder members; Henry Degacher had been its first Adjutant. George Paton and William Degacher joined the battalion as Ensigns within a year of its establishment. In 1860 the 2/24th was sent to Mauritius on a tour of duty that lasted six years. During this period, Mostyn, Much, Rainforth and Younghusband were added to its officer complement. The Battalion's next posting was Burma, then India. In 1873, after thirteen peaceful years in the colonies, the 2/24th returned to England. Cardwell's new military districts had come into existence and the 2nd Battalion was moved to Brecon. Most of the 'long-service' men, by that time, had completed their obligations to the Queen, and over the next five years were replaced with 'short-service' recruits from the surrounding districts. By 1878, the 2nd Battalion had acquired a decidedly Welsh character.

On 28 January, Henry Degacher received an urgent telegram instructing him to prepare his Battalion for immediate departure to South Africa. Four days later twenty-four officers and eight hundred and fifty men together with their wives and children boarded the *Himalaya*. The military commentator who had found so much to criticise about the 90th, considered the 2/24th a 'marked improvement'. He was dismayed, however, by the 'shortage of virile moustaches' and thought them novices at rifle-drill. The men created a better impression in Cape Town, where the *Cape Times* described them as 'stout, healthy, well-built lads, with plenty of beef in their muscles, and as likely fellows as could be found to turn into soldiers of the best type. Their only fault is youth, a fault which will mend with every day'.

The *Himalaya* anchored off Buffalo Mouth on 9 March, having passed H.M.S. *Active*, with Cunynghame and Coghill on board, the previous day. The infamous East London surf allowed two companies to be put ashore without mishap. Conditions then underwent a sudden change and made it impossible for the remainder of the Battalion to land. Two days were to pass before the sea calmed sufficiently to allow all the men to be brought out. The biggest indignity was saved for the Battalion band. The hawser, along which their lighter was being hauled, snapped and the boat turned broadside over the bar, dumping Bandmaster Henry Bullard, bandsmen and instruments into the surf. One of the soldiers disembarking at East London that day was the Adjutant of the 1/24th. Teignmouth Melvill, unable to find a place on the Staff College course, had returned, after an absence of four months, to serve with his battalion for the remainder of the year.

The 2nd Battalion was taken to 'King' as quickly as trains could be procured. Lieutenant-Colonel Henry Degacher found the town he last had seen two years before, a changed place. Wartime overcrowding and close-quartered living, aggravated by a serious water shortage, had strained the rudimentary public health facilities. The once pleasant town on the banks of the Buffalo River had become a foul-smelling pest hole. Its outskirts were polluted with putrid animal carcasses, rotting vegetable matter and carelessly disposed waste, while dysentery and typhoid were reaching epidemic proportions. A scene reminiscent of the Great Plague was the 'dead cart' which did a daily round accompanied by two constables with fixed bayonets. Fortunately for the newcomers they were not long delayed in King William's Town. As each company came in, it was dispatched to a healthier environment in the Amatholes.

The highland known as the eastern Amatholes consisted of the Gwili Gwili, Sidenge and Buffalo ranges. Its tallest peak, Mount Kempt, was clearly visible in King William's Town. The heights formed a well-watered plateau from which many rivers took origin, and the rugged valleys through which the rivers flowed were heavily forested. Dense vegetation grew on the slopes of the hills, and at the foot of the steep kranses that formed the Buffalo Poort stretched a formidable barrier o trees and undergrowth called the Pirie Bush. To the south the bush gave way to undulating glades studded with bushes and small trees. Cattle grazing in this verdant lowland could be driven, readily, into the nearby forests and concealed from view. The whole area was a vast, natural hiding place in which the entire Ngqika nation could find concealment for itself and its herds. An officer who fought against Maqoma in the previous frontier war left a graphic description of the Amathole bush: 'this all but impenetrable forest, studded throughout with enormous masses of detached rock, overgrown with wild creepers, so strong and so thickly interlaced as almost to put a stop to our advance; covered moreover with dense thorny underwood, concealing dangerous clefts and crevices, and strewn with fallen trees in every stage of decay, while the hooked thorns oft the 'wait-a-bit' clinging to our arms and legs, snatching the caps off our heads and tearing clothes and flesh, impeded us at every stage'. His account referred to the campaign in the Waterkloof district. But Evelyn Wood, who had read a great deal about that war, thought it could not compare with the Pirie Bush as a 'natural stronghold for our black man'.

Such was the 'Amathole fortress' in which Sandile grew up, survived two major wars, and had returned to, to wage war yet again.

14

War in the Amatholes

General Thesiger had to act quickly if he wanted to confine the Ngqikas to the kloofs, kranses and valleys in which they had taken refuge. He chose Colonel Wood, his most experienced staff officer, to throw a cordon around the eastern Amatholes. The first two 2/24th companies to arrive in King William's Town were ordered to accompany him to the Amatholes. He left one company at Bailie's Grave,* a low earthwork situated on a ridge near the south-western buttresses of the Buffalo Poort. The other accompanied him to the village of Keiskamma Hoek, where he intended to set up his headquarters. Rupert Lonsdale, an ex-officer of the 74th Regiment, who commanded a Mfengu contingent, was already there with the news that his force had narrowly escaped disaster after a brush with some Ngqikas on the hills overlooking the village.

Lonsdale's Mfengu, 'C' Company 2/24th, and two hundred mounted farmers from Grahamstown and Cradock made up Wood's Keiskamma Hoek command. On his right the line was prolonged southwards by a large Mfengu contingent which arrived from Komga a few days later. It was led by Frank Streatfeild, a boisterous adventurer who had given up an unsuccessful farming venture to command levies. On Wood's left Commandant Frost concentrated five hundred volunteers near Fort Merriman, and further east, near Stutterheim, Commandant Schermbrucker gathered together two hundred and seventy mounted colonials and four hundred Mfengu. To prevent a Ngqika breakout in the southwest, Thesiger asked Commandant Edward Brabant, who knew the Pirie Bush intimately, to place a volunteer detachment near Bailie's Grave.

The arc-shaped line from Bailie's Grave to Stutterheim was meant to converge on the Buffalo Poort and squeeze the Ngqikas out of their

*The post, abandoned after the last frontier war, had acquired its sinister name in 1835, when a colonial patrol led by a Lieutenant Charles Bailie was ambushed and massacred in a nearby kloof.

mountain hideout. The Pirie Bush, their likely direction of flight, was guarded by five companies of the 2/24th disposed in a straight line from Ntaba-ka-Ndoda (the hill that looked like a man's head) to Izeleni Post, the place where the waters of the Buffalo, Cwengwe and Izeleni rivers came together. One company had to be stationed close to the Pirie Mission because its converts were suspected of siding with the rebels; another took up a position at Hayne's sawmill where the Buffalo River emerged from dense thickets and flowed past the wild, overgrown cliffs that formed the Buffalo Poort. Henry Degacher commanded the southern exit from the Amatholes. Thesiger, about to conduct his first military operation, made Hayne's mill his headquarters. It was a position from which he could do little more than gaze up at the forested heights that towered around him and try to surmise what was happening on the heights above. His force, which numbered almost three thousand men, was estimated to have a marginal superiority over Sandile's army in manpower, and an overwhelming one in weapons.

The drive was to start at daylight on 18 March, but Colonel Wood had received information that there were over a thousand warriors on the Gwili Gwili Heights, and he decided to move out at night in order to lesson the risk of ambush while his men negotiated the difficult ascent onto the highland plateau. Walking in single file it took his men till dawn to complete the seven mile climb. When the sun rose Wood gazed out on an empty landscape, and with no other troops in sight, settled down to await the arrival of Streatfeild's Mfengu.

Brabant, too, had taken his men out during the night and had reached the plateau before Wood. His men, however, had spotted some cattle grazing in a glade below them, and falling for the oldest Xhosa trick in frontier warfare, chased after them. The pursuit had led them into a thicket where hundreds of Ngqikas were waiting. Streatfeild's levies had climbed the Rabula Heights and were about to move onto the plateau, when word reached them that Brabant was in trouble. Streatfeild abandoned his advance and turned south to help the beleaguered colonials. It took him the best part of the day to bring them out, and cost him one of his best officers. Wood, for lack of support, was forced to remain in the position he had occupied at sunrise.

At Hayne's mill all was quiet. The Xhosas' stampede that Thesiger had hoped to witness, failed to materialise; so, for that matter, did his troops. He spent the day in anxious ignorance, oblivious of what was happening on the heights above him. In the evening, he sent messengers galloping in all directions with instructions for the columns to spend the night in the positions they had occupied, and to re-commence the drive on the following morning; but the surprise he had hoped to achieve, was lost.

Brabant's misadventure had a demoralising effect on Wood's volunteer contingent; when he moved out in the morning, they refused to enter the bush because they felt 'it was not a fit place for Europeans', preferring to leave it to Lonsdale and his Mfengu. It was not until Wood started to lead his company of youthful soldiers into the bush that they relented. The Mfengu, moving in front, had some light skirmishes on the plateau, but they reached the edge without having encountered any serious opposition. They were joined, after a short while, by Frost's and Brabant's men. The area above the poort was encircled, and a large group of rebels emerged from the bush with their hands in the air – a group composed entirely of women and children.

At the sawmill, Thesiger heard the noise of gunfire, and minutes later saw his mounted men appear on the heights above him. He was convinced that the Xhosas were about to rush out of the poort, and ordered his two artillery pieces to shell the bush. After a few dozen salvos had been fired, it dawned on him that there was little activity on the plateau and that the bush at the foot of the cliffs looked singularly undisturbed once the shells stopped exploding. He could not understand the inactivity on the plateau, and ordered his ADC to take a small detachment of Mfengu and soldiers through the bush of the Buffalo Poort to the plateau above. Fortunately for the soldiers and the Mfengu someone pointed out to Thesiger that it was insane folly to send men into the Xhosa infested forest merely to satisfy his curiosity.

A confusing day was followed by a memorable night of wind, driving rain and freezing temperatures. In the Pirie Bush regulation sentry duty was abandoned; the men were broken up into silent groups of four, one man keeping a lookout while his companions tried to sleep. Sentries were instructed not to patrol or get separated from their group. It was impressed upon them that the bush was full of cunning warriors, and that their only hope of not being taken by surprise was to rely on their ears. Morning brought a heavy mist that covered the plateau and hid the cliffs; by late afternoon Thesiger was no wiser about the situation on the plateau than he had been the day before. He decided there and then to move his headquarters onto the Sidenge range, and Degacher was ordered to take two 2nd Battalion companies onto the heights. The only feasible route for the infantry with their heavily-laden wagons was a circuitous wagon-track past the village of Frankfort. The march was begun that night, and for the inexperienced young soldiers, who had been on constant alert for forty-eight hours, it was the start of a toughening-up process that was to continue for four months and turn Degacher's boys into seasoned campaigners.

The next morning, Captain Gosset, who was attached to Schermbrucker's staff, rode down from their encampment near Mount Kempt in time to guide the General up the shorter route through the Cwengwe valley. Thesiger was, at last, in a position to see what was happening on the plateau. From Mount Kempt he watched Colonel Wood's men break camp, and after they had gone, he watched, with doleful eyes, the Xhosas come out of the bush and take possession of the deserted camp site. The troops on the plateau had spent the previous day enveloped in mist. Wood had consulted with Frost and Brabant, and they had agreed on a drive down the Buffalo Poort when the mist lifted. Thesiger spotted them as they were about to begin the descent. The headlong scramble to Hayne's mill proved so arduous that their men had little energy left to search for Xhosas. From the General's vantage point on Mount Kempt it soon became apparent that his offensive had left Sandile's warriors in unhampered occupation of the lower plateau.

The results of the four-day offensive had not, in Wood's opinion, been 'commensurate with the discomfort we underwent'. The lessons learnt were noted down by Thesiger's Military Secretary; the General, in future, would occupy a position where he could observe the movement of his troops, he would not leave too much to the discretion of his column commanders, and he would introduce flag signalling as soon as possible.

Conscious that his performance was being watched by critical colonial eyes, Thesiger made immediate preparations for another offensive. Degacher's men were put to work cutting a path from Mount Kempt to the Cwengwe valley in order to speed communications between Headquarters and the troops guarding the Pirie Bush. The lower plateau could be dominated by artillery placed on the Sidenge range, and the Band of the 1/24th was brought from King William's Town to make good the shortage of trained artillerymen. Taking the field-pieces up the narrow, winding track that led to the Sidenge Heights, posed a problem. It was solved by inspanning three mules in tandem fashion. The driver ran alongside the hind mule holding the reins, while another man guided the lead mule. Because the low carriages were unstable over rough ground, and inclined to turn over, two men had to cling to the handles on either side of the limber.

The second offensive began on 28 March. Degacher's men on Sidenge joined forces with Frost's commando in a drive onto the Gwili Gwili plateau. There they linked up with Wood's column, which had again made the ascent from Keiskamma Hoek. Brabant had been placed under Wood's immediate orders and given the task of clearing the Rabula Heights. This operation was better co-ordinated than the first, but the Ngqika avoided any confrontation with the troops. They forsook the highland plateau for the safety of the Pirie Bush. Thesiger's forces again had little to show for their exertions, but this time they kept possession of the lower plateau. Their one consolation, as they bivouacked in the cold and the rain, was that the Xhosas, confined to the sunless forests, were even more uncomfortable.

The burgher volunteers examined the results of eleven days campaigning and came to the conclusion that they represented a poor return for all their discomfort. Three volunteer officers had been killed and less than two hundred head of cattle had been captured. It was a prohibitive price by frontier standards, and compared poorly with the performance of Schermbrucker's commando, which had captured three hundred cattle and killed fifty-five of Matanzima's men in the two days preceding the General's offensive. The concensus of opinion was that the man who had replaced Cunynghame was more considerate of colonial feelings, but did not inspire as a 'Kaffir fighter'. The volunteer units began to disintegrate, and the unconfortable work of holding the plateau was left to the infantry and the FLH. The flight of the Ngqikas into the Buffalo Range had freed the latter from the necessity of patrolling the supply-route to the Transkei. Fred Carrington, who had been promoted to a vacant captaincy in the 2nd Battalion, had returned to the Transvaal, and command of the FLH had passed to Major Redvers Buller.

Thesiger grasped the importance of using large Mfengu detachments to clear the Pirie Bush. An urgent telegram was dispatched to Colonel Glyn at Ibeka asking him to send all the levies he could spare. On 3 April, James Ayliff arrived with a thousand Mfengu. Two days later they commenced a sweep from Mount Kempt to Hayne's mill. Thousands of rounds were expended in the operation. A few elderly Xhosas and a large number of bushbuck fell victim to the fusillade, and a large batch of women and children was captured. The result merely confirmed the fact that the rumour about Sandile having vacated the Buffalo Range was true.

Hunted by a powerful enemy and with a £500 reward on his head,

Sandile was capable still of firing old loyalties. Jali, the easy going chief of the Ndlambes, forsook his kraal to be with him. Reinforcements arrived from the Kama clan, and the veteran warrior Siyolo broke out of his reservation to join him. Siyolo had fought alongside Maqoma in the war of 1835, and with Sandile in the two subsequent frontier wars. He had been wounded, mauled and imprisoned, but had not lost his fighting spirit. Age had neither changed his habits nor taught him prudence: he had left the lower reaches of the Keiskamma River with two thousand warriors in a bid to reach Sandile in the Lotutu Bush. His force was spotted near Debe Nek by a Diamond Field Horse patrol. Siyolo's instinctive response was to cut off the patrol and destroy it. But he quickly discovered that his men were no match for well-armed horsemen in flat country. He lost two of his sons in the skirmish and his followers had to scatter into the bush around Ntaba-ka-Ndoda.

As soon as the news of the encounter with Siyolo reached him, Thesiger sent Ayliff's Mfengu to reinforce the single infantry company near Ntaba-ka-Ndoda. The remainder of the 2/24th was ordered to concentrate at Bailie's Grave as quickly as possible. Wood and Brabant were instructed to work their way along the Rabula River and search the northern perimeter of the Lotutu Bush. At the Burnshill Mission, Wood discovered two companies of the 90th, and promptly added them to his force. The arrival of the two FLH squadrons and Lonsdale's Mfengu gave him sufficient men to place a thin line on the northern and western boundaries of the Lotutu Bush. Degacher's infantry, in the meantime, had been grouped near Bailie's Grave for an attack on Ntaba-ka-Ndoda.

The hastily mounted offensive in the Lotutu Bush merely emphasised the superiority enjoyed by an enemy who knew the area intimately and was prepared to exploit the natural cover that the forests provided. The Transkeian Mfengu, who spearheaded the attack, were driven from the unfamiliar terrain no less than four times, and lost two of their officers in the process. To make matters worse, Streatfeild's and Lonsdale's levies were mistaken for Xhosas by Degacher's troops and were fired upon with rifles and artillery. After the failure of Ayliff's Mfengu it was the turn of the white forces to probe the bush. The troops at Bailie's Grave were strung out in a line that stretched to Debe Nek, and told to converge on Ntaba-ka-Ndoda from two directions. The men were so widely separated that they could barely see the helmet of their nearest comrade above the long grass. Few of them had more than an inkling of what was happening about them. Some heard the enemy, but few saw him. One who did, when it was too late, was Private Michael Collins, the first member of the 24th Regiment to be killed in action in South Africa. Degacher's young soldiers were lucky that day, but they remembered, for a long time afterwards, the ugly noise of the Xhosa muzzle-loaders at close range and the deadlier silence of their assegaais. They were made aware of their own clumsy conspicuousness and felt the impotent loneliness of their vulnerability.

The day's operations proved no more successful than the previous one; and to complicate matters, a heavy rain began to fall in the late afternoon. Thesiger decided to suspend further operations in the Amatholes until his troops were rested and the Sprigg Ministry raised fresh burgher forces. Three companies of the 2nd Battalion were left behind to guard the Pirie Bush while the remainder returned to King William's Town. The first phase of a frustrating campaign was over.

Black levies were indispensible for the war in the Amatholes, but the Transkeian Mfengu had proved a disappointment. They had become near-rebellious after their thrashing in the Lotutu Bush and even their trusted leaders had difficulty persuading them to obey orders. The men who had fought bravely against the Gcalekas were unwilling to risk their lives in the Amatholes. Their own kraals were no longer threatened and they had little enthusiasm for what, to them, amounted to foreign service. Ayliff's contingent had to be sent home. The Ciskei Mfengu, who served under Streatfeild and Lonsdale, had impressed the General with their enthusiasm. The answer, it seemed, was to recruit in the kraals and villages in the Ciskei. The hardships that the Mfengu clans in the Amatholes were suffering from Xhosa raids lent impetus to enrolment and a large contingent was raised in the Alice and Middledrift district. A very useful addition to Thesiger's mounted strength was the arrival of Commandant von Linsingen with three hundred volunteers. They had put down a rising near the lower reaches of the Keiskamma River and their morale was high. The General was ready to plan his next offensive. He visited Fort Beaufort and learnt that Tini had vacated the Waterkloof and joined forces with Sandile and Siyolo in the Lotutu Bush. Colonel Palmer, a recent convert to a pacifist sect, readily handed over command of the 90th Regiment to Wood, who moved them immediately to Burnshill.

The new plan was to ring the Lotutu Bush with large forces and converge on it from four directions. The columns were to link in a steadily tightening noose while a battery of artillery, under the command of Major Harness, turned the wooded Xhosa refuge into a death trap. Redvers Buller was to drive down the Gongqo and Zanyokwe valleys from the north. The assault from the south was to be made by von Linsingen's volunteers reinforced by a contingent of Mfengu and *loyal* Ngqikas. He was to start out from Debe Nek, clear the southern approaches to Ntaba-ka-Ndoda and ascend the Lotutu plateau.

The movements of Buller and von Linsingen were designed to drive the Xhosas towards the west where Evelyn Wood, with the largest concentration of men, would be waiting. His force was divided into two columns; one was to head east to the high open ground overlooking the bush, the other was to take a more southerly course towards the lower Zanyokwe valley and gain the Lotutu plateau by climbing the Makabalikele ridge. The operational area was less than sixteen square miles, and Thesiger's army numbered something over four thousand men; it was confidently predicted that this time Sandile would not escape.

The advance began at six o'clock on the morning of 30 April. Von Linsingen, sensible, reliable and religious, treated his men to a prayer and a ration of brandy before leaving Debe Nek. He encountered some opposition at the foot of the unassailable southern face of Ntaba-ka-Ndoda, and killed seven of Siyolo's scouts. The mountain itself was unoccupied. His column then took a circuitous route towards the lower Zanyokwe valley, where they halted to await the arrival of Wood's Makabalikele column.

Colonel Degacher's forces reached the heights overlooking the eastern perimeter of the Gongqo and Zanyokwe valleys without meeting any resistance. His guns, two of them manned by bandsmen from the 1st Battalion, began a bombardment of the bush. The bursting shells had the desired effect. Tini's men scattered and Siyolo ordered his men to attempt a break-out in the south-west. Thesiger, on a suspicion that there were Xhosa spies in the telegraph office in Alice, had deliberately transmitted false plans to Wood. Acting on his misinformation Siyolo directed his warriors to the Makabalikele ridge.

Wood's columns had the greatest distance to cover and were late getting started. The Right Column, which he personally commanded, neared the Makabalikele ridge at about the same time that Siyolo's vanguard approached it from the opposite direction. A mile-long stretch of dense bush guarded Wood's approach to the ridge. The trees, vines and creepers were so closely intermingled there that the infantry had to enter the thicket in single file. Dragging two 7-pounders through this arborescent barrier greatly slowed the column's progress. The leading company of infantry had gone about a thousand yards into the bush when a hail of fire poured into them from all sides. Siyolo, unable to estimate the size of the column, urged his warriors to close in for the kill. One warrior got close enough to the Company Commander to fire at almost point-blank range. A Lieutenant Saltmarshe immediately took command. He advanced a mere fifty yards before receiving the full discharge of a musket in his chest. There was another rush of warriors and four more soldiers fell. Under a shower of leaves the men stumbled against trees, got snagged up in the bushes and collided with each other as they tried to fall back through the smoke-filled thicket. Panic was averted when a stocky colour-sergeant, bellowing orders and curses with equal facility, rallied the company and prevented a fatal bottleneck from developing. They held back the Xhosas long enough for the 7-pounders to be dragged up. The guns were loaded with case and fired at random into the bush. The warriors were caught off balance by the unexpected appearance of the big guns. Siyolo finally realised what he was up against and told his men to vacate the ridge. They disappeared into the bush of the Zanyokwe valley. By the time Wood's column finally established itself on the plateau, von Linsingen had linked up with Streatfeild's Mfengu and sealed off the western perimeter of the Lotutu Bush.

In the north Buller's column had worked its way down the Gongqo River and had crossed the dividing ridge that separated it from the Zanyokwe. His men had been involved in almost continuous skirmishing with a near invisible foe. At one point, as they were about to close with the enemy, a long line of unarmed women appeared as if from nowhere and formed a human screen behind which their men escaped. At about this stage the death occurred, under the strangest circumstances, of a 2nd Battalion NCO.

Sergeant Stratton, while directing the fire of his section, suddenly turned to the soldiers nearest him and yelled a quick, cheerful farewell. He then placed his rifle barrel in his mouth and blew his head off. Stratton had appeared quite happy that morning, but some of the men later recalled a remark he had made about shooting himself rather than fall into Xhosa hands. Yet when he shot himself, it was the Xhosas who were in danger of being taken prisoner. Stratton was buried in a shallow grave where he fell. The following morning his body was discovered sitting bolt upright in its grave, as if regretting a hasty decision. It turned out that someone had thought it a great waste to bury a good pair of boots along with the sergeant.

Most of the kloofs, ravines and watercourses in the Zanyokwe valley had been scoured by the middle of the first afternoon. Nearly a hundred

Xhosa dead were counted, but it was a disappointingly small number for an operation of this magnitude. The following morning Degacher's troops entered the bush in a sweep towards the west. They found it deserted. In the night, the Xhosas had made their way stealthily past Ntaba-ka-Ndoda, and were once again in the Pirie Bush. Thesiger's frustration was as great as his brooding silence, but he was still not willing to abandon his strategy of planned offensives. He returned to King William's Town to prepare, in secrecy, one last drive on the Buffalo Range. He kept away from the Pirie Mission and Hayne's sawmill until his preparations were complete, because he believed that both places abounded in spies. The offensive was set for 8 May. Its aim was to occupy the western ramparts of the Buffalo Poort, surround the Pirie Bush and seal off the escape route to the Lotutu plateau.

The evening before the drive was to commence, a force under Wood, dragging two 7-pounders, ascended the heights near Bailie's Grave in heavy rain. They were joined in the morning by Buller's column. As an exercise in moving men and equipment in bad weather across difficult terrain, it was a commendable success; but as a surprise tactic it proved a dismal failure. All they found were a few stragglers beating a hasty retreat into the bush of the Buffalo Poort.

The columns that had been chosen for an ascent through the Pirie Bush, fared even worse. Degacher was delayed for hours near Hayne's mill by the late arrival of his Mfengu auxilliaries, and von Linsingen, at the Pirie Mission, was held up by false reports about Xhosas concentrating near Ntaba-ka-Ndoda. Thesiger found little to console him after the first day of his fifth Amathole offensive. In one of the very few engagements with the enemy, a detachment of the FLH was surprised and mauled by a Xhosa rearguard. In meeting his death where he did, the leader of the detachment, Captain McNaghten, gave his name to the krans on the western side of the Buffalo Poort.

The following morning Buller, determined to avenge the death of his men, lined his force up on the edge of McNaghten's Krans for a thrust into the Buffalo Poort. The Mfengu led, followed closely by the FLH and two 2nd Battalion companies in open order. During the descent, Captain Godwin-Austen, commanding 'B' Company, was nearly killed when a soldier behind him accidently triggered off his loaded rifle. The bullet ripped his tunic open and tore an ugly gash in his back. The wound removed him from active duty for many months, and the command passed to a subaltern with eleven years service called Gonville Bromhead.

SCENE OF OPERATIONS IN THE EASTERN AMATHOLES

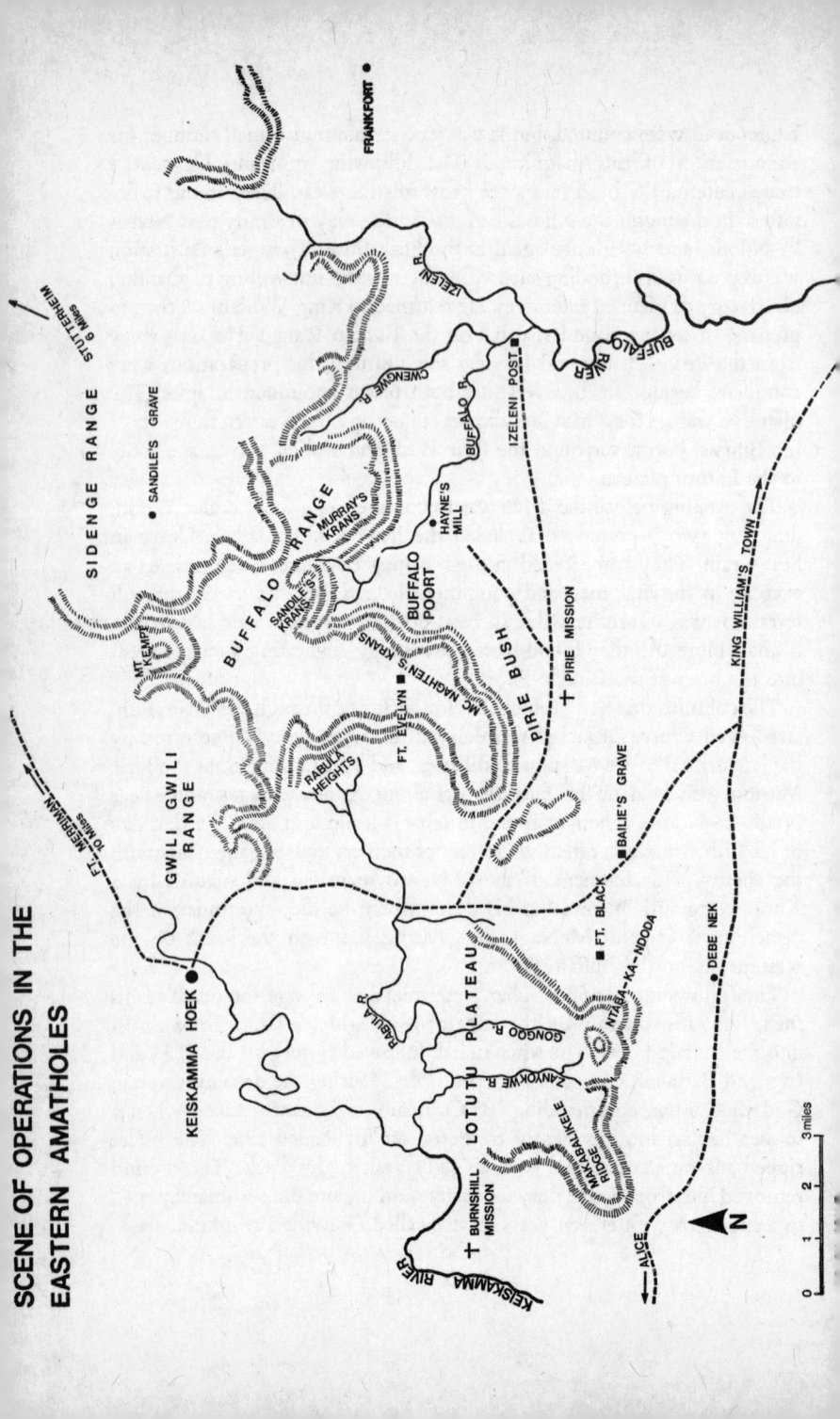

Buller's unopposed descent into the very heart of the Buffalo Poort meant that the drawbridge into Sandile's fortress was now permanently down. Thesiger's troops were in almost complete control of the territory through which, two months before, only the Xhosas had moved freely. But the General had had enough. It was no secret that his planned offensives were becoming the 'laughing stock of the Colony', and he finally acknowledged the futility of trying to trap the wily 'Tiger of the Forest' in his stronghold. It was also clear, however, that the Ngqika army no longer posed a threat to anything larger than an isolated farmstead or a small Mfengu kraal. Thesiger was ready to adopt the strategy which the colonial commandants had been urging for weeks.

The eastern Amatholes were divided into eleven military districts. In each one a mounted force was stationed. If any Xhosas were discovered they were to be pursued until they crossed into the district of a neighbouring commandant who in turn would take up the chase. In this manner pursuit and harassment would be uninterrupted, and no detachment need be drawn far from its base. In addition, Thesiger ordered the construction of two earthworks to command the well-trodden path between the Buffalo Range and the Lotutu Bush. Fort Evelyn was erected on McNaghten's Krans, and Fort Black near the foot of Ntaba-ka-Ndoda. The last was named in honour of Major Wilsone Black of the 2/24th.

The plight of the Xhosas was becoming desperate. They were no longer capable of operating as an army, and only small foraging parties ventured out of the bush. For the third time in his life Sandile found it necessary to ask the white man for terms. But his emissaries were told that this time surrender would have to be unconditional. The war in the Amatholes had reached the stalemate that Colonel Glyn had had to contend with for almost four months on the other side of the Kei. General Thesiger decided that the time had come to visit the Army of the Transkei and see how it was being tackled there.

15

Frontier settlements

Since the arrival of Thesiger and his team colonial attention had been focused on the Amathole show. Only during the lulls between the General's offensives did the press exhibit any interest in the Transkei and Colonel Glyn's forgotten army. Few notable successes had been chalked up against the fugitive Sarhili, and to make up for the dearth of news, the newspapers composed sarcastic accounts about the 'social life' Her Majesty's Officers enjoyed in the Transkei. They reported that Sarhili had become so concerned about the lack of a military presence in the territory that he had personally called at Ibeka to inquire after the soldiers' welfare. Suggestions were put forward that the Colony subscribe for a billiard-table for the Officers' Mess because the weather had become too windy for smoking outdoors. One newspaper, with mock solemnity published the results of the 'Ibeka Autumn Handicap'. These articles ultimately led to an outcry against the soldiers who did 'nothing but eat, drink and fill out returns at colonial expense.'

The Army of the Transkei, however, was enjoying anything but a luxurious existence. Isolated detachments, holed-up inside earthwork fortifications, were scattered throughout the territory. These men, living in primitive conditions, were deterring the Gcalekas from attempting a re-organisation of their broken army. By the middle of April, all eight companies of the 1/24th had moved to the Transkei. Upcher and Heaton were isolated in a God-forsaken spot near the mouth of the Shixeni River, Captain Henry Harrison's company garrisoned Fort Nixon, and Rainforth's men guarded Upcher's original camp site at Centane. When Thesiger's Military Secretary visited the Transkei, he marvelled at the 1st Battalion's proficiency in throwing up earthworks.

The General arrived at Ibeka a few days after yet another carefully planned operation to trap Sarhili in Bomvanaland had failed. His own experiences in the Amatholes and Colonel Glyn's less than spectacular achievements against the Gcaleka chief resulted in a decision to abandon large-scale operations in the Transkei. Small mounted detachments, capable of a quick strike at short notice, it was decided, would have the best chance of success against a foe that would not be brought to battle. On 14 June, orders were given to vacate most of the fortified positions in the territory; within a few days the four 1/24th companies that had been in the Transkei since December of 1877 were back in King William's Town.

The remainder were concentrated at Ibeka under the command of Henry Pulleine. The Battalion's senior field-officer had received, at last, a field command. His two months at Ibeka were to be characterised by an inactivity that did little to further his experience of war. Such operations that did take place were limited in scope and masterminded by Teignmouth Melvill, who had set his heart on capturing Sarhili. He followed up every clue to the chief's whereabouts with relentless vigour; with ten mounted men and a platoon of infantry he searched the Dwessa Forest, crossed the Bashee and scoured Bomvanaland. All his information pointed to a hide-away on the lower Bashee, but the Gcaleka chief stayed one jump ahead of his pursuers. Melvill remained in the Transkei until the middle of August when colonial contingents arrived to take over the hunt.

The Xhosa chiefs in the Amatholes fared worse than Sarhili. In the last week of May, Tini kaMaqoma was captured by some Mfengu while trying to make his way back to the Waterkloof. Siyolo forsook the Amatholes and was killed in a chance encounter with a colonial patrol. Sandile, with a shrinking band of followers, was holed up deep in the forests of the Buffalo Poort where relentless probings by Buller, Schermbrucker and Lonsdale kept him confined. Many prisoners were taken, but none would reveal the exact hiding place of the 'Tiger of the Forest'. But the determined operations eventually paid off. Sandile was forced to vacate his stronghold, and events, a few days later, would confirm the importance of this achievement.

It started when a detachment of Lonsdale's Mfengu on patrol in the Sidenge hills surprised a small party of Ngqikas. The outnumbered Xhosas had stood their ground until half their number lay dead. A week later, a Ngqika warrior, who surrendered to a colonial patrol near Frankfort, told his captors that one of the men wounded in the encounter with Lonsdale's Mfengu had been Sandile. He described how the Chief's bodyguard had tried to take him to the Thomas River where his sons Edmund and Matanzima were hiding, and that he had died in the bush near Fort Merriman. A party set out immediately to search for the body. It was found and identified by the withered leg. The flesh on the right arm and part of the left side of the face had been gnawed away by a wild animal, but the features were still recognisable. There was an ugly hole in his right side which had been caused by the passage of a Snider bullet through the upper abdomen. The body was taken to the farm of a certain Mr Schuss where Commandant Schermbrucker had his headquarters.

On Sunday 9 June, a detachment drawn from 'A' and 'B' Companies of the 2/24th, was marched to the Schuss farm and paraded on either side of a freshly dug grave. The officers present were Major Dunbar, Captain Tongue and Sub-Lieutenant Thomas Griffith. At eleven o'clock the body of Sandile was brought to the graveside on the guns of eight Mfengu pall-bearers. The head and face had been almost denuded of hair by people who wanted a memento of the notorious Xhosa chief. The sermon, delivered by Schermbrucker, took the form of a warning about the fate that befell those who chose to rebel against the Queen. It was addressed to the black onlookers. The dirge was a Mfengu chant in praise of their own prowess. After the funeral the officers retired to the farm-house for lunch. A considerable quantity of beer was consumed – some of it, perhaps, in tribute to the chief who had been dismissed as a useless drunkard, but had died a hero.

Sandile's sons were captured early in July and committed to trial a few days after the Government announced an amnesty for all rebels who came in to surrender their arms. The Ngqika rebellion was over.

The 2nd Battalion was kept in the Amatholes until the middle of July when it was relieved by colonial volunteers. The weather for the past month, had been exceptionally cold, particularly in the highlands, and the battalion suffered many casualties from exposure: seven men died in the closing weeks of the war. To the Commander-in-Chief of the British Army, Thesiger wrote: 'Degacher commanding the 2/24th deserves great credit for the efficient state of his battalion, which contains a large proportion of young soldiers ... The battalion had borne their trial remarkably well'. On 24 July, Degacher's men sailed for Natal, leaving their wives and children in King William's Town.

In August, the Ninth Frontier War was declared, officially, to be over.

The Xhosas had finally comprehended the futility of matching themselves against the technological might of a nineteenth-century European power with a colonial mission. The relevance of the Xhosas (the first blacks to confront the white man in South Africa) as a military power, had ended with their defeat in 1853. Its subconscious realisation a few years later had resulted in the national convulsion which became known as the 'great cattle-killing'. The older chiefs like Sarhili and Sandile had come to accept this unpalatable truth, but a new generation, reared on the heroic legends of a past so recent that some of its leading figures were still alive, had never known the bitter taste of defeat.

Kimberley, and the emergence of an industrial economy had allowed the young Xhosas glimpses of a less restrictive white society, and had put in their hands a hitherto undreamed of number of guns. They had not, however, comprehended what advantage the other technological triumphs of the age had afforded the white man. In the Ninth (and last) Frontier War the largest Xhosa armies ever to have taken the field tied up fewer soldiers than had any of the previous wars. The Xhosas had been defeated by steam-transportation, the telegraph and the breech-loading rifle – all used for the first time in a South African conflict. The white troops had been led by uninspired commanders, but Cunynghame and Thesiger were, nevertheless, the inheritors of the accumulated experience of eight frontier wars and had not had to wrestle with the problem of adapting tactics learnt in the Peninsular War to the South African bush. Another unexpected development had been the willingness of the Mfengu to defend their homes. They had proved a very useful adjunct to the Colony's forces and the military had exploited their skills to the full.

War between white and black might have been avoided had Frere not arrived on the frontier when he did. Had Molteno been allowed to handle the situation in his unhurried and cautious way, the wedding-feast fracas might never have developed the proportions it did. The state of tension and mistrust which Frere had discovered on the frontier had its origins in the credence given to rumours of a countrywide black conspiracy. The Burgers-Sekhukhune War had given rise to these rumours the year before, and they had endured because Eastern Province politicians had sought to exploit them for their own ends. The rumours had found too easy acceptance in the Colonial Office because they were seen to promote the benefits that might be derived from confederation. Frere believed that union of the white states in South Africa could be brought about more readily if they were freed from the bogey of black independence. He had welcomed the opportunity to settle decisively the Cape Colony's long-troubled frontier and impose, to his way of thinking, the only solution for lasting peace – the incorporation of the Transkei into the Cape Colony. He may have accepted war too readily as a means of furthering his mission, but the acceptance was tempered by the sincerely held belief that British justice and the liberal Cape Constitution would, in time, permit the Transkeian blacks to obtain a full share in the Colony's future.

For the Xhosas the immediate consequence of the war was total subjugation. The Ngqika Reserve was divided up into farms and sold by public auction. The population was disarmed and relocated in Gcalekaland, even the clans that had remained loyal to the Colony. Those who strove to remain near the Amatholes could do so only by becoming farm hands or domestic servants. Gcalekaland was divided into magisterial districts, and the power of the hereditary chiefs was inherited by appointed magistrates. Bomvanaland lost its independence and was incorporated into the Magistracy of Thembuland. The conquered territories were administered by the Cape Secretary for Native Affairs until 1885 when formal annexation to the Cape Colony was proclaimed. Sarhili gave himself up three years after the war ended; he was, by then, no longer of interest to the Colony and ended his days in peaceful obscurity.

It might also be said that the Ninth Frontier War accelerated the rise of Afrikaner nationalism. To help pay for the war which had cost the Colony £1 750 000 Sprigg introduced an excise duty on spirits. The burden fell largely on the Western Province farmers, most of whom were 'Old Colonists'. Their outrage led to the formation of the Farmers Defence Union and the election to Parliament of its organiser, Jan Hofmeyer. His objective was to inculcate in the Afrikaners a sense of national self-respect. It was to lead to the founding of the Afrikaner Bond, and prepared the ground for Anglo-Boer confrontation.

The defeat of the Xhosas left the Mpondo as the only independent nation of consequence in the Transkei. Their territory was divided into an eastern and a western half by the Mzimvubu River. The river mouth formed a natural habour which the Portuguese navigators had named Port St. Johns. For thirty years various Cape Colony Governors had tried, unsuccessfully, to persuade the Mpondo to cede the port to the Colony. Frere thought that the triumph of British arms in the Transkei afforded him an excellent opportunity to convince the Mpondo chiefs of the inevitability of cession. In July he sent Major Elliott on a mission to Nkqwiliso, the Chief of western Mpondoland. Elliott, by accusing

Nkqwiliso of giving sanctuary to the Gcalekas and their cattle, persuaded the chief to cede his rights over the navigable waters of the Mzimvubu together with a nine mile strip of land along the west bank of the river to the Cape Government. The presence of the 90th Light Infantry and the FLH on the border of Mpondoland had added might to Elliott's arguments. The troops, destined for Natal, had been sent overland deliberately, to awe the Mpondos with the High Commissioner's power. Colonel Wood had halted his column in Kokstad on 27 July. They were to remain there for a month as a warning to Mqikela, the ruler of eastern Mpondoland, who was a much less tractable man than Nkqwiliso.

After Elliott prepared the way for a British presence in Port St. Johns, Frere persuaded the British Government of its desirability. A warning that an unguarded port on the South African coastline was an open invitation for foreign powers to establish themselves on the mainland did the trick. The Colonial Office agreed to protect the Mpondos from the alien influence of Germany and Russia. Lest Exeter Hall mistake his actions for aggressive imperialism, Frere carefully explained that the Mpondo were the most backward of the Transkeian people and that their territory was a hotbed of witchcraft and cruel pagan rites.

The occupation of Port St. Johns was to be effected by 'B' Company of the 1/24th. On 17 August, Captain Harrison, Lieutenant Spring and Lieutenant the Hon. Ulick de Rupe Burke Roche, together with eighty-five rank and file, boarded H.M.S. *Active*. Two weeks later, General Thesiger raised the Union Jack and proclaimed nine miles of the west bank of the Mzimvubu British territory. While 'B' Company unpacked its picks and shovels and began the construction of yet another earthwork in the Transkei, Thesiger and his Military Secretary departed in haste for Natal. Captain Harrison and his men were to watch the waters of the Mzimvubu for one long and lonely year – far removed from the ferment and tragedy that were about to overtake the country and their battalion.

16

The Mounted Infantry

Forty-seven men from the 1/24th had no part in the war against the Xhosas. They were the soldiers Cunynghame had sent to Natal in May 1877 to become the nucleus of a mounted infantry squadron that was to serve in the Transvaal. They were joined at a training camp on the outskirts of Newcastle by thirty-six men from the Buffs. Fred Carrington was entrusted with the organisation of the squadron, and Lieutenant Edward Browne and Sergeant Fitzmaurice of the 1st Battalion were made responsible for the training.

The drill devised for them was extremely basic by regular cavalry standards, but it proved more than adequate for the general duties that the men were called upon to perform. They were taught to work in groups of four – three men dismounted and one on horseback holding the reins. Getting in and out of the saddle had to be executed at the double on all occasions; and to avoid confusion, exercises were performed in a single extended line. Their seat would have turned a cavalry-master purple with embarrassment, but by the time Carrington moved them to the Transvaal all the men were secure in their saddles. The squadron retained the white helmet and red tunic of the infantry, but the dark-blue trousers were replaced by brown corduroys and gaiters. The men called themselves 'Carrington's Horse' but Shepstone preferred a more prestigious title for his escort; he named it the Transvaal Mounted Infantry.

In August 1877, the squadron escorted Shepstone on an extended tour of the eastern Transvaal. The rough, informal people of the goldfields, who had warmed to Cunynghame's hearty manner, disliked the Administrator's stiff and formal style; it was the good fellowship of Carrington and Browne that saved the visit from being a social disaster. A few months later they accompanied Shepstone to Utrecht for a meeting with King Cetshwayo's indunas. Shortly after their return to Pretoria, Carrington left for King William's Town to organise the Frontier Light Horse, and Edward Browne took command of the squadron. A few weeks later he was joined by a small contingent from the 1/13th and forty men from the 80th Regiment. And while war raged in the 'Old Colony' the mounted infantry patrolled a seemingly subdued Transvaal.

Towards the end of June 1878, Shepstone asked Browne to provide an escort for his son, Henrique, the Transvaal's Secretary for Native Affairs. Henrique was to undertake a special mission for his father on the Transvaal's western boundary. Theophilus Shepstone wanted to extend the border to the Harts River, recover the lands President Pretorius had lost, and re-establish Transvaal authority in the District of Bloemhof. The scheme was calculated to enlarge his dominion and regain the goodwill of his Boer subjects. The time seemed opportune: Griqualand West was in the throes of a rebellion.

Some of the rulings of the Land Court, which Henry Barkly had established after Southey's dismissal, had given rise to anger and discontent amongst the Griquas. In attempting to establish the validity of the titles held by the many land-claimants, the court had faced a gargantuan task. It was inevitable that some of its decisions should have been received with hostility. Moreover, Judge Andries Stockenström's personal feelings about the Keate Award had made it even more difficult for a Griqua to prove his claim to a disputed title. The Griquas had soon discovered that any white man who made a pretence at farming and could afford the services of a smart lawyer could dispossess them of their lands, while they in turn, were classified as nomads with no right to land ownership. In time, the half-caste inhabitants of Griqualand West came to realise that they had ceded far more to Britain than the diamondiferous lands.

Among the growing list of discontented individuals was Botlhasite Gasebonwe, the senior chief of the Batlhaping. The Keate Award had deprived him of his territory between the Vaal and the Harts. To make matters worse the Griqualand West Administration had chosen to recognise Mankurowane, a lesser, but more cooperative chief, as spokesman for the Batlhaping. Gasebonwe had set about collecting compensation in the manner he understood best – cattle raids across the border. In December 1877 Major Owen Lanyon, the Administrator of Griqualand West, struck back at him. His kraal was surrounded by an armed force and a large cattle-fine was levied. Angered by the humiliation, Gasebonwe took an oath to exterminate all whites in Griqualand West. His bold cry for vengeance became a rallying call for the disgruntled Griquas and Koranas in the territory.

The first hint of rebellion, however, came from Koegas on the Orange River. Donker Malgas, the leader of the 'Pramberg Kaffirs', a community of refugee blacks who had fled from the Transkei at the time of the *Mfecane*, had heard reports of great Xhosa victories in the Transkei, and had been inspired to try a little cattle-lifting in his neighbourhood. In April, Major Lanyon took a small punitive expedition to Koegas, and to his great surprise found himself threatened by a combination of 'Pramberg Kaffirs' and Griquas. He was forced to withdraw from what could have become a dangerous situation.

Within days a large mob surrounded Griquatown. It required the combined efforts of Lanyon's force and a hastily organised relief column from Kimberley to break the siege. There was, by then, little doubt that the Colony was threatened with widespread rebellion. Lanyon sent an urgent telegram to King William's Town demanding the immediate return of the Diamond Field Horse. The poorly organised Griqua rebels were no match against the combined forces of Lanyon and Warren. They were brought to battle on four different occasions and defeated each time. They suffered their greatest setback in the Langeberg, an arid mountain range on the Colony's western border. But while Lanyon and Warren were occupied with Griquas, Gasebonwe's followers went on a rampage along the Colony's northern border. Three whites (the Burness brothers and the wife of the younger brother) were shot down in front of their store in Danielskuil while attempting to reason with their attackers. The ensuing panic sent all the whites in the district flying to the Moffat Institute in Kuruman for protection.

With the Griquas seemingly subdued, Lanyon and Warren hurried to the invested mission station. It was the turn of Gasebonwe's followers to taste the wrath of the Kimberley volunteers. They were chased up the dry Kuruman valley and whipped in an engagement at Gamopedi. From there they fled to Takoon, a natural mountain stronghold honeycombed with caves, which had been a popular refuge at the time of the *Mfecane*. But on 24 July, Lanyon's forces broke through the defences. From Takoon Gasebonwe fled to his lost lands between the Harts and the Vaal, where the only authority was the detachment of Mounted Infantry under Lieutenant Edward Browne.

Henrique Shepstone's escort of fifty Mounted Infantrymen (twenty-three from the 1/24th) had arrived in Christiana, a squalid little village on the west bank of the Vaal, on 8 July. Shepstone's mission was to treat with the independent clans in the district and persuade them to place themselves under Transvaal protection. While he waited for Korana and Barolong emissaries to arrive, his escort found picks and shovels, and attacked the abandoned claims on the river. Three days of hard digging yielded one diamond which fetched thirty shillings at the magistrate's office. On their fifth day in Christiana, the soldiers sold their implements of prospecting.

By the time Lanyon crossed the Harts River his volunteers were tired of chasing the elusive Batlhaping chief and were clamouring to return to Kimberley. He called off the chase and left it to Mankurowane to prove his worth as a recognised chieftain by capturing Gasebonwe. The Mounted Infantry troop was asked to guard the territory between the Harts and the Vaal rivers and Lanyon returned to a hero's welcome in Kimberley. Browne did not stay long in Christiana. A message reached him from Pretoria requesting his return. Command of the Mounted Infantry detachment at Christiana was handed over to Lieutenant Nathaniel Newnham-Davis of the Buffs.

Even while the white mining community was celebrating the successful outcome of the campaign against the insurgents, reports began arriving which indicated that the spirit of rebellion was still alive in the territory. On 22 September a reorganised field-force, divided into two columns, moved out of Kimberley. The smaller one headed for Griquatown, the other one, under Warren, took the road to Likatlong, the principal village of the southern Batlhaping. After he had crossed the Harts River and turned west, Warren learnt that the smaller column had been attacked by a mixed force of Griquas, Koranas and 'Pramberg Kaffirs' and had fallen back on Griquatown.

As soon as the rebels heard that Warren was hurrying to intercept them, they abandoned the environs of Griquatown and headed for the Langeberg. But Warren was determined not to allow so strong a rebel force to get away. He divided his column into three detachments and went after the retreating horde as fast as he could. He also dispatched a messenger to Christiana requesting the Mounted Infantry to ride to Kuruman by way of Taung to serve as a red-coated deterrent to Gasebonwe. If Kuruman was not threatened, the troop could join him in his drive to the Langeberg.

The rebels had chosen to make a stand in a rocky canyon where the Gamayana, an insignificant river that took origin in the Langeberg, emptied itself into the sands of the Kalahari. Over one thousand three hundred rebels with their cattle, sheep and horses had crowded into the dry river-basin. The only approach was along a shallow valley from the west, and there the Griquas had constructed a barricade of rocks and boulders.

On 11 October, Warren made his first assault on the stronghold. His plan, which involved an attack up the Gamayana valley by part of his force, failed. The Griquas ensconced behind their fortifications and protected on three sides by high cliffs could not be dislodged. The attacking force had to spend most of the day behind cover.

The day's events showed Warren that a divided force could not hope to breach the rebel defences. His only hope of success lay in an attack against one point by his entire force. The rebels had expected the attack to come up the Gamayana valley and had prepared for it. He resolved to attack them from the direction they least expected, the Gobatse Heights which overlooked their encampment.

The gruelling ascent began in the early hours of 14 October. The climb, which involved dragging a 7-pounder with its limber and ammunition, took seven hours. By the time the gun was in position on the Gobatse Heights it was mid-morning. The sun was high, but Warren had achieved complete surprise. The troops could see the rebels behind their barricade, facing out towards the desert. Suddenly pandemonium broke out in the encampment. Someone had looked up and seen Warren's entire force arrayed on the heights behind them. A frantic about face was followed by a scramble to some boulder-covered rises that faced the attackers. So good a cover did these positions appear to afford the Griquas that the soldiers felt their night of toil had merely compelled the rebels to exchange one set of impregnable defences for another.

As soon as Warren saw the commotion below, he extended his line and ordered the attack to begin. Two dismounted troops of the Diamond Field Horse were sent down a ridge on the extreme right to outflank the rebels behind the nearest rises. At the same time the field-piece started shelling the canyon floor behind the defenders to discourage reinforcements from coming forward. The remainder of Warren's force then began the descent, troop by troop; the Mounted Infantry were in the centre, the Diamond Light Infantry on their left and a detachment of black levies from the mines of Kimberley on the extreme left. The Griquas were well-armed and many were competent shots. Within minutes Drummer Burley of the 1/24th was bowled over by a bullet that flattened his bugle, and two mounted infantrymen had their helmets knocked off.

The descent turned into a series of crouching rushes from boulder to boulder. Some of the men from the Diamond Field Horse, who had fought in the Amatholes, found it a more dangerous experience than facing Xhosas: it was 'more like fighting experienced and desperate white troops'.

The initial advance soon settled down to an exchange of fire from behind cover. The fighting reached a stalemate which was to last for almost five hours. Then, inexplicably, the defenders seemed to lose heart, and began to retire onto the slopes behind them. As soon as the return fire weakened, the whole of Warren's line rose up and charged forward. The rebels were forced off the slopes and down the canyon. The retreat became a rout with the Griquas fleeing blindly into the desert, leaving cattle and possessions behind.

A few days after the battle a message reached Lieutenant Newnham-Davis which stated that the Mounted Infantry was 'required on the Zulu border'. In a report of the action on the Gobatse Heights, Private John Power of the 1/24th received a special mention for gallant conduct.

The short-lived rebellion of the mixed-breed people that had settled Griqualand West was over. It had been an uncoordinated reaction to the dispossession that had begun with the arrival of the first white farmers and had been easily put down. But it was to provide Frere with an excuse for re-arranging the affairs of Griqualand West in a way that would make the Colony a more acceptable partner in a South African confederation. Less than a week after the victory in the Langeberg, he drew up plans for the tribes on the Transvaal's western border to permanently 'ensure a friendly supply of labour to the diamond fields'. To settle the vexatious land question as quickly as possible he ordered Warren to deal with the disputes as he judged best, and to see that the whites, in whose hands the future of the Colony lay, were satisfied.

It was left to Richard Southey to speak up in defence of the defeated rebels: 'So gross was the injustice sustained by these people in the Land Court that had I been a Griqua, I too would have rebelled'.

Lieutenant Browne had been recalled from Christiana to take command of the mounted infantry in Pretoria. Relations with Sekhukhune had deteriorated to such an extent that a punitive expedition was in the process of being organised against him.

The troubles had begun almost eight months before, when the Administrator of the Transvaal returned empty-handed from his meeting with King Cetshwayo's indunas. Because of his vaunted reputation in native affairs, Shepstone had found it difficult to reconcile himself to the Zulu rebuff, particularly as his white subjects had witnessed his failure. The Boers had not had any dealings with his administration since the annexation. The only official communication he had received from them was a complaint about the guns that were finding their way into Sekhukhune's hands. He desperately wanted to gain the adulation of the people whose country he had taken over, and had resolved to supplant the diplomatic setback against Cetshwayo with a triumph over Burgers's vanquisher.

In terms of the treaty which had brought President Burgers's war to an end, Sekhukhune had undertaken to pay the Transvaal two thousand head of cattle in compensation. By January 1878, the obligation had not been fulfilled. Shepstone had demanded immediate payment. But he had chosen an unfortunate time to become intransigent. The drought which had brought war to the Cape Colony's eastern frontier was causing hardship throughout the country, and the threat of famine also loomed over the Bapedi. Sekhukhune had collected two hundred emaciated animals and had handed them over in part payment. The contribution had been rejected out of hand. Poor crops, a shortage of grazing and the peremptory demand for reparations had made Sekhukhune re-examine the benefits of British rule in the Transvaal. The land on which Fort Burgers stood, and which he claimed as his own, had not been returned; instead, a garrison flying the British flag had been stationed there to uphold Transvaal sovereignty. The small garrison in Fort Weeber, on his western border, was another irritation. Yet the visible might of the British Empire on his borders was represented by nothing more than a few hundred *Amacafula* ('Natal Kaffirs'), who had been fashioned into a police force by Captain Marshall Clarke of the Royal Artillery. Sekhukhune decided that the time had come to reassert his authority over those clans that had indicated a willingness to come under Transvaal protection.

In February, his warriors had attacked a kraal under the protection of Fort Weeber. Hopelessly outnumbered, the twenty-five man garrison had been forced to stand by helplessly while the villagers were slaughtered and their cattle driven off. From attacks on recalcitrant kraals, Sekhukhune had turned to raids on white farms in the Waterfall River valley. In one of the raids a farmer had been killed. Shepstone had sought to make a popular cause out of the incident, and had appealed to the Boers to come forward and assist Clarke and his policemen. But the men who had refused to help their own President against Sekhukhune had shown less inclination to assist an English Administrator and his black police. Rejected by the Boers, Shepstone had tried next to convince Frere that Sekhukhune's belligerence was the work of Zulu agitators and that a general uprising of the Transvaal tribes was imminent. He had called for a display of British Arms to suppress Sekhukhune and impress the Boers.

General Thesiger had his hands full in the Amatholes when Shepstone made his appeal for help. All he could spare the Administrator of the Transvaal was the services of Colonel Rowland and Captain Fred Carrington, who was to utilise his personal popularity to raise yet another troop of volunteer cavalry. Colonel Hugh Rowland V.C., the Commanding Officer of the 34th Regiment, was one of the special service officers who had accompanied Thesiger to the Cape Colony. Thesiger had found little employment for his talents in the Xhosa war, and as compensation, appointed him to lead an expedition against Sekhukhune.

Without the support of the Boers, the Transvaal Administration had hesitated to commit itself to a sustained campaign against him. It was not until the war in the Cape Colony ended that troops were made available for the expedition. When the 2/24th arrived in Natal, it released the 80th Regiment for service in the Transvaal. By the middle of August, Rowland was ready to begin the preparations for his invasion of Sekhukhuneland.

His first act was to surround Sekhukhuneland with a series of forts. Fort Burgers, twenty-five miles south-east of Dsjate, Sekhukhune's town, was made the main base. But it was not until the end of September, when Buller arrived with the FLH, that Rowland moved his headquarters to Fort Burgers. By delaying the expedition until the beginning of summer, Rowland wasted the best months of the year for operations in the eastern Transvaal. Temperatures in the Spekboom valley were topping ninety degrees, and the infrequent watering-places were drying up fast. And with the hot weather came the 'horse-sickness' that could fell a healthy animal in two days. Transportation in that part of country, in the summer, depended largely on 'salted' horses and mules. Immune animals were hard to come by and fetched high prices, particularly at a time of unusual demand. The Colonel had been warned by the local farmers that unless he acted quickly, he could expect to lose sixty per cent of his horses and mules.

By the time Rowland was ready to move he had under his command some one thousand two hundred infantry, six hundred mounted men and two mountain guns. Carrington commanded the Transvaal Mounted Volunteers which was made up of men he had recruited and troops of irregular horse. Like the Transvaal Mounted Infantry and the FLH, the Transvaal Mounted Volunteers also came to be known as 'Carrington's Horse'. And for a few weeks in October, three mounted units that owed their existence to the efforts of an infantry officer from the 24th Foot, campaigned together in Sekhukhuneland. Edward Browne's men were now known officially as the 1st Squadron, Imperial Mounted Infantry. Thesiger had given command of the squadron to Major John Russell, a regular cavalry man from the 12th Lancers. Russell had been horrified by the unorthodox drill of the foot-soldiers on horseback, and brought in a drill-sergeant from the Lancers to knock some style into them. Neither Russell's criticisms nor his pompous manner were welcomed by the men, and Edward Browne, who stayed on as second-in-command, was soon at odds with him.

On Thursday 3 October, Colonel Rowland set out from Fort Burgers with one hundred and thirty infantry, three hundred and eighty-eight horsemen and two 7-pounders for Sekhukhune's stronghold. The greater part of his force was scattered in fortified posts around the chief's rapidly shrinking domain. Shepstone was impatient for a triumph in the Transvaal; Thesiger thought it 'absolutely necessary that decisive results be obtained at once': Rowland gave them a 'reconnaissance in force'.

The road to the capital village of Sekhukhuneland was a broken wagon-track that wound between rocky hills. The grass was withered from months of unrelieved drought; tall aloes, their once fleshy leaves shrunken and blackened, stood in their thousands, grotesquely stark on the burnt slopes. Less conspicuous than the aloes were Sekhukhune's warriors. Their inaccurate but annoying fire from behind cover, constantly harassed the slow, winding column. The soldiers tried to retaliate out of sheer frustration, but the Bapedi never stayed in one place for long. A few determined attempts were made to dislodge the snipers but they simply withdrew to a position ahead of the column and waited for it to reappear. Casualties were negligible, but the harassment added to the miseries of the march.

Heat and lack of water were a greater threat to the column. On the second day out, after a particularly distressing march, they reached a watershed that fed the Olifants and Steelpoort rivers and found nothing but dried-out watercourses. The soldiers were forced to dig deep in the river-bed to find enough water to slake their thrist; there was none for the animals. That same night the camp was attacked on three sides in a diversionary tactic that distracted the troops while their oxen were driven off. In the morning, a thirsty, dispirited column assembled for the final push to Dsjate. Four perspiring miles along a sandy gully brought them to the place where President Burgers's commando had been repulsed. The defences impressed Rowland as much as they had Burgers's men two years before. He decided against an assault. His artillery pieces lobbed a few futile shells onto Sekhukhune's mountain before he ordered his troops to turn about for the march back.

The return journey was even more gruelling. The infantrymen suffered the most, but the mounted men were discomfited when the 'horse-sickness' made its unwelcome appearance. The symptoms developed rapidly: the horse's head would begin to droop, he would stagger from side to side, froth would well up in his mouth and he would sag to the ground. On the march, the only therapy was a bullet in the head. With his mounted troops in danger of being reduced to infantry, Rowland was a very worried man. But he had made a lucky decision when he chose a different route back in the hope of finding water. He did not find water, but he eluded a large force which Sekhukhune had concentrated ahead of him. At the base camp the situation was also serious. Horses were dying at the rate of five a day, the weather stayed aggressively hot and cases of fever had begun to appear. Supplies from Lydenburg were held up by a shortage of draught animals and the troops had to be put on short rations. Rowland decided against another expedition, and Fort Burgers was abandoned.

Colonel Rowland's achievements against Sekhukhune were uninspiring, even by comparison with Burgers's effort. The Queen's loyal subjects in Pretoria thought he had made 'a pretty kettle of fish of the Sekhukhune campaign', and the Boers were decidedly unimpressed. Messengers from Sekhukhuneland went out to all the important chiefs, and the message they carried described how the 'red-coats' came to Sekhukhune's Great Place, gazed at his might and turned tail. Shepstone felt that Britain's prestige, and by implication his own, had never stood lower in the Transvaal. Frere, too, was greatly disappointed. He agreed with Shepstone that a convincing display of Imperial power had to be made as soon as possible for the sake of the Transvaal and confederation.

Part Three

September 1878 to August 1879

17

September days

The soldiers who returned from the Transkei had the look of experienced campaigners. Their faded uniforms were held together by patches and their bronzed faces, under their yellowed, dirt-begrimed helmets, were covered with bushy beards; even their colonel sported an aggressive grey beard. More than half the 1st Battalion had been under fire and the men had acquired a reputation as steady shots – about the best regulars in South Africa, a distinction earned at the cost of twenty-one deaths from sickness and exposure. There had been no casualties as a result of enemy action. Equally remarkable was the fact that in eleven months of war, only one man had deserted.

For his services in the Transkei Colonel Glyn was made a Companion of the Bath. Russell Upcher was recommended for the same award. His commendation described the battle of Centane as one 'which had proved more disastrous to the enemy than any previously on record in South Africa'. Coghill, Anstey, Hodson and Atkinson were mentioned in despatches, a special note was made of the exceptional services of Carrington and Pulleine in the raising of volunteer forces, and Francis Porteous, who had served as garrison adjutant in King William's Town, was commended for his musketry instruction. From Sir Bartle Frere the officers received a silver cigar-box for their Mess – 'a souvenir' of the 'trying months' when he shared accommodation with the officers in the Military Reserve.

September saw the return to South Africa of Captain William Degacher. He had considered leaving the army after his marriage, but the war on the Cape Colony's frontier and the prospect of hostilities in other parts of South Africa had persuaded him to return to active duty. Captain Reginald Younghusband, who had missed the more hectic months of the war, also returned that month with a wife. But Coghill, who arrived in Cape Town on 12 September, had escaped the snares of matrimony.

Coghill was met on the docks by colonel Forestier Walker with an invitation to become the Governor's ADC. The offer was tempting, but Coghill had heard that the more permanent position of Battalion Adjutant would become vacant when Melvill returned to England to enter Staff College. He had heard also that Colonel Glyn wanted him to succeed Melvill. General Thesiger solved Coghill's dilemma. He prohibited Melvill from leaving South Africa because he would soon need the services of every experienced officer in the country. Nine days after arriving in Cape Town Coghill was on his way to Natal to join Sir Bartle Frere.

The likelihood of a war against the Zulus was the main topic of conversation in the Colony; but the 1st Battalion seemed destined to resume the routine duty in King William's Town which the Gcalekas had interrupted the year before. Among the disappointed officers were Edward Hopton Dyson and William Whitelock Lloyd, the first subalterns in the Battalion to hold the new rank of Second Lieutenant. Both men had arrived in King William's Town in the closing stages of the Xhosa war and had missed most of the excitement. The first indication that some members of the 1/24th might participate in a campaign against the Zulus was a request for Lieutenant Clements and his seventeen mounted infantrymen to move to Natal. They were to join Colonel Pearson's command as part of the Second Squadron, Imperial Mounted Infantry. Two weeks later, on 24 September, fifty men under the command of Henry Pulleine, also sailed for Durban. The day they marched out of the Military Reserve, Private George Morris of 'E' Company wrote his mother, 'I am greatly afraid that we are going to Natal where they expect another outbreak of the nations and I am afraid that we shall have some very hard and sharp work up there as the disaffected tribe are a very numerous one and well-armed and are very large made people and some say a brave lot ...' Within a few days of landing in Cape Town Coghill wrote: 'war with the Zulus is not imminent but I still am of opinion that it must take place'; a week later he added, 'I think I can smell sulpher [sic] ...'

In military circles the organisation of the Zulu Army had been a subject of discussion for many years. The soldiers knew that the military system created by Shaka had been devastatingly effective against the other tribes, but in its only important contest with whites (a small Boer force armed with muzzle-loaders), the Zulu Army had suffered so decisive a defeat that for the next thirty years it avoided any confrontation with white settlers. Since the accession of Cetshwayo, however, the Zulu military machine had been revitalised, and fire-arms had been added to its weaponry. But what intrigued Her Majesty's officers most about the Zulu military organisation was the celibate condition of the army. Every Zulu male was brought up to be a warrior, and none was permitted to take a wife until he had proved himself in battle or achieved veteran status. The restriction that white settlement had imposed on the once freely ranging impis, had reduced drastically the number of intertribal tussles, and thereby the opportunities for matrimony, a situation that conjured up visions of grizzled old warriors being rewarded with young virgins after endless years of service. It led the British officers to conclude that the Zulu army was made up of frustrated warriors eager to qualify for the ultimate reward.

Cetshwayo had demonstrated vividly the importance he attached to military tradition only two years before. A group of maidens, chosen to become the wives of two veteran regiments, had tired of waiting for the stipulated term to expire, and had taken lovers from among the young men. When the King heard about it, he ordered the immediate execution of all the girls. The incident had so horrified the settlers that Sir Henry Bulwer had found it necessary to issue a reprimand. Cetshwayo's reply had made it clear that as he did not interfere in the Colony's affairs, he expected to have the same courtesy extended to Zululand. He had gone on to remind Sir Henry Bulwer, Governor of Natal, that the customary 'washing of spears', which should have taken place after the death of his father, Mpande, had been deferred only to please the English.

Fifteen years before Mpande died, Cetshwayo gave the Zulus and Natal an inkling of how willing he was to cater for military traditions. To strengthen his claim to the Zulu throne, he eliminated the followers of his nearest rival in one of the bloodiest battles ever fought in Zululand. The valley where it took place became known afterwards as the 'Place of Bones'. This bloody episode in the fight for succession was never forgotten and many of the settlers believed that it was only Shepstone's influence over Cetshwayo that prevented him from launching his impis against the Colony. Many whites feared that Cetshwayo embodied the cruelty of his uncle, Dingane, with the military aspirations of his uncle, Shaka, and were convinced that he was behind every disturbance in the country. In the doings of Langalibalele, Sekhukhune, Sarhili, Sandile and Gasebonwe they perceived the 'evil influence' of Cetshwayo.

It was three years since Wolseley had declared that sooner or later the Zulu military system would have to be destroyed. Commodore Sullivan had warned the Admiralty in December 1877 that Zululand would be the next likely scene of operations. General Thesiger when he arrived in South Africa had little doubt that the Xhosa War was merely the prelude to a campaign against the Zulus. After Centane, Coghill had written, 'one thing is clear that Cetshwayo wants a beating and sooner or later he must get it'. The mood of the Military was one of inevitable confrontation. A cynical member in the Colonial Office had remarked that the army would scarcely let pass an opportunity which would furnish them with decorations and brevet promotions. But other considerations also influenced the feelings of Her Majesty's soldiers; some genuinely believed that it was their Christian duty to rid the land of a barbarous tyranny.

If in September 1878, the notion of a war against Cetshwayo had become the preoccupation of the Military in South Africa, in London, the Government was more concerned with rising tension in Afghanistan. When the new Secretary of State for Colonies thought about South Africa at all, it was with the fervent hope that Frere would desist from further military adventures. He had, in fact, proscribed specifically against another Kaffir war. But despite Hicks Beach's wishes, the country, by then, was well along the road to war. Drought, the personality of Shepstone, and Frere's driving ambition to succeed in confederating South Africa had made armed conflict inevitable.

The dry years had begun in 1875, and before the year was over reports had come in of crop failures in the northern part of the Ciskei and Transkei. The summer rains had failed to appear the following year or the year after, and by the middle of 1878, old-timers in Natal were saying that they could not recall a drought of such severity in fifty years. The country's economy was almost wholly agricultural, its rivers were seasonal, cultivation and grazing were dependent on the annual rainfall and the rains set the temper of the land. The drought had awakened old grievances. The Sekhukhune War of 1876, the unrest on the Eastern Frontier and the war that came in 1877 were all symptoms of the dehydrating sickness that afflicted the land. It had moved Coghill to write, 'If the drought lasts many a farmer will be ruined – there was and is no feeding for stock in most parts – the ground is hard as rock, what grows there will hardly provide nourishment for a goose and the general appearance of the country is a universal brown with nothing to relieve the eye'.

Zululand had not been immune. As the streams dried up and the grass withered, the Zulus had to drive their herds further and further afield in search of grazing, and they thereby increasingly exposed their cattle to the endemic 'lung sickness'. To watch his wealth, his precious herds, being decimated by disease and starvation, had added irrationality to the black man's mood of depression. For the rain-makers, sooth-sayers and witch-doctors it was a time of full employment; and to replenish their own herds, the chiefs encouraged the 'smelling-out' of witches. The victims of superstition soared and the barbaric side of native life was glaringly emphasised. Its greatest publicists were the missionaries, especially those who had made no headway in Zululand.

Cetshwayo regarded the missionaries as competitors for the loyalty of his young men and treated Zulu converts as outcasts. He incensed the men of God by forbidding adult males from settling on mission stations. The drought, inevitably, focused the attentions of the heathen king on those converts who were the possessors of healthy herds, and a few black 'martyrs' were created. In missionary writings Cetshwayo became Satan's representative in Zululand. The King had made an enemy of a vocal and influential group. Exeter Hall was almost ready to condone a war that would lift the yoke of tyranny from the Zulu people.

An expanding population and the search for grazing had forced more and more clans to move onto the healthier, high grassland of northern Zululand. Their presence had brought renewed tension to a territory which had been under dispute for sixteen years. What Cetshwayo regarded as his kingdom was bounded by the Assegaai River (in part) in the north, the Tugela River in the south and the Buffalo River in the west. But between the headwaters of the east-flowing Assegai and the south-flowing Buffalo was a fifty-mile gap devoid of any natural landmarks. Over the years, farmers from the Transvaal had drifted through this undefined border, settled on the grasslands to the east of the Buffalo and established the village of Utrecht. The settlement had been tolerated by Mpande, and in time, the Blood River, some thirty miles to the east of the Buffalo, became the unofficial boundary.

When Cetshwayo first began to establish his right to succession, two of his brothers fled to Utrecht for safety. To get them back he had offered the Boers in the district grazing rights on the east bank of the Blood River. They had assumed that the offer included the right to farm. The arrangement had been confirmed by Mpande, and in 1864, a new boundary had been beaconed-off some twenty miles east of the Blood River. But after his brothers escaped to Natal Cetshwayo regretted his offer to the Boers, and thereafter resisted all further attempts at encroachment. In his opposition to the Boers he had been encouraged by the then Natal Secretary for Native Affairs.

At the time of Mpande's reign Shepstone had been disturbed by the extension of Boer influence into Zululand and had conceived the notion of ingratiating himself, on Natal's behalf, with the likely future king. He had gone to Mpande's kraal, and in the name of Queen Victoria had acknowledged Cetshwayo as the rightful heir. When his father died, Cetshwayo had thought that another endorsement by the representative of Britain's Queen would not be amiss, particularly as Mpande's favourite son had slipped into the Transvaal to seek support against him. He had wanted his friend 'Somtseu' to be 'archbishop' at his coronation, and Shepstone, despite Colonial Office opposition, jumped at the chance of becoming king-maker of the Zulus.

In 1875, while Burgers was in Europe negotiating his railway loan, the Acting-President of the Transvaal had proclaimed the disputed lands on the Blood River part of the Province of Utrecht. Cetshwayo had reacted with angry threats, confident that his friend and ally, the Natal Secretary for Native Affairs, would be sympathetic to his cause. Garnet Wolseley who was in Pietermaritzburg at the time, had thought it a marvellous opportunity to kill two birds with one stone. Had the Colonial Office agreed, he would have encouraged a Zulu invasion of the bankrupt republic. His plan had envisaged Britain stepping in after both contestants had exhausted themselves to offer the Transvaal salvation through confederation and to dismantle the Zulu military system.

When Shepstone rode out with his police escort to 'conquer' the Transvaal, Cetshwayo offered his old ally the services of the Zulu Army. Forty thousand assegaais could not have been interpreted as an act of friendly persuasion, and Shepstone turned the offer down. He had not been averse, however, to having a few impis stationed near the disputed border. What better demonstration could have been had of the advantages of British rule, as personified by the power of the Natal Secretary for Native Affairs, if those impis had departed at a wave of his hand?

What the Republic had needed most, however, was an expert in financial matters and an experienced administrator; what it received was an authority on native tribal lore. As the months went by, Shepstone realised that the Boers not only refused to look upon him as their saviour, but disregarded his very presence. He was a sensitive man, very conscious of his status. Prestige meant more to him than he would have cared to admit. He had earned a knighthood, was the Queen's official representative in the Transvaal and nominal head of the Boers, but the adulation was missing. He had risen to prominence by his clever manipulation of Natal's black population, but his white charges were not behaving like the *Amacafula*. Shepstone's impassive face hid a distressed heart.

He had been most cooperative when Wolseley came to change the Natal constitution. Sir Garnet had been grateful for his assistance, but had thought him 'a very cunning, underhand fellow', and 'a hard unfeeling man, who had he been a Roman Emperor, would never have hesitated to commit any amount of cruelty in the coolest manner if by so doing he gained his ends'. If he could not gain the respect and affection of the Boers by popular government, Shepstone resolved to achieve it through his talent for 'Native Affairs'.

He had set out from Pretoria on 16 August 1877, 'to communicate with the most important and formidable native powers on the boundaries of the territory, such as Sekhukhune, the amaSwazi, and the Zulus'. His tour had brought him to the Province of Utrecht in October and he had found it gratifying to see his popularity with the Boers on the Zulu border soaring. In his letters to Carnarvon he had emphasised 'the pinnacles of peril which the Republic, and South Africa generally, had reached at the moment when the annexation took place. A single shot, an untoward but untrue report, might have overwhelmed us all in an irretrievable calamity'. In Shepstone's mind the annexation had ceased to be an act of political chicanery, it had become an act of deliverance. In Utrecht he had intended showing the Boers how tame 'the elephant' (Cetshwayo) would be in his hands.

The Zulu King had expected 'Somtseu' to promote his interests when he became ruler of the Transvaal. Instead, he received orders to withdraw his men from the disputed territory. These lands, to Cetshwayo, were no longer a matter of mere national pride: good grazing was becoming scarce and their ownership had become an urgent necessity. A conference with Shepstone had been arranged for 19 October. Cetshwayo's delegation had been made up of senior indunas led by Mnyamana Buthelezi. Shepstone had conducted the meeting in the ceremonial manner at which he excelled, but his customary long pauses for deliberation had not helped the Zulus understand the policy change that had taken place when the Natal Secretary for Native Affairs became the Administrator of the Transvaal. They had expected a generous settlement in which two allies divided the spoils. They had expected to receive the territory between the Blood and the Buffalo rivers while their good friend and neighbour, the English Colony of Natal, took the lands to the west of the Buffalo. Their quarrel, after all, had been only with the Boers.

In his formal, didactic manner, Shepstone had informed them that the interests of Natal were now the same as those of the Transvaal, that only the strip of land on the east bank of the Blood River was negotiable, and that his decision was final. Cetshwayo had taken a while to adjust to the changed situation. His reaction had been the dispatch of two thousand men to establish a kraal on the north bank of the Pongola near the new settlement of Luneberg. The warrior force could threaten the lines of communication between the Transvaal, Natal and the Swazi country, and command Utrecht. Shepstone had regarded it as a deliberate attempt at intimidation and a personal insult: 'an act which I was scarcely prepared to expect'. For once in his life, Shepstone lost control of his emotions: he ordered his escort of mounted infantry to ride into Zululand and demonstrate his displeasure. Carrington had been aghast at so irrational an order, for 'to do so was to march to certain death'. Luckily for the mounted infantry, Shepstone had calmed down in time to cancel the order. He had then set about countering Cetshwayo's action with his own military deployments. Three companies of the 1/13th were sent from Pretoria to Utrecht, and Sir Henry Bulwer, the Lieutenant-Governor of Natal, had been requested to place the troops in Newcastle at his disposal. Bulwer, who was not given to hasty actions, had let him have two companies of the 80th on the strict understanding that they were coming to reassure the farmers in the Province of Utrecht, not to start a war.

The kraal had turned out to be more a cattle-kraal than a military one; but Cetshwayo's next move made the schism with Shepstone irreconcilable. The King, without consulting him had had the temerity to send a deputation to Bulwer to give his version of the meeting on Conference Hill. This had been followed by the announcement that two Pietermaritzburg lawyers had been appointed Cetshwayo's diplomatic agents in the boundary dispute. Shepstone had contemptuously dismissed them as 'two irresponsible private gentlemen ... neither of whom it is believed can speak or understand the Zulu language or knows anything of the Zulu King, people or country'. He jealously guarded his reputation in native affairs, and refused to recognise the credentials of his usurpers.

Shepstone had lost face both in Zululand in the Transvaal. The painful realisation that he could not be the protector of the Boers and retain his influence over Cetshwayo decided him that the King would have to go. His official correspondence, thereafter, became one long diatribe against Cetshwayo. He alleged that Cetshwayo had sent £2 000 in gold to Sekhukhune to start a war in the Transvaal; that his troops were 'extremely defiant' and clamouring to be 'led to war'; that he was taking advantage of the Cape Colony's troubles to make unreasonable demands; and that conditions in Zululand were untenable because all manner of cruelties were being perpetrated on the people by the army. In a letter to Carnarvon and Frere, written in January 1878, he had stated, 'only when the Zulu Government is changed will the peace of South Africa rest on a saner basis'. Cetshwayo's military machine had to be broken so that the Zulus might enjoy the happier condition of the 'Natal Kaffirs'. It was a sentiment that appealed to the humanitarian High Commissioner for South Africa.

Frere regarded the Colony of Natal as a stronghold of reaction, but hoped that if the settlers were freed from their fear of the barbarian army on the other side of the Tugela, and if their situation was improved by union with the other white states, then the legislators might be persuaded to enact the liberal laws of the Cape Colony. Destroy the cruel despot in Ulundi, and the Zulus, too, would share in the benefits of an enlightened Empire. The Kingdom was an obstacle to the important social and economic changes that would follow on confederation. His views on the tyrant, Cetshwayo, moreover, had been endorsed by Theophilus Shepstone, the unchallenged authority on black people. Sir Bartle was ready to extend his Transkeian solution to Zululand.

There was, however, one complication. In December 1877, when he thought Shepstone might precipitate a war, Bulwer had proposed the setting up of an independent boundary commission. Cetshwayo had accepted the offer, and so, much more reluctantly, had Shepstone. At the insistance of the Secretary of State for Colonies, Frere had agreed to act as final arbitrator in his capacity as High Commissioner. Until the Commission had made its findings known, no action could be undertaken.

The Commissioners were Michael Gallwey, the Natal Attorney-General, John Wesley Shepstone, Theophilus's brother and his successor as Natal Secretary for Native Affairs, and Lieutenant-Colonel William Anthony Durnford R.E. The appointment had been gazetted in February, and they had begun taking evidence in March. The final draft of their report had been completed at the end of June, and to Frere's dismay, had upheld all Cetshwayo's claims east of the Blood River. The High Commissioner, at that time, had been preparing for a visit to the Transvaal; it had been his intention to offer the Boers a measure of self-government in return for cooperating in a confederation. The disputed territory could have made a useful gift, but the Commission's findings would have been a slap in the face. Under the circumstances, Frere decided to cancel the visit and withhold publication of the award until he judged the time more opportune.

He would wait and see what gains Colonel Rowland's expedition would bring the Transvaal, and retain in South Africa the extra battalions that the Xhosa War had called forth. Recognising Cetshwayo's right to the lands on the Blood River would not persuade him to dismantle his warrior army, but a strong build-up of troops might. The Colonial Office would have to be convinced that reinforcements were needed in Natal, even if it involved manufacturing a crisis. A few minor incidents that could be exploited to bring about a showdown with Cetshwayo had occurred recently on the Natal-Zululand border, and the means would justify the end – if the end was a secure Natal, a contented Transvaal, and Zululand under an enlightened administration watched over by Westminster. The time had come for Frere to transfer himself to Pietermaritzburg. On 23 September, a detachment of the 2/24th welcomed him ashore in Durban; a few days later, his new ADC arrived from Cape Town.

Thesiger, in the meantime, had moved most of his troops in Natal nearer to the Tugela River. Evelyn Wood's column had reached Utrecht, a detachment of the 2/24th was guarding Middle Drift and the Buffs were encamped near the Tugela mouth. The Durban garrison had been depleted by the deployment and Colonel Glyn was asked to send two companies to Natal. On 5 October, 'C' and 'D' Companies under Pulleine and Upcher landed in Durban. Pulleine became the Military Commandant of Durban, but all the excitement was fifty miles further north in the Colony's capital. It looked as if Henry Pulleine would once again exercise little more than his talent for public relations.

18

All roads lead to Natal

Pietermaritzburg, with a population of less than five thousand, became, in September 1878, the headquarters for the direction of South African affairs. The pretty little town with its neat houses and rose-planted gardens was jolted out of its easy-going, sub-tropical languour by the arrival of the General and his staff. Fort Napier, the home of the Natal Command began to bustle with purposeful-looking officers – 'there never was a time when such a number of Colonels, Majors and Captains were to be seen about', commented one awed burgher. The business of the Military brought contractors and entrepreneurs into town; the social activities of the Military attracted the colonial ladies. Pietermaritzburg had never known such a plethora of eligible young men: it was even more exciting than the 'reign' of Sir Garnet and the Ashanti Ring. But the season really got underway when the High Commissioner moved into Government House.

The arrival of Frere was made the occasion for the most important social event in years – a grand ball in the Theatre Royal. Tickets were an exorbitant fifty shillings a couple, but colonial beauty and fashion paid up gladly for the privilege of being presented to Sir Bartle. The extravagantly decorated theatre was a little too draughty for comfort and the guests had to squirm inelegantly at the overcrowded supper tables, but the ladies were enthusiastic dancers and Her Majesty's officers recalled, with hopeful anticipation, the amorous adventures in Natal of Wolseley's aides. An astute wife of an officer from the 90th Regiment, however, found time between dances to reflect on the Guest of Honour 'as a person whose efforts were largely calculated to aid promotion' in her husband's profession. For the 1st Battalion's sole representative at the ball it proved an occasion to celebrate, together with Lieutenant-Colonel Forestier Walker and Captain Francis Grenfell, the reunion of General Cunynghame's old staff.

A few days later, Coghill, sporting a reddish beard, found zestful employment in a farce staged for the benefit of dependants of men killed in the Xhosa war. His nights in Pietermaritzburg were a round of dinners and parties, but his days were filled with the business of the High Commissioner. Frere had to convince Sir Henry Bulwer and Bishop Colenso (the hesitant and the querulous) that the war with King Cetshwayo was necessary. But even more important was the compliance of the British Government, who would have to foot the bill. A copy of the Boundary Commission's findings had reached the Colonial Office by then, and in an attempt to discredit its recommendations, Frere resuscitated Stockenström's argument in the Griqualand West Land Court about nomads not being entitled to settled boundaries. He followed it up with a strongly-worded attack on the Zulu King and elevated two minor incidents into a pretext for war.

The more serious of the two had begun as an adulterous liaison in the kraal of a senior Zulu chief called Sihayo. While the chief was attending his king in Ulundi, his sons discovered that two of his wives had taken lovers and resolved to kill the erring women. The wives, both of whom were pregnant, got wind of the fate that was about to overtake them and fled to Natal. Sihayo's sons were determined to avenge the stain on their father's honour, and ignoring diplomatic niceties, crossed the border and seized the wife who had taken refuge in the police-kraal of Field-Cornet Robson. According to one witness, they knocked out her front teeth, tied leather thongs around her wrists and neck and dragged her screaming to the Zululand side of the river. There, in full view of the people who had given her asylum, she was bludgeoned to death. The following day Sihayo's sons crossed the Buffalo again, found the other wife, and carried her back to Zululand where she was shot. The details of the slayings varied with every telling, but to the warmongers the Sihayo family vendetta represented a premeditated border violation. The incident had occurred in July, and Bulwer had been pressurised into asking King Cetshwayo to hand the murderers over for trial in Natal. Cetshwayo had responded with an offer of £50 as compensation for what he considered, at most, a technical breach of Natal's sovereignty.

The other border provocation took place near Middle Drift. A white surveyor and his assistant, who were inspecting a crossing on the Tugela, rode through the shallow waters to the Zululand side of the river. They were apprehended by a small warrior party and detained for about an hour. Neither man was molested, but they were made to empty out their pockets before being released.

In Frere's hunt for proof of Cetshwayo's belligerency, the Sihayo affair became an 'invasion of Natal territory', and the incident with the surveyor, the 'kidnapping' of two British subjects. The Secretary of State for Colonies, however, was unimpressed by these transgressions. Reinforcements were refused on the grounds that they were needed in Afghanistan. A faction hostile to Frere's policies had surfaced in the Colonial Office; meanwhile in Natal, Bulwer was obstructing him with his insistence on maintaining legal formalities while the General was attempting to put the Colony on a war footing. Next came the news that Rowland had abandoned the campaign against Sekhukhune, and with it the fear that the exultant blacks were telling each other that 'if the bull calf (Sekhukhune) has to be left alone, what will happen when the elephant (Cetshwayo) attacks the white man?'. To Frere, a victory in Zululand had become a matter of urgency, yet officialdom was resisting him at every turn. It was the settlers, demonstrating their faith in his policies, who helped restore his sense of mission. Their reasons for favouring a war were varied: some thought the conquest of Zululand would open up a vast, new source of cheap labour, others were attracted by the immediate profits that might be made from the sale of transport and provisions to the expeditionary force; a few had even begun speculating in real estate on the other side of the Tugela; but most feared for the safety of Natal should the troops be withdrawn before the Zulu Army was tamed. They felt that the actions of Thesiger and Frere had provoked Cetshwayo to an extent that future cordial relations would be impossible. To Frere, the situation in Natal was the Eastern Frontier all over again – the settlers crying out for protection and strong leadership, while petty-minded politicians with limited vision did their best to obstruct him.

General Thesiger, who on the death of his father had succeeded to the title of Second Baron Chelmsford, was a willing instrument in the High Commissioner's hands. He ignored all the political disputations and devoted himself to building up a military presence on the Zululand border. By the beginning of October he had troops stationed at three places along the two hundred mile border. Greytown, more centrally located than Pietermaritzburg, was made the advance base, and the five 2/24th companies in Pietermaritzburg together with Major Harness's battery of artillery were moved there.

With the Pietermaritzburg garrison totally depleted, Pulleine was asked to bring up 'C' company from Durban and take command of Fort Napier. Pulleine had made many friends in his short stay in Durban and the local newspapers expressed the hope that the 'Colonel's services in Natal will meet their reward'. Lord Chelmsford was going to need all the volunteers he could get and Pulleine must have had little doubt that his likely duties would be those of the Army's public relations man in Pietermaritzburg. Appeals had been made for men who had led volunteer parties in the Xhosa war to come forward and demonstrate their expertise against the Zulus. The redoubtable old Schermbrucker was one of the first to respond. He brought a small, German-speaking contingent calling itself the 'Kaffrarian Vanguard' to Natal. Chelmsford with his passion for keeping cognate groups together sent them to reinforce the German settlers in Luneburg. By mid-November, most of the freebooters and adventurers whose appetite for fighting had not been satiated by the Cape Colony's war, had found their way into Natal. But there were four regular battalions in South Africa that were outside the borders of Natal: the time had come to reunite the 1/24th.

The news that the Headquarters of the 1st Battalion was leaving King William's Town and was to be replaced by the 'Connaught Rangers', raised a cheer in Cape Town. The city was delighted to be rid of a regiment whose 'disorderly conduct' had made it a 'terror to the citizens'. On the other hand the imminent departure of the 1/24th was noted with regret in King William's Town; the Battalion was described as 'one of the best behaved regiments' ever stationed there. On Sunday 10 November, the men and their families attended a farewell church parade in the Military Reserve. The service was conducted by the Reverend John Gordon, and Band-Sergeant Gamble led the choir. The Reverend's concluding words were: 'probably we would next meet at the bar of God on the final day of account'.

A few days later, four hundred and sixty-three officers and men were marched to the King William's Town railway station. The wives and children were left behind, as was Captain George Paton, who had been assigned to staff duties in the Military Reserve. The Battalion had been re-equipped and the men marched with the relaxed smartness of a well practised team. The band struck up with a music-hall song that was the current rage, and the men joined in its popular chorus:

> We don't want to fight, but by jingo if we do,
> We've got the ships, we've got the men, and got
> The money too.

The song was to give a designation to the imperialism that would characterise the sunset years of Victoria's reign; and the soldiers, on their way to Natal in the closing weeks of 1878, were about to inaugurate that age.

When the Headquarters of the 1/24th reached Pietermaritzburg they found Pulleine occupied with organisational duties; the army's goodwill ambassador was about to set off on a horse-purchasing trip. 'F' Company (under the command of William Mostyn), took over garrison duty and freed 'C' Company for the march north. Captain Younghusband took charge of 'C' Company. On the last day of November, to the strains of 'I'm leaving thee in sorrow, Annie', Colonel Glyn led his men out of Pietermaritzburg. Included amongst those whom they were leaving behind was their Bandmaster, and Major Logan. The same morning, two Boer notables in a humble post-cart also left the Natal capital. Paul Kruger was returning to the Transvaal after his second failed mission to London. The new Secretary of State for Colonies had refused to restore independence to the Transvaal, and had referred him back to Frere.

During their short stay in Pietermaritzburg, Colonel Glyn and his senior officers attended a dinner given in Kruger's honour. The Boer leader, despite his coarse manners, had proved entertaining company. His description of a balloon ascent at the Paris Exhibition, and his mistrust of the new-fangled bicycle, had made for amusing listening; but they had found him a trifle tiresome when he insisted on lecturing them about the Zulus. He had warned them that the impis moved quickly and stealthily, and had advised them to send out scouts far ahead and not to camp without forming a laager. But Kruger was speaking to men who a few months before had triumphed over the Xhosas, men who were confident of their ability and their arms, men who considered the black man's reluctance to join battle the biggest travail of 'Kaffir warfare'.

The road to Greytown was heavy with mud, and it took the 1st Battalion four days to cover the fifty miles. The rain would not let up. It had poured almost continuously from the time they set foot in Natal. The long drought was broken. The Tugela had risen so high and was flowing so swiftly, that it had become a near impassable barrier. The dried-up rivers and the forgotten streams were running again, the grass was springing up green, sweet and abundant, and the earth was soft for ploughing. It was the time for planting next year's crops, for fattening the herds – it was the time for peace.

James Sivewright, the manager of the telegraph company and a friend of the 1st Battalion from the King William's Town days, had just returned from a visit to the Blood River territory; he described it as 'the loveliest bar none ... well-wooded – well-watered', with grass as green 'as that of an English meadow in June', and added that if he was in King Cetshwayo's place he would 'fight to the death for it'. Glyn and his officers knew that on 11 December Sir Bartle was to meet Cetshwayo's representatives and announce the findings of the Boundary Commission. Sivewright, whose control of the telegraph gave him access to secret information, hinted that it had gone in favour of the Zulus; but Coghill was confident that there would be war, and had asked Glyn to find him a place on his staff should Frere release him from his duties as ADC.

The High Commissioner's meeting with Cetshwayo's indunas was to take place near the Tugela Lower Drift. A month before the meeting, Coghill had intimated in a letter home that he knew the findings of the Boundary Commission, and had laid great stress on the failure of Rowland's expedition – as if that was going to influence the terms of the award. Frere's recognition of the Zulu claim to the Blood River territory was to be accompanied by an ultimatum he had drawn up in consultation with Theophilus Shepstone. According to Sivewright, Shepstone had complained that not a man on the Boundary Commission was qualified to adjudicate on the issue, and that the award had been 'torn into tatters' by him. Shepstone had also assured Frere that in the event of war, Cetshwayo, whom he knew to be a coward, would be easily broken. In his opinion, the King was a blusterer whose real power lay in 'finesse and diplomacy'.

Frere and his staff arrived at the agreed meeting-place two days early. When Cetshwayo's representatives turned up, the sailors from the Naval Brigade had to ferry them across the swollen Tugela to the Natal side of the river. There, under the shade of a wild fig tree, John Shepstone read out the findings of the Commission to the assembled indunas. The territory to the east of the Blood River was confirmed as belonging to the Zulus, but white farmers already settled there were to be allowed to stay on if they chose to do so, and compensated if they left. The chiefs seemed reasonably satisfied with the award. The bombshell came after lunch. It began as a long, rambling diatribe against Cetshwayo that took nearly three hours to read. One of the conditions attached to the award related to the grievances of Natal: Sihayo's sons had to be surrendered within twenty days to stand trial in the Colony. In addition, a fine of five hundred head of cattle was imposed for not handing them over when first requested. For the insult to the surveyor and his helper another one hundred head of cattle was demanded. Cetshwayo might feel humiliated by the addendum to the Commission's award but it was not sufficiently humbling to drive a cautious man to war. So there followed a series of demands that were nothing less than blatant interference in the internal affairs of Zululand.

The Zulu Army was to be disbanded and its warriors sent back to their kraals. Enforced celibacy had to cease. A British Resident had to be accepted into Zululand to look after the interests of whites and converts in the kingdom. Missionaries were to be allowed in and given a free hand, and there was to be no interference with Zulus who wanted to attach themselves to mission stations. Cetshwayo was given thirty days in which to comply with the terms of the ultimatum. If he failed to carry them out the British Army would march into Zululand. There was to be no further discussion, either at the meeting or at a later date. Full compliance was required by 11 January.

The indunas were stunned by the ultimatum; none seemed to have grasped the details; and no one was willing to take the report back to their King. Eventually, after a long delay, a messenger with an approximate verbal paraphrase of the day's proceedings, set off in the general direction of Ulundi.

The details of the ultimatum reassured the Military that they would have their war; their preparations would not have been in vain. No one was disturbed unduly, when two days after the ultimatum a despatch arrived from the Colonial Office specifically prohibiting war with the Zulus. Of much greater interest to Chelmsford's staff was an enclosure announcing the dispatch of the 2/4th (the King's Own Royal Regiment), and the 99th (the Duke of Edinburgh's Regiment) to South Africa. The proviso that forbade the use of these Battalions in aggressive actions could be accommodated by using them to guard the supply-lines, and thereby freeing the troops already in South Africa for active service.

Chelmsford's strategy for the forthcoming war involved the simultaneous invasion of Zululand by multiple columns, all thrusting towards Ulundi. He was confident that if he concentrated all his forces they would be more than a match for the Zulu Army; but a column of that size would of necessity move at a snail's pace along the wagon tracks that served for roads in Zululand. But the border with Zululand was long and for the most part mountainous. The fast-moving impis of Chief Mnyamana Buthelezi (the Commander-in-Chief of the Zulu Army) could easily bypass so cumbersome a column, cross the border at any one of a dozen different fords and make a retaliatory strike into Natal or Transvaal. Instead, Chelmsford decided to launch his invasion from four or five widely separated bases. Smaller columns would be more mobile and more likely to invite a Zulu attack. They might also tempt the Zulu Army to divide its strength. With such a plan Chelmsford had to accept the risk of being outnumbered at least five to one in any engagement, but he was confident that discipline and superior arms would triumph in the end. His original plan had called for five columns each with a regular battalion as its hard core, one battalion in reserve and another to protect the supply lines. The seven battalions called for equalled the total number stationed in South Africa. He was prepared to entrust the protection of Simonstown to colonial volunteers, but the Cape Colony's frontier districts and the Transvaal could not be denuded of troops. There were two battalions in the Transvaal, but Rowland's failure against Sekhukhune, and the unpredictable attitude of the Boers, necessitated keeping at least one battalion north of the Vaal; that left him with five battalions for use against the Zulus.

The British Government's initial refusal to send out two additional regiments of infantry, and the discovery that Natal could not supply anything like the number of wagons and teams necessary to transport five columns and their supplies into the heart of Zululand, had made him revise his original plan. The number of columns was reduced to three. One column would cross the Tugela near its mouth and drive up the coast, another would march from Utrecht, and a central column would enter Zululand at Rorke's Drift. The Buffs had been brought up to full strength by the arrival of its three companies from Mauritius, and together with the Naval Brigade made up Colonel Pearson's infantry force on the lower Tugela. Colonel Glyn was given the command of the Central Column. His infantry was to consist of the 2/24th and those 1st Battalion companies that could be spared from protecting the long supply line to Rorke's Drift. The Left Column, under the command of Evelyn Wood, was to have the 90th Regiment and the 1/13th as its hard core. Chelmsford's reserve battalion was the 80th Regiment; it was to be kept in the Transvaal, but conveniently close to the Zulu border. Colonel Rowland was to command the reserve force.

The General's request for a regular cavalry regiment had been turned down; which meant that his columns would have to depend largely on mounted colonial detachments. His infantry had provided him with a second mounted squadron which he attached to Colonel Pearson's column. There was Buller with his two hundred campaign-hardened FLH, and Natal boasted a permanent mounted police detachment modelled on the FAMP. It numbered a little more than one hundred men, and was commanded by Major John Dartnell, an ex-army officer who had fought in the Indian Mutiny. The remainder would have to come from militia units and privately organised commandos. Chelmsford had hoped for one thousand volunteer horsemen – he got less than half that number. His most optimistic projections gave him a white field force of six thousand men – an estimated ratio of one soldier for seven Zulus. The Boers, with a few exceptions, had given little indication of willingness to fight alongside the British. An auxiliary force, drawn from Natal's large black population, was an absolute necessity. It was Anthony Durnford who came to the rescue.

Two months after he had ruled in favour of King Cetshwayo in the Blood River dispute, the quixotic engineering officer drew up a detailed memorandum for the recruitment and training of an indigenous contingent to fight against Cetshwayo. The stumbling block had been Henry Bulwer, without whose permission the scheme could not be put into operation. The Lieutenant-Governor had been reluctant to take the step that would put the Colony on a war footing and antagonise the Zulu King. By the time consent was wrung from him, all plans for the meaningful instruction of Durnford's black volunteers had to be abandoned. The seven thousand *Amacafula*, who were persuaded to fight for the Colony, created a need for experienced leaders. Men like Rupert Lonsdale, who had commanded Mfengu in the Amatholes, were much in demand. But many had been absorbed into administrative posts in the Cape Colony's newly conquered territories and were not available for Natal's war. Chelmsford did have a surfeit of detached-service officers and gentleman-adventurers who had been attracted to South Africa by the prospect of a colonial campaign, men new to the country with little understanding of local customs and no knowledge of the black man's language. It was from their ranks that he had to find the officers for his three black regiments. The non-commissioned officers, the men responsible for basic instruction, were even less suited for the task. Drifters, down-and-outs and misfits from the disbanded Pulleine's Rangers were the ones that were prepared to join the Natal Native Contingent (NNC). They were intolerant, contemptuous of their charges, and equated instruction with bullying. Misunderstandings were common, and harsh punishment was meted out as a matter of course. Unmotivated and poorly armed, the NNC came to be regarded as little more than a labour force.

Durnford's personal command was the notable exception. Thanks to his limitless energy, his men ended up being the best armed, best clothed and best drilled in the NNC, and his NCOs had been carefully chosen. He had hoped to command the entire contingent, but his very friendliness with the natives, his close ties with Bishop Colenso and his place on the Boundary Commission, had given rise to a suspicion that he was soft on black people and not to be relied upon in a war against a black nation. Nor, for that matter, did certain members of Chelmsford's staff approve of an engineering colonel having command of so large a field force. He was given one regiment (the 1st NNC) consisting of three battalions of a thousand men each. He added to his command five troops of experienced native horsemen, and chose their officers from amongst the most dependable colonials. Every man in Durnford's Horse was issued with a uniform and a breech-loading carbine.

Chelsmford could not help but be impressed with the calibre of Durnford's force. He decided to strengthen it with a rocket-battery, and allow it to operate as a separate column. Eight men, drawn from Captain Mostyn's company in Fort Napier, were placed under Major Francis Broadfoot Russell of the Royal Artillery and given instruction in the handling of a rocket-tube. The column was ordered to assemble at Middle Drift, a crossing on the Tugela which Wolseley had considered a suitable jumping-off place for an invasion of Zululand. The rugged terrain on the Zulu side of Middle Drift could best be negotiated by lightly equipped infantry like the 1st NNC, but Chelmsford could not rid himself of the reservations he had about the black composition of the column, and its commanding officer, and finally relegated it to the role of a reserve for the defence of a gateway into Natal.

19

The Central Column

Helpmekaar (help each other) consisted of two dwellings and a ramshackle store that served the Umsinga Native Reserve. The corrugated iron structure stood on a featureless plain near the eastern rim of the Biggarsberg plateau. On those days when the rain let up and the clouds lifted it was possible to look down upon the rugged Buffalo valley and glimpse the swollen river on its twisted journey to the Tugela. Beyond the river, turned a deceptive gentle green by the young grass that had sprung up everywhere, stretched the hills of Zululand.

The importance of Helpmekaar lay in its freedom from the 'horse-sickness' and its nearness to Rorke's Drift; and there Chelmsford chose to assemble the Central Column. Situated some fifty miles to the north of Greytown, it was reached by a seldom-used road that scarcely deserved the name, an uphill wagon-track that forded two rivers in a tortuous bid to ascend the Biggarsberg. The recent rains had washed away what meagre resemblance it had to a road, but in December 1878, it became a major highway for the legions of Sir Bartle Frere.

By the middle of December 'A', 'C', 'E' and 'H' Companies of the 1/24th were under canvas at Helpmekaar, and an officer's mess had been constructed out of biscuit tins and empty crates.* A generous supply of rum and 'Square Face' (gin) helped dissipate the ever-present damp under the stretched tarpaulin that served as its roof. The only other luxury on that sodden plateau was the ration of fresh bread that Cook-Sergeant Field unfailingly provided despite the daily thunderstorms – '... we meet every night with heavy rains, accompanied by thunder and lightning, which continue until six o'clock in the morning!', wrote Private Owen Ellis of the 1st Battalion; and sometimes it was hailstones 'as large as a fist'.

---

*Captain Rainforth's 'G' Company had been detached in Greytown to guard the supply line, and Lieutenant Archer Morshead had been seconded district adjutant to Major Hopton of the 88th, the new Commandant of Greytown.

But every morning the men were mustered on the wet veld and made to practise advancing in attack *with the distance between files doubled*, because the General, influenced by his Amatholes experience and in disregard of the stress laid on the Zulu practice of charging home in mass, had ordered that formation adopted. When the weather permitted Lieutenant Porteous and Sergeant Chambers conducted rifle practice, but the occasions were few.

It was not long before the dispiriting weather began to take its toll. Constant exertion in wet clothes and unseasonably cold nights brought on chills that progressed to pneumonia; chafed feet in soggy boots developed infected sores that refused to heal; and the rudimentary sanitary arrangements introduced dysentry in the camp. One of the casualties was Brevet-Major William Much, who had to be sent, protesting, to Pietermaritzburg to convalesce. By Christmas, few were busier than Surgeon-Major Peter Shepherd and his orderlies. The festive season was no joyous occasion, and Private George Morris found much to complain about. The Christmas dinner consisted of 'nothing but some boiled beef and onions and biscuits'. He remembered, too, that he had not received prize money or field pay after the Xhosa War and hoped that the Zulu campaign would bring greater rewards. He wrote wistfully of making his fortune in South Africa as a civilian, and concluded his letter – 'I trust God will bring me safe out as he has before'.

The encampment grew rapidly throughout December. Assistant-Commissary Dunne erected three large sheds for the Column's supplies, and as the various units that were to constitute Glyn's command began to arrive, a village of tents sprang up on the plateau. Fifty-eight Natal Carbineers, commanded by Shepstone's lawyer son, 'Offy', pitched camp about a quarter-mile from the 1/24th. They were joined by about thirty volunteers who called themselves the 'Newcastle Mounted Rifles', and a group of twenty-two that went under the name of 'Buffalo Border Guard'. The largest colonial contingent to reach Helpmekaar was Major Dartnell's one hundred and twenty strong Natal Mounted Police. A few days before Christmas, four companies of the 2/24th (Major Dunbar's wing) marched in.

The black regiment attached to the Central Column assembled near Sandspruit some ten miles to the south of Helpmekaar. The two thousand men in Rupert Lonsdale's 3rd NNC were divided into two battalions. No. 1 Battalion was commanded by Hamilton-Browne, a tough, intolerant, adventurer who had commanded Pulleine's Rangers in the latter part of the Xhosa war. The ranks of the 3rd NNC were filled with an uninspiring motley of farm-labourers and domestic servants. Their uniform consisted of little more than a loin-cloth and a red headband. Each man carried the blanket he had been given as a reward for coming forward to defend the Colony. Two hundred breech-loading rifles had been distributed to the regiment. The remainder had to make do with knobkerries, assegaais and an assortment of muzzle-loaders. Those fortunate enough to be entrusted with a rifle were never issued more than five rounds at a time, and even this quantity was considered a waste by their scornful instructors. Musketry instruction was not undertaken and the infrequent attempts at drill merely led to explosions of temper and assaults. It would have been a near miracle if experienced NCOs had turned these men into a disciplined force capable of standing up to a determined enemy in the time available. But no one expected the *Amacafula* to fulfil this function. Their role, as their instructors who had fought on the Eastern Frontier understood, was to enter the bush ahead of the troops and force the enemy to show himself.

Colonel Glyn throughout this time was fully occupied with the organisation of the column and the establishment of an advanced base on the Buffalo. His staff included Major Cornelius Clery, a theoretical tactician who had been a lecturer at Sandhurst, Captain Alan Gardner of the 14th Hussars assigned to General Duties, and Captain Edward Essex of the 75th Foot as director of transport. All of them were newcomers to South Africa; only Captain Henry Hallam Parr of the 1/13th and Major Henry Spalding, the Quartermaster-General on the Headquarters Staff, were known to Glyn from the time of the Xhosa war. The position of Orderly Officer he reserved for Coghill.

The last days of the year saw the arrival in Helpmekaar of Lieutenant-Colonel Henry Degacher with the other wing of the 2nd Battalion. It was the first time that both battalions of the 24th Foot were to campaign as a regiment; and with William Degacher in temporary command of the 1/24th, the battalions were led by brothers. The New Year, which was heralded in by more thunderstorms, brought the General and four of his staff officers to Helpmekaar. Chelmsford had decided to attach himself to the Central Column for the invasion of Zululand. It spelt the end of Colonel Glyn's hopes for an unfettered command. He would be left with the administrative headaches while the General decided on the strategy. A few days later, the one hundred and thirty men and six guns of N Battery, 5th Brigade, Royal Artillery were led in by Lieutenant-Colonel Harness.

Among the last to reach Helpmekaar was the 1st Squadron, Imperial Mounted Infantry, from the Transvaal. Twenty eventful months had passed since Browne and his men last saw their comrades from the 1st Battalion, and a great deal of reminiscing had to be gone through. Chelmsford had proposed putting Major John Russell, the squadron's unpopular commander, in charge of all the mounted men, and had given him the local rank of Lieutenant-Colonel. But the colonial volunteers quickly demonstrated that they preferred Dartnell to the opinionated cavalry officer and refused to accept the General's ruling. Russell's position in the Central Column was left undefined.

The ultimatum was about to expire; it was time for the Central Column to move down to the Buffalo River. The mounted volunteers and two companies of the 1/24th were the first to leave. The 3rd NNC came up from Sandspruit and were afforded the same welcome by the band of the 1/24th as the 2nd Battalion had received. The night before the troops moved to Rorke's Drift, the officers of the 1st Battalion invited their counterparts in the 2nd Battalion to a dinner in their boxwood mess. The date was a few days short of the thirtieth anniversary of Chillianwala, and William Degacher and Francis Porteous recalled that disastrous afternoon in India when they proposed the toast: 'That we may not get into such a mess – and have better luck this time'.

It was twelve precipitous miles from the top of the Biggarsberg to Rorke's Drift. The road to the drift skirted the hill at the foot of which James Rorke had built his house and his trading store, and continued for another half-mile before reaching the place where the banks of the Buffalo had been flattened to allow for an easier crossing into Zululand. Rorke had faced his buildings towards the setting sun. Behind them towered the hill the Zulus called Shiyane. After Rorke's death the property passed into the hands of the Swedish Missionary Society. The present incumbent had turned the store into a rude church and had moved his family into Rorke's house. He had renamed the hill Oskarberg in honour of Sweden's King – the change in name was about the only impression he had made in the district.

Before the Central Column descended on Rorke's Drift, Assistant-Commissary Chermside had turned the church into a storehouse and the missionary's eleven-roomed house into a much-needed hospital. The arrival of four thousand five hundred men, three hundred wagons and carts, and one thousand five hundred oxen, transformed Rorke's remote corner into a noisy waste of trampled grass, mud and garbage. At the drift,

Lieutenant Francis MacDowel, the Column's only engineering officer, had his hands full constructing a barrel-raft and enlarging the existing pont. MacDowel, who had refurbished Fort Burgers for Rowland, had been attached, originally, to Wood's column, but Colonel Glyn had spotted him when he came to Helpmekaar to inspect some engineering stores, and as the Central Column was without engineers, had co-opted his services. A company of Royal Engineers had landed in Durban on 4 January, and with Colonel Glyn crying out for engineers, Lieutenant John Chard, the senior subaltern, was sent ahead in a light cart. He arrived at Rorke's Drift barely a day before the Column crossed into Zululand.

There was an air of impatience at Rorke's Drift. Everyone was eager for the invasion to begin, and bring to an end a life under dripping canvas. There was much grumbling about the formality of having to wait for an ultimatum to expire. On the day before the invasion was to begin, a subaltern rode into the camp with his soldier servant, his black groom and a spare horse. Frere had given Coghill permission to join his battalion; he had completed the journey from Pietermaritzburg in three days. The spare horse was for his Colonel.

Reveille on the morning of 11 January was sounded at 2 : 00 a.m. As the men came on parade they were startled to find themselves searched by their officers. A contractor, who had arrived at Rorke's Drift the day before with a wagonload of brandy and cigars at unpatriotic prices, had had his merchandise stolen during the night. So woeful had been his plaints that Colonel Glyn was forced to order a search for hidden liquor before the business of crossing the Buffalo began.

The guns of N Battery were moved in the dark to a rise overlooking the drift and unlimbered with their muzzles pointing towards Zululand. First light brought a heavy mist to the river valley and a light rain began to fall on the assembled troops. The swift-flowing Buffalo was an uninviting pea-green colour and no one was too eager to test it. The native contingent, whose uniforms and arms were unlikely to suffer from immersion in water, were cajoled with threats, curses and blows, to enter the river and build a human chain to the far bank. The mounted men rode their horses into the water and were the first across. They immediately fanned out in a wide semi-circle and waited for the 'red-coats' to be ferried across. As soon as the infantry reached the Zululand side of the river they were formed up in 'Receive Cavalry' squares. Skirmishing parties were sent out and it was quickly established that the crossing was going to be unopposed. The men were put to work erecting a new camp along a curve on the river. Zululand had been breached, but for the time being there was to be no further advance. The Buffalo, however, had exacted its toll from the invaders. Several blacks were drowned, and a private in the Mounted Infantry had a narrow escape when his horse lost its footing and was swept away by the strong current.

For the rest of the day the troops were employed ferrying supplies and putting up tents. When at the end of the day the inevitable thunderstorm broke, nothing seemed changed to the weary soldiers. They had crossed a river, advanced a few hundred yards, and established another camp in the mud. In Pietermaritzburg the event was commemorated with a special edition of the *Times of Natal*. It carried an announcement from the High Commissioner, in the diplomatic format reserved for such occasions: 'The British forces are crossing into Zululand to exact from Cetewayo reparations for violations of British Territory committed by the sons of Sihayo and others, and to enforce compliance with the promises made by Cetewayo at his coronation for the better government of his people. The British Government had no quarrel with the Zulu people'.

Encouraged by the ease with which his forces had established themselves in Zululand, Chelmsford left immediately for a meeting with his favourite column commander. The Left Column had crossed the border the day before the ultimatum expired, and Colonel Wood had ridden south with Buller and the FLH for the prearranged meeting. The rendezvous site lay some ten miles up river from Rorke's Drift, and the exchange of pleasantries lasted three hours. The FLH used the time to round up a herd of cattle grazing nearby – cattle which Sihayo had collected to fulfil the conditions of the ultimatum.

The General's party was back at Rorke's Drift by early afternoon, and found a visitor in the camp. Anthony Durnford had ridden up from the Middle Drift at Chelmsford's bidding. The arrival of the two infantry battalions from England had resulted in a change of plan. The defence of Natal and the supply lines to Pearson's and Glyn's columns could now be secured by the newcomers; Durnford's command was to act in combination with the Central Column. His move into Zululand was to coincide with the departure of the troops from Rorke's Drift; but before that, the Central Column had to settle scores with Sihayo.

The camp on the Buffalo had been pitched in Sihayo's domain, and his kraal, Sokexe was situated a few miles away, under the western buttresses

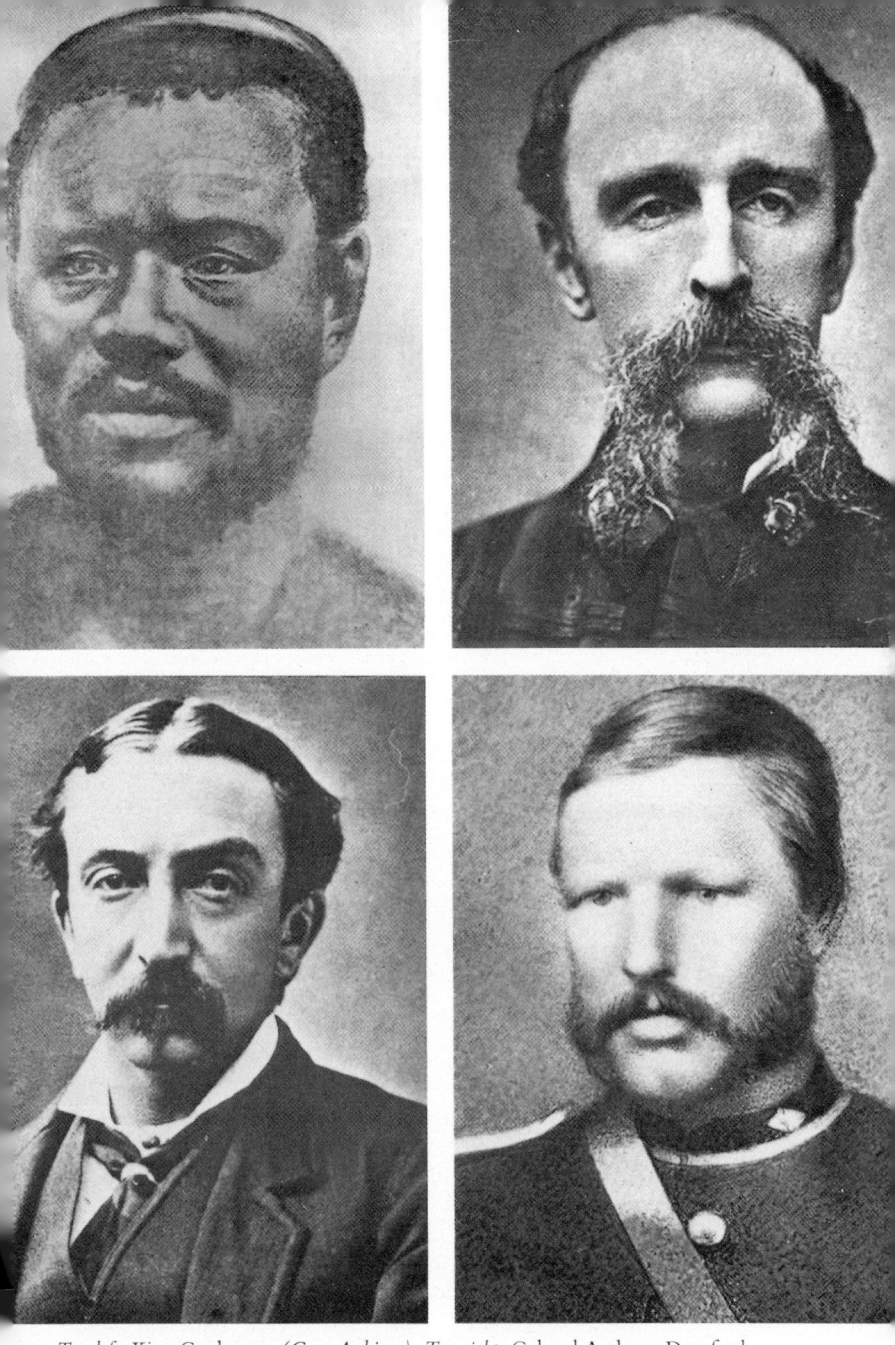

Top left: King Cetshwayo *(Cape Archives)*. *Top right:* Colonel Anthony Durnford R. E. *(Courtesy J. B. Hayward & Son, Piccadilly)*. *Bottom left:* Captain William Degacher, Commander of the 1/24th at Isandlwana *(Courtesy J. B. Hayward & Son, Piccadilly)*. *Bottom right:* Quartermaster James Pullen *(Courtesy J. B. Hayward & Son, Piccadilly)*.

Top: Burck and the ill-fated Band of the 1/24th. *Bottom:* Corporal Harry Richardson and the Pioneers of the 1/24th *(Both photographs: Album of Bandmaster Burck).*

Top left: Captain William Mostyn. *Top right:* Captain Reginald Younghusband.
Bottom left: Lieutenant Charles Cavaye. *Bottom right:* Lieutenant Francis Porteous
(Courtesy J. B. Hayward & Son, Piccadilly).

Top: Coghill standing over Melvill's body *(From the painting by C. E. Fripp).*
Bottom: Isandlwana ... the end. A view from the camp-site of the 1/24th.
(Africana Museum, Johannesburg).

of the Nqutu Range. The Chief was at Ulundi, but sufficient followers, it was believed, had remained behind to pose a threat to the Column's lines of supply. There was, in addition, moral justification for destroying the home of the murderous clan which had outraged the Colony and had helped bring on the war. Military necessity and righteous indignation combined to seal the fate of Sihayo's kraal.

The main assault was to be undertaken by Hamilton-Browne's battalion with three companies of the 1/24th in support. The bayonets of the infantry, it was hoped, would ensure that the *Amacafula* did their duty. The force would attack along the eastern shoulder of the gorge in which Sihayo's village was located. The other NNC battalion and the 2/24th would set out a few hours later, take a different route and come round the western side.

The attacking force set out at five o'clock the following morning. Major Wilsone Black of the 2/24th commanded the NNC because Rupert Lonsdale had fallen off his horse and was concussed. Chelmsford would not be left out of the affair, and rode out with Major Black and Captain Degacher. When a mounted troop, which had ridden ahead, reported that the Zulus were preparing to put up a resistance, Chelmsford had second thoughts about delaying the departure of the support column. He sent Coghill back to hurry them on. His message delivered, Nevill galloped furiously to catch up with his battalion; he had no intention of missing a fight if he could help it. It was 12 January, the day before the anniversary of his baptism of fire at Nyumaga.

Near Sihayo's gorge, Hamilton-Browne stopped his men and ordered the defenders to lay down their arms. He was greeted with a volley of rifle-fire and an avalanche of rocks. The result was an immediate evaporation of ardour in the ranks of the NNC. But an inclination to retire was corrected by the loaded rifles of the red-coated infantry and the example of three hundred Zulu expatriates who were fighting for the Colony because of a grudge they bore King Cetshwayo. The Zulus spearheaded the assault. A short, sharp fight took place on the slopes of the gorge. The NNC had two killed and eighteen wounded while Sihayo's followers left twenty dead. William Degacher's men had little part in the action. But Colonel Glyn had a narrow escape when a Zulu sharpshooter took deliberate aim at him. It was the shouted warning of an officer of the NNC that saved his life.

The other Degacher's troops, in the meantime, had reached the mouth of the gorge and were close to the knoll on which Sihayo's village stood.

Chelmsford rode over to them, formed the companies into a line, and ordered a charge. The 1/24th, at the other end of the gorge, had climbed unopposed to the top of Sihayo's Krans, and from this vantage point watched the 2nd Battalion expend its energies in a furious assault on huts which only they on the krans could see were deserted. The kraal was levelled to the ground and five hundred head of cattle were confiscated in the practised Gcalekaland manner. The day's successful outing was spoilt, somewhat, by a heavy thunderstorm that overtook the troops on their march back to the Buffalo.

The continuous rains had caused the small river which flowed near Sihayo's kraal to overflow its low banks. Its shallow valley, which was traversed by the wagon-track into the interior, had become a quagmire, and in its present condition it presented a formidable obstacle for the wagons and carts that accompanied the Central Column. Lieutenant Francis MacDowel estimated that it would take at least a week to repair the road, and an encampment was established near Sihayo's Krans. Four companies of the 2/24th were sent to protect the working party. Their camp on the 'Bashee' (the name they gave to Sihayo's river which is now known as the 'Batse'), like the main camp on the Buffalo, was neither entrenched nor fortified. Only when word reached the General that three impis had left Ulundi to attack 'Somtseu's Column' (the Zulus believed that Shepstone commanded the troops at Rorke's Drift), were attempts made to fortify the camps. Major Dunbar's wing on the 'Bashee' built a low stone wall on two sides of their encampment and Glyn had 'small entrenchments' dug 'just outside the exposed portions' of the main camp.

An elderly Boer, whose father and brother had been killed fighting the Zulus, visited Rorke's Drift at about this time and was horrified by the sight of the unprotected, sprawling camp. He gave solemn warning against underestimating the Zulu army. Chelmsford, however, was full of confidence. His mounted troops had ridden twenty miles into Zululand and had returned without encountering any opposition. He dismissed the old Boer as an 'alarmist' who, like some 'Natal officials', saw 'danger where really there is none . . .' Colonel Glyn felt less complacent. He had wanted to fortify, at least, the depots at Helpmekaar and Rorke's Drift; but the General had preferred to leave such exhausting work to the permanent depot troops. He had thought the fortifications could wait for the arrival of the 2/4th, and overruled Glyn. The same mood of optimism was to be found in a letter, written a few days earlier by Private Owen Ellis: 'This war will be over in two months' time and then we shall be hurrying towards England. We are about to capture all the cattle belonging to the Zulus and also burn their kraals; and if they dare to face us with the intention of fighting, well, woe be to them!' Such was the temper in the camp when, on 17 January, Henry Pulleine rode in and took command of the 1/24th.

Lord Chelmsford, by then, had prepared his plans for the next advance. The Column was to move ten miles into Zululand and establish a temporary camp that was to serve as a base for an attack on the stronghold of Chief Matshana, whose kraals were scattered along the Mangeni River valley. It was Chelmsford's intention to employ one of Durnford's battalions in the operation. The battalion was to move up to Sandspruit and cross the Buffalo at a point less than ten miles south of the Mangeni River. But a few days before the move took place, Durnford marched his column to the Tugela River with the intention of crossing into Zululand. He had reacted to unsubstantiated rumours that the Zulus were planning to invade Natal across Middle Drift. Chelmsford only just managed to stop what he considered to be a hasty act of imprudence. He severely reprimanded Durnford and threatened him with replacement. Major Bengough of the 77th Foot, the senior regular-army officer with the Middle Drift Column, was placed in command of the force that was to cross at a place called Elandskraal, near Sandspruit, and Durnford himself was ordered to join Colonel Glyn's column with his Native Horse, the Rocket Battery and three companies of infantry. He reached Rorke's Drift on the evening of the twentieth and found the campsite on the Zululand side of the Buffalo River deserted. The Central Column had pulled out that morning.

20

The 'Little Sphinx'

If you stand on the banks of the Buffalo River, near the drift where James Rorke used to moor his pont, and look at the hills of Zululand, one hill with a distinctive outline (not unlike a lion *couchant*), stands out from all the others. The men of the 24th Foot thought it resembled the brass sphinx on their tunic-collars, and – because the hill is not a large one – named it 'the little Sphinx'. The hill is about seven miles from Rorke's Drift, but the winding wagon-track to Ulundi that used to pass beneath its southern face added another three miles to the journey. The plain in front of the hill was to be the Central Column's next camp site. The Zulu name for the hill is Isandlwana.

Left behind at Rorke's Drift when the Central Column broke camp were thirty-six men too ill to make the move, an unattached NNC company and the 2nd Battalion's 'B' Company. The latter was entrusted with the protection of the depot until the 2/4th arrived. Since the time when Captain Alfred Godwin-Austen received his wound in the Ama-tholes, 'B' Company had been commanded by Lieutenant Gonville Bromhead. A sergeant and nine men from the 1st Battalion were also left at Rorke's Drift; five of them were patients in the hospital.

The road out of the 'Bashee' valley rose gradually towards the ruins of Sihayo's stronghold, skirted the western buttresses of the Nqutu Range, then turned east in the direction of Isandlwana. About a mile before the hill it crossed the gully through which the Manzimnyama stream flowed on its course to the Buffalo. From the gully it was a steep haul to the Nek, the stretch of ground that formed a saddle between the precipitous southern wall of Isandlwana and a stony kopje. The companies guarding the road-works on the 'Bashee' were the first to reach the new camp site. Behind them stretched a line of men, wagons and oxen almost five miles long. When the vanguard reached the Nek they found Major Clery waiting to lay out the camp. The ground at the foot of Isandlwana was hard and stony and the camp-line had to be drawn about a hundred yards in front of its eastern slope, where the soil was more yielding. Column Headquarters was established at a point midway along the hill, and the area in front of it was allocated to the 2/24th. On the left of the 2nd Battalion, extending in a line towards a nearby low plateau, Clery placed the two battalions of the 3rd NNC. The artillery and the mounted contingent were allocated a place to the right of the 2nd Battalion. The Nek was left clear and the 1/24th camp was sited on the right flank in front of the stony kopje. Water from the plateau trickled through two dongas a few hundred yards in front of the camp. For sanitary reasons it was the usual practice to place native contingents downstream, but because the stony kopje commanded the Nek and the road to Rorke's Drift, Clery thought it prudent to locate reliable troops there. The right or 'downstream' flank was also the one nearest the Mangeni valley: the most likely place, it was believed, from where a threat to the camp might originate.

The line of the camp stretched for almost a thousand yards in front ot Isandlwana. It faced a plain that sloped gently down to a large donga (gully) about half a mile away, then continued uninterrupted for another twelve miles to the flat-topped silhouette of the Siphezi hill. To the left front of the camp the plain was bounded by the plateau escarpment; but on the right it extended southwards for almost five empty miles to the Malakatha and Hlazakazi hills. A conical kopje, about a mile and a half in front of the camp was given undue prominence by the surrounding flatness, but its highest point was well below the level of the plateau. The only signs of previous habitation were two small abandoned kraals on the far side of the donga.

Chelmsford rode into the camp at lunch time, and declared himself well satisfied with the layout. He was happy to see that it commanded seventy square miles of open ground. Someone observed that the camp was a little too close to the plateau, but he was assured that vedettes posted on the plateau would guard against the unlikely event of a surprise attack from the north. After a quick lunch, the General and his staff galloped off in the direction of the hills that hid the Mangeni valley. Before they left, Inspector Mansell of the Natal Mounted Police was told to take some of his men on to the plateau and establish vedette posts.

The procession of tired men and lumbering ox-wagons continued throughout the afternoon, and by the end of the day the ground in front of Isandlwana had come to resemble a huge wagon-park. Not all the wagons, however, reached the camp before nightfall. The corduroy road of logs through the mud of the 'Bashee' valley had broken down, and the Manzimnyama had proved a greater obstacle than had been anticipated. With night coming on, it was decided to establish a small encampment for the stragglers near the Manzimnyama crossing. A detachment drawn from the 2/24th was sent back to guard the camp. In the failing light of dusk another company of infantry marched into the encampment. It was Mostyn's 'F' Company. They had left Pietermaritzburg on 9 January, and Helpmekaar that morning. Sergeants Ballard, Cooper and Upton had pushed their men hard, and everyone was grateful when a halt was called on the Manzimnyama. 'Thank goodness, here we are at last', was Mostyn's relieved comment.

The General and his staff returned to the main camp at about six-thirty. On their way back from the Mangeni they had spotted some fowls scampering about in an abandoned kraal. The thought of a roast-chicken dinner had spurred some of the junior officers to give chase; but a nimble chicken had caused Coghill to stumble and wrench his troublesome left knee. He had managed the ride back, but could barely walk. In front of Isandlwana fires were being lit for the evening meal. Excited yells and the bellowing of cattle indicated that the daily ration was being slaughtered.

Picquets were posted for the night in a semi-circle that extended from the edge of the plateau to beyond the stony kopje. The vedettes were about a half a mile further out. Inspector Mansell had been rebuked by one of Chelmsford's staff officers for posting them too far out and had been sent back to draw them in. One of Mansell's vedettes had apprehended an elderly Zulu on the plateau who told them that the big impi would not be coming from Matshana's district but from the north. Sub-Inspector Phillips brought the information to the General as he was about to start his dinner. He listened politely but did not think the old Zulu's tale merited a change in his plans for the following morning. He was going to send out two strong reconnaissance forces to probe Matshana's stronghold. Rupert Lonsdale, who had returned that morning sufficiently recovered from his head injury to command his regiment, was to take both NNC battalions past Malakatha to the Mangeni valley and follow the river eastwards. A large mounted detachment, under Major Dartnell, was to scout the terrain between the Hlazakazi and the Magogo hills. In the afternoon he was to rendezvous with Lonsdale on the Mangeni. Two members of Chelmsford's personal staff were to accompany Dartnell to see that no rash action was taken. The campaign was getting under way at last. Supper was a 'merry affair that night'.

Dawn on the morning of the 21st found the 3rd NNC mustered and ready to depart. One company from each battalion was to remain behind to look after their camp and provide men for picquet duty. Early risers saw Lonsdale leading his men past the stony kopje in the direction of the Malakatha peaks. By the time the mounted men had saddled their horses and drawn their rations, the whole column was awake. Dartnell's detachment was made up, almost entirely of police and volunteers. There was a brief commotion in the camp when one of them discharged his pistol too close to his pony's ear and was violently thrown by the startled animal. His place was taken by a young trooper who had come off vedette duty a short while before. An hour after the departure of the NNC, Dartnell's contingent cantered off in the direction of the rising sun.

Chelmsford had heard that a big impi had left Ulundi three days before, and estimated that it might be nearing the Tala Heights by now. He thought its likely route would be over the Magogo to the Mangeni valley, but could not discount the possibility of it swinging north, past Siphezi to the Nqutu Range, as the old Zulu had predicted. He ordered Edward Browne to take out four mounted infantrymen on a patrol behind Siphezi. Shortly after breakfast 'F' Company arrived with the wagons from the Manzimnyama. Mostyn made his report to Pulleine, while Edgar Anstey and Pat Daly strode over to the 1st Battalion kitchen for their 'belated morning meal'. They told their fellow officers that Upcher's 'D' Company from Durban was expected in Helpmekaar that very day and that Rainforth's men ('G' Company) would, in all likelihood, catch up with the Column the following evening.

The sun was high and the clouds were scattering when Browne's men rode out across the plain. It looked as if the day was going to turn into a real scorcher and there would be no shade away from the camp. The infantrymen were starting to go about their duties when a lone figure, leading his mount, walked in from the south. It was Dr Frank Bull, the surgeon with the 3rd NNC, who had been forced to turn back when his horse went lame. He told Colonel Glyn that so far Lonsdale had encountered nothing more formidable than a few old women and some goats.

Shortly before mid-morning Chelmsford rode out with a small escort to visit the kraal of Sihayo's older brother, Chief Magumdana, who had approached Henry Fynn, the Magistrate at Umsinga, with an offer of submission after the sacking of Sihayo's kraal. The General's party, however, found the village deserted; the inhabitants had fled into the hills at the approach of Lonsdale's battalions. Chelmsford was back at Isandlwana in time for lunch. The meal was scarcely over when the old chief arrived with Henry Fynn. He agreed to the General's terms and promised to surrender all the arms in his kraal. Chelmsford, by then, was confident that whatever enemy forces lurked in Matshana's district could be easily dealt with by the Central Column. He had reservations about the wisdom of allowing Bengough's battalion to ford the Buffalo near Elands Kraal and act independently on the Mangeni. The matter was discussed with Captain George Shepstone, one of Durnford's staff officers, who had ridden in from Rorke's Drift. He took an order back for Bengough to join Durnford at Rorke's Drift.

A short while after Magumdana left, Browne returned with the first report of hostile forces. He had run into a party of about thirty warriors near Siphezi and had exchanged shots with them. The Zulus had been moving towards the north and Browne did not think they were part of a large impi. Chelmsford then decided to reconnoitre the high ground to the north of the camp. He rode up the half-mile long spur that linked the rump of the 'sphinx' with the plateau, and was rewarded with a fine view of the open camp. It was obvious that the higher ground of the plateau could afford advantage to an enemy equipped with firearms and artillery, but the Zulus scarcely fell into that category. Further north, as far as Chelmsford could see, the terrain was featureless, undulating grassland. He turned east and rode along the plateau's edge to the furthest vedette, stationed on a knoll over two miles from the camp. The General was satisfied with the disposition of the sentries on the plateau and made no changes.

The defence of the camp was Colonel Glyn's responsibility. Both Frere and Cunynghame had praised him for his reliability and willingness to follow orders, and in the normal course of command he would have carried out the instructions laid down in the manual for field operations in Zululand. A cattle laager would have been drawn up and trenches dug regardless of the nature of the ground; but the presence of the General had placed him in an invidious position. Lord Chelmsford and his personal staff tended to dominate the decision-making and Glyn found himself acquiescing increasingly to the opinions of the man who physically towered over him and was his ranking superior. He was later to admit, 'As regards outposts and the ordinary precautions for the safety of the camp, I consider for all these arrangements I was wholly responsible', but went on to add that the only intelligence department in the column was entirely at the disposal and under the control of the General and his staff; and knowing that Chelmsford had to consider the movements of all the other columns, was 'very diffident in volunteering an opinion adverse to a movement' he considered hazardous. Nor did Glyn feel obliged to speak out if his 'judgement dissented from a movement the General had ordered'.

Chelmsford had thought that entrenchments at Isandlwana 'would take a week to make', and were not really necessary. The question of drawing up a laager was dismissed because some of the wagons would be returning to Rorke's Drift for supplies, and it was far more convenient to outspan them on the Nek close to the road. In the opinion of many of the officers at Isandlwana, the camp was well sited for a defensive action; and the line of vedettes could give ample warning of an approaching enemy. But there were some who felt uneasy about the total lack of defences and the disposition of the picquets. Major Dunbar was one of them, Melvill was another. On the evening of the 20th, Dunbar had complained to the staff officer on duty about the absence of a picquet behind Isandlwana, and had received the reply, 'Well Sir, if you are nervous, we will put a picquet of the pioneers there'. The same officer was later to admit that never in all his life had he 'experienced so strong a presentiment of coming evil ...' Some NNC officers had also lamented the unprotected condition of the camp, and had commented on the lack of respect Chelmsford and his staff accorded the Zulus. According to Hamilton-Browne, Colonel Glyn had looked depressed and had shaken his head when the extended nature of the camp was pointed out to him.

Isandlwana was casting its late-afternoon shadow over the camp when the General rode down from the plateau. He had been with the advanced vedette when a party of mounted Zulus was noticed about a mile away, and had assumed that they belonginged to the group Browne had encountered. On his way back to camp Chelmsford was overtaken by the two staff officers who had ridden out with Dartnell that morning. They told him that the mounted detachment had stumbled on a sizeable Zulu force near the Mangeni River about twelve miles from the camp, and that Dartnell had decided to spend the night on the near side of the river rather than return to camp. It was his intention to attack the Zulus in the morning with the help of Lonsdale's force. Dartnell's suggestion that the native regiment also spend the night on the Mangeni had been conveyed to Lonsdale. The staff officers riding back to the camp carried Dartnell's request for the assistance of a few companies of regular infantry.

Chelmsford's return to the camp coincided with the arrival of two

NNC companies driving a herd of captured cattle. Captain Murray, the officer commanding the detachment, knew nothing about Dartnell's plans; he knew only that Lonsdale's men were tired and hungry. It was almost dark when another group from the 3rd NNC rode into camp. It consisted of officers and NCOs who had disagreed with Lonsdale's decision to join Dartnell. They had refused, allegedly, to spend the night in the veld without food or blankets; but it was obvious to everyone that the proximity of a large Zulu force had been the influencing factor. Chelmsford liked Dartnell's plan even less when he learnt about the disagreement in the NNC command. But by then, it was too close to nightfall to bring the troops on the Mangeni back to camp. He ignored Dartnell's request for an infantry reinforcement, but sent a mounted detail with food and greatcoats to Dartnell's bivouac. Lieutenant Walsh of the 1/13th, the officer in charge of the detail, also carried the General's consent for an attack in the morning, provided the odds were not too great. Lord Chelmsford sat down to supper a worried man. The thought that he might have endangered the men on the Mangeni by not sending the reinforcements requested, disturbed him all evening.

He was woken shortly after one o'clock by Major Clery with the news that a messenger had come in from Dartnell's camp. The man had lost his way in the dark and the report he made was hours old. It appeared that just before sunset Dartnell's scouts had discovered another Zulu force (estimated at over two thousand warriors), and that he was still determined to attack them in the morning. The message repeated Dartnell's earlier request for two or three companies of regular infantry. What Chelmsford now feared, was that the Natal volunteers were confronting not merely Matshana's followers, but the vanguard of the big impi. He knew, only too well, that what Frere dreaded most, was the demoralising effect a Zulu success might have on the colonists. Frere had repeatedly stressed that a Zulu victory 'would bring them out openmouthed, in a revolution – anti-military and anti-imperialistic – with the Lieutenant-Governor and Colonial Service at its head'. And at this precise moment, it was the colonial boys on the Mangeni who were exposed to that very danger. Earlier in the evening, Chelmsford had comforted himself with the thought that if it came to the worst, Dartnell's horsemen and Lonsdale's blacks could easily outdistance an enemy almost three miles away from them. But in the early hours of the morning, this line of reasoning no longer seemed convincing.

If Dartnell had indeed stumbled on the big impi it would be tactically correct to order the immediate recall of the troops on the Mangeni, fortify the camp, and receive the Zulu Army from behind prepared positions. But Chelmsford was beginning to mistrust Dartnell's judgement. The Commander of the Natal Mounted Police might disregard his orders and expose the volunteers to hopeless odds in a foolhardy attack. He might even have miscalculated the size of the enemy's forces. He felt as he had that day at Hayne's mill, when he waited endless hours ignorant of the mismanagement of his first offensive in the Amatholes. At the back of his mind was another doubt (also based on his Amatholes experience) which made him wonder whether the Zulus would avoid a confrontation with a large, prepared, military force. The Xhosas had made that mistake at Centane; the Zulus might be more cunning. He could foresee a situation where he was compelled to continue his advance on Ulundi while the Zulu Army harassed his slow-moving column with hit and run tactics. It had become imperative that he find out for himself what was waiting for Dartnell and Lonsdale on the other side of the Mangeni. He would take out a force large enough to risk an engagement with the big impi, and attempt to reach Dartnell's bivouac before breakfast. The Zulus might be tempted into an attack.

The General's staff was roused and sent scurrying in all directions with messages. The strongest infantry battalion, numerically, was to accompany him, and Henry Degacher was instructed to parade his men without noise or lights. Colonel Harness was ordered to bring four of his six guns, and the NNC pioneer detachment was to go along to clear a path for the guns. Lieutenant-Colonel Russell was to ride ahead with the Mounted Infantry. Not wishing to offend Colonel Glyn, Chelmsford offered him command of the force.

The 2/24th was instructed to turn out in light marching order with one day's supply of preserved rations. The men were to draw seventy rounds each, but their Quartermaster was to remain in camp with his ammunition wagons. It was at first decided to leave the battalion band behind; but at the last moment someone remembered that there would be no ambulances with the column, and Degacher ordered his bandsmen out as stretcher-bearers. Bandmaster Bullard and four young drummer-boys, too small to carry stretchers, were left at Isandlwana. When the battalion was paraded it was discovered that Lieutenant Pope's company was to have supplied sentries for picquet duty that day, and the decision was taken to leave 'G' Company in camp.

All the activity had been confined to the camp centre. On the far right,

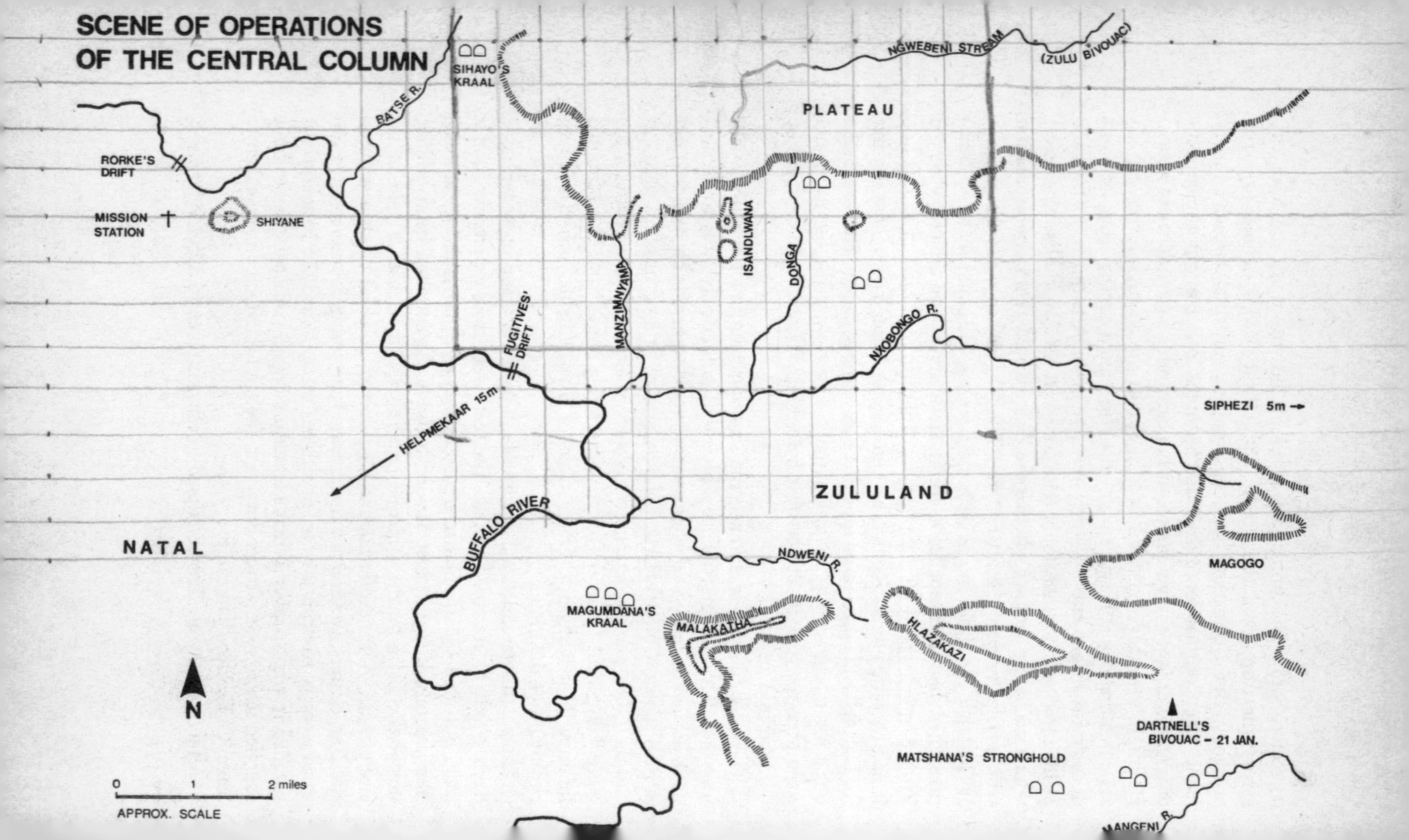
SCENE OF OPERATIONS
OF THE CENTRAL COLUMN
SIHAYO'S
KRAAL
BATSE R.
NGWEBENI STREAM
(ZULU BIVOUAC)
PLATEAU
RORKE'S
DRIFT
MISSION
STATION
SHIYANE
ISANDLWANA
DONGA
MANZIMNYAMA
FUGITIVES'
DRIFT
NXOBONGO R.
HELPMEKAAR 15m
SIPHEZI 5m
ZULULAND
BUFFALO RIVER
NATAL
NDWENI R.
MAGOGO
MAGUMDANA'S
KRAAL
MALAKATHA
HLAZAKAZI
DARTNELL'S
BIVOUAC – 21 JAN.
MATSHANA'S STRONGHOLD
N
0
1
2 miles
APPROX. SCALE
MANGENI R.

in front of the stony kopje, all was quiet. The 1/24th, with the exception of 'C' Company, which was also on picquet duty, continued its slumber. Only the Battalion Headquarters was awake. On Colonel Glyn's instructions, Major Clery strode over to Pulleine, and in Melvill's presence, informed him that he was to take charge of the camp. He was advised to keep his vedettes far out, but to draw in his line of picquets. The wagon convoy that was to have returned to Rorke's Drift in the morning, was to remain at Isandlwana to spare his troops the chore of escort duty. Richard Glyn was leaving his battalion's most senior officer in command of the camp, a man who in twenty-four years service had never heard a shot fired in anger. Glyn had known Pulleine for nine years, and was fully aware that the Major's talents found their best expression in an office. But he was not overly disturbed because Pulleine, in all likelihood, would have nothing more exacting to attend to that day than striking camp.

Chelmsford, however, remembered that Durnford was at Rorke's Drift. His mounted troops would make a useful adjunct to the camp's strength. Lieutenant Horace Smith-Dorrien, a junior transport officer, was given a message to take to Durnford. It read:

'You are to march to this camp *at once* with all the force you have with you of No. 2 Column.
Major Bengough's Battalion is to move to Rorke's Drift as ordered yesterday, 2/24th Artillery and mounted men with the General and Colonel Glyn move off at once to attack the Zulu force about ten miles distant.
P.S. If Bengough's Battalion has crossed the river at Elands Kraal it is to move up here (Nongweni* Valley).'

In the Headquarters camp Coghill enviously watched his tent companion getting dressed. He had been laid up with his injured knee since the previous evening and there could be no question of his riding out with Colonel Glyn. Captain Henry Parr waved him a hasty good-bye and left to join the column.

By three-thirty the troops were assembled and ready to march. The night was black, and the few camp lights at the foot of Isandlwana looked startlingly bright by contrast. As the hushed column moved off towards the south-east, the General hoped that somewhere in that inky wildnerness he would surprise King Cetshwayo's 'man-killing gladiators', and demolish their vaunted military reputation.

*Possibly the Nondweni – a small north-flowing river taking origin from the Magogo heights, but more likely the Mangeni.

21

Wednesday 22 January

i

The first light of the Zulu dawn showed faint and watery behind the mist-shrouded Siphezi hills when the day's duties began in the camp at Isandlwana. Pulleine's first task was to push out the vedette perimeter. There were over a hundred mounted men in the camp from whom he could draw his horse sentries, and he decided to establish two posts on the plateau and one on the conical kopje. The furthest was to be stationed on the escarpment edge, about two miles in front of the camp. Because the General's column was operating in the south-east, he considered it prudent to concentrate the camp's sentinels in the north-east. South of camp he placed only one mounted lookout, on a kopje overlooking the Nxobongo stream. Captain Barry's company of the 2/3rd NNC was sent up the spur and spread out a short distance from the edge of the plateau. Below them No. 9 Company of the 1/3rd NNC extended the picquet line towards the big donga.

The road to Rorke's Drift needed repairing in parts, and because Lieutenant MacDowel and the NNC pioneer detachment had accompanied the General, Edgar Anstey was asked to take a fatigue party to the Manzimnyama. It was full light when they set out. The clouds, which had dispersed the day before, had returned, and the morning sky was grey. Rain in the afternoon was a possibility. When George Hodson brought 'C' Company back from sentry duty, the cooks were starting to prepare breakfast for the one thousand two hundred men in the camp.

Breakfast-call was sounded shortly after seven-thirty. The men drifted towards their kitchens and began to form casual lines. Suddenly, the sound of distant gunfire was heard, and everyone wondered whether the General had made contact with the big impi. Minutes later an NNC officer was seen urging his horse down the escarpment. He did not stop until he reached the camp headquarters. Coghill came out to meet him. They spoke for a few seconds, then Coghill hobbled back to report to

Pulleine. A few minutes later Melvill emerged from the tent and ordered a bugler to sound the 'Fall-in'. It was followed almost immediately by 'Column Call'. Breakfast was abandoned and the men scattered to their respective parades. A few minutes later a messenger ran over to the 1st Battalion camp with orders from Captain Degacher for his five companies to march to the deserted ground in front of the 2/24th and the artillery camps. The men from the 2nd Battalion's 'G' Company were returned to camp and formed up on the right of the 1st Battalion. While the artillerymen were harnessing their horses, Melvill rode up with orders for the infantry to form a line facing the escarpment. They marched to a point below the NNC camp and formed up in column. Someone asked Pulleine for permission to bring in the NNC picquet behind Isandlwana; and it was remembered that Lieutenant Anstey's work-party was even further back and, in all probability, had not heard the alarm. A chary officer noticed the civilian wagon-drivers idling in the camp and ordered a sentry posted outside the Officers' Mess.

The message Pulleine received had been carried from an advanced vedette by the Honourable Standish Vereker, a civilian commissioned in the NNC. It merely stated that a large body of Zulus had been seen moving along the plateau in the north-east. Vereker was unable to say whether they were heading towards the camp or away from it. Pulleine pencilled a hasty note and gave it to a police trooper to take to the General. The message revealed his lack of precise information: 'Staff-Officer – report just came in that Zulus are advancing in force from left front of the camp. 8.5 A.M.'. Half an hour later he was still no wiser. Through their fieldglasses neither Pulleine nor Melvill could see anything unusual on the escarpment. Vereker had ridden back and no further messages had been received from the vedette. Captain Krohn's NNC company was due to go on picquet duty, but Pulleine ordered them to stay in camp. Instead, one of Krohn's subalterns, a Lieutenant Adendorff, was asked to ride to the outlying vedette and bring back the latest intelligence. Adendorff returned shortly after nine to report that the warrior-party Vereker described had divided into three groups; that two were retiring to the north-east and that the third had moved off in a westerly direction.

Very little of what Pulleine had been told threw light on the objectives of the Zulus on the plateau. His men had been standing in line for over an hour and their uneaten breakfasts had grown cold in the deserted kitchens. They were hungry, restless and hot. The sky was overcast but the morning was becoming progressively more oppressive. He must have felt that he had over-reacted to the misinterpretations of inexperienced civilians. He had heard often enough how difficult it had been to draw the Xhosas into open battle; perhaps the Zulus were no different. He was about to dismiss the men, when a party of warriors was noticed on a knoll on the escarpment edge about half a mile beyond the conical kopje. They lingered for a while before disappearing. Pulleine felt uneasy, and asked Krohn's other subaltern, Walter Higginson, to take an NCO with him and ride up to the plateau for more information.

At about this time, a solitary rider appeared over the Nek. It was Lieutenant John Chard from Rorke's Drift. The engineering officer had learnt from Lieutenant Smith-Dorrien about the General's early morning departure, and bored with his duties at the drift, had ridden over to hear what developments had taken place. He told Pulleine that there was no news from Upcher or Rainforth, but that Durnford was on his way to Isandlwana. He heard about Adendorff's report, but was told, that in the opinion of the officers on the staff, the danger from the north-east, in all probability, had been overestimated. The warrior group which allegedly had moved towards the west disturbed Chard, and he decided to return to Rorke's Drift with the information. Pulleine made up his mind to keep his troops under arms until Durnford arrived. To two dedicated whist players like Pulleine and Melvill, it might have seemed an appropriate moment to relax for a while over a game of cards.

While Chard was making his way out of the camp, two officers from Hamilton-Browne's battalion approached Pulleine for permission to send rations to their commander who had been away from camp for more than twenty-four hours. James Daly and Edgar Anstey overheard the request and added two bottles of whisky to the rations and an explanatory note stating that they had eaten his dinner the night before and wanted to make amends. Pulleine was distracted next by a small party of peaceful Zulus approaching from the south. They had come to deliver the arms Chelmsford had demanded from Magumdana. The surrendered arsenal amounted to eight or nine ancient muskets.

At about half past ten, Lieutenant-Colonel Durnford reached the camp. His escort of Native Horse drew looks of undisguised astonishment from the soldiers. They were well-mounted, fitted with uniform dress and carried Martini-Henry carbines. After the ragtag Mfengu levies and the near naked NNC, the appearance of the Natal Native Horse was a startling experience for the soldiers. A short distance behind the horsemen came a company of 1st NNC infantry and Major Russell's Rocket Battery. While Durnford and his staff wheeled left towards Pulleine's headquarters, his command halted in front of the wagon-park on the Nek.

Durnford was the senior officer in the camp. He had held the rank of lieutenant-colonel for over five years and had not as yet heard that he had been promoted full colonel in December. Pulleine was a major with a brevet of lieutenant-colonel, and the younger man by eight years. The two men differed as much in temperament as they did in physical appearance. Pulleine, who was of shorter height than average, had a genial disposition that had made him many friends; but even his most loyal well-wishers found it hard to visualise him in the role of a dashing military leader. Durnford was tall, lean and intense. His paralyzed arm testified to his combat experience and few doubted his courage. But his strongly held and unorthodox views about the blacks had made him a contentious person in colonial circles. And where Pulleine was cautious, Durnford was impulsive.

Pulleine was happy to see Durnford. He told him about the gunfire at breakfast time and mentioned that he had not as yet heard from the General. About the Zulu force on the plateau he could tell him little more than that the estimated number was between five and six hundred. The 'estimated' enemy strength did not impress Durnford. He had earlier made the remark that in South Africa 'one believes half of what one sees', and less of what one hears. The report of a Zulu party moving towards the west, however, puzzled him and he ordered Lieutenant Wyatt Vause to take his troop of Native Horse back along the Rorke's Drift road to protect his baggage wagons. Durnford could see no threat to the camp and suggested that the infantry, who by then had been standing in line for nearly three hours, be returned to their private parades for an early lunch. For the first time since breakfast Henry Pulleine felt relaxed. His anxiety over the enemy movements on the plateau had been allayed by an experienced superior who would soon take over responsibility for the safety of the camp.

Lunch was a hurried affair that ended when Lieutenant Higginson rode down from the plateau. His report, disjointed to begin with, became more jumbled as Durnford insisted on precise answers. All that Higginson could say was that he had found Captain Barry and Lieutenant Vereker watching a large body of Zulus. When asked where they were, he made a vague gesture towards the left. Durnford became irritated by the confused reports emanating from the plateau, and decided to send his own men on a thorough reconnaissance in the direction of the Nqutu Range. Lieutenant Roberts's troop of Native Horse was directed to explore the north and west, while Lieutenant Charles Raw's troop searched the north-east. To ensure an accurate assessment of the Zulu strength on the plateau he ordered two of his staff officers, Captain Barton and Captain George Shepstone, to accompany them.

The horsemen had barely reached the plateau's edge, when a messenger passed them with a note stating that the Zulus were retiring towards the east. Durnford saw an immediate correlation between the movements on the plateau and the route taken by the General's column. Six days before, Chelmsford had stated that Durnford's Native Horse and Bengough's battalion were to cooperate with the Central Column in a drive through the Mangeni valley. Durnford still regarded himself as the commander of an independent column. The notion that the General wanted him to command, merely, the camp at Isandlwana, was inconceivable to him. The man who had galloped to Pretoria to rescue Shepstone from imagined dangers, who had almost invaded Zululand to thwart a rumoured attack on Natal, reacted according to his nature – he would leave the camp to Pulleine and cooperate with the General in the Mangeni valley as previously planned; but in view of a possible threat to the General's left from the Nqutu Range, he would interpose a force between the Zulus on the plateau and the column on the Mangeni. Anthony Durnford was ready to assume his favourite role of knight-errant. According to Higginson, Durnford's immediate comment on hearing about the retiring Zulus, had been, 'Oh! is that so? Well, we will follow them up'. He then asked Higgingson to ride after Shepstone with instructions to scour the plateau in an easterly direction and drive any Zulus he might find down to the plain. Turning to Pulleine, Durnford suggested that his own force should be supplemented by two companies of infantry. Henry Pulleine tensed up. The camp was about to become his responsibility once again; and his orders were clear – the troops at Isandlwana were to stay in camp. Durnford must have been amazed at Pulleine's inability to grasp the fact that the threat was not to the camp, but to the General on the Mangeni. Pulleine had the equivalent of almost seven companies of regular infantry and a squadron of horse plus two fully-manned artillery pieces at Isandlwana, not to mention the four hundred black levies: a force large enough to deter even the big impi. But Pulleine was regulation-minded and preferred to act on clearly stated instructions – only an official order from Durnford would make him relent. Even as he turned down Durnford's request Pulleine looked to Melvill for support. The latter understood his dilemma and warned the engineering colonel against the removal of troops from the camp. Durnford dropped the matter, and Pulleine, feeling that he had offended his superior, agreed to come to his aid if he got into difficulties,

Durnford was impatient to get started. He had two troops of Native Horse in the camp (the Edendale troop under Lieutenant Harry Davies and the Hlubi troop under Lieutenant Henderson) as well as Captain Nourse's company from the 1st NNC and Major Francis Russell's Rocket Battery. He was not prepared to wait for his wagon-train and its escort to arrive. The 1/24th soldiers attached to the Rocket Battery heard Durnford order Major Russell to head towards the right front because he wanted to try and outflank the Zulus. He himself would ride ahead with the mounted troops; the Rocket Battery was to follow with Nourse's company of infantry in support.

The message Higginson carried to Shepstone recommended that he enlist the help of the NNC picquet company on the plateau. Pulleine would have to see to it that they were replaced by troops from the camp. William Degacher was asked to send one of his companies onto the plateau. He chose 'E' Company, commanded, since Captain Much's illness, by Lieutenant Cavaye.* The men had been belted and buckled up with water-bottle, haversack and ammunition-pouches since breakfast. Sergeants Edwards, Bennet and Fay checked that the men had drawn their seventy rounds and that the 'lunger' was in its sheath. It was an easy climb from the NNC camp to the rim of the plateau – they made it in fifteen minutes. Cavaye spread most of his men out in a line facing north. A platoon under Second-Lieutenant Edwards Dyson was moved a few hundred yards to the left, to cover the north-west. Their field of view was almost uninterrupted: in the distance they could see a detachment of Native Horse riding in extended formation towards the north-east.

Cavaye's men had been in position about twenty minutes when the

---

*There are a number of contradictions on this point. Captain Edward Essex at the Court of Inquiry (*The Times*, 17 March 1879) repeatedly referred to 'Cavaye's Company'. Privates J. Williams and J. Bickley in their testimony called it No. 5 (E) Company. Private G. Wilson spoke of ' "G" Company, Lieutenant Cavaye in charge'. The *Kaffrarian Watchman*, 5 February 1879, printed the names of the officers and sergeants in each company. William Degacher and Cavaye were put in 'A' Company and Porteous and Dyson in 'E' Company. The Nominal Roll of the men killed at Isandlwana in *Historical Records of the 24th Regiment*, 1892, listed Cavaye as the only officer in 'A' Company and Porteous and Dyson as the officers of 'E' Company.

Perhaps Essex, a relative newcomer, mistook Porteous for Cavaye.

quiet on the plateau was broken by the noise of rapid rifle-fire. A few minutes later they saw a rider spurring his horse down the escarpment. George Shepstone galloped into camp headquarters with news that his men had stumbled across a huge Zulu horde packed into a large gully. Shepstone's breathless arrival was followed a few minutes later by the imperative notes of the 'Fall-in'. Once again the red-coated infantry formed up in front of Isandlwana. As they were getting into position the dull morning sky grew ominously darker. Everyone looked up expecting to see a sudden accumulation of black thunderclouds; and at Helpmekaar, Lieutenant Wilfred Heaton of 'D' Company noted in his diary that the eclipse of the sun began at 11 : 51.

The attention of the people in camp was next drawn to a group of horsemen riding in from the south. The party consisted of Captain Alan Gardner, Major Stuart Smith of the Artillery, Lieutenant MacDowel, two NNC officers, two red-coated subalterns and an escort of ten mounted infantry. Gardner was carrying orders for the removal of the camp at Isandlwana to a new site on the Mangeni River. The subalterns in the party were Thomas Griffith and Henry Dyer. Griffith, who was on comissariat-duty for the 2/24th, had been sent back to supervise the transfer of his battalion's baggage, and Henry Dyer, the Second Battalion Adjutant, had offered to asist him.

Pulleine found himself confronted by an agitated volunteer officer shouting that his mounted troops were falling back before a massive Zulu force, and a staff officer from the General ordering him to strike camp. It was crucial for Pulleine's assessment of the situation that he know what the gunfire at breakfast time had signified; and when Gardner informed him that it had been the forces of Dartnell and Lonsdale dispersing a few hundred of Matshana's warriors, there seemed little doubt that what Shepstone's men had blundered into was the big impi. Despite the chilling realisation Pulleine still had some reservations. Earlier that morning he had made the whole camp stand to arms for hours on what had turned out to be a false alarm. He had sent a message to Chelmsford stating that Zulus, who never materialised, were advancing towards him in force; and Colonel Durnford, moreover, had dismissed the reports on which his actions had been based as unreliable exaggerations. Henry Pulleine must have realised that he might soon be engaged in his first military action, but he was determined, probably, not to behave like an excited subaltern. His reply to the General was brief. He wrote that he was unable to move camp at present; and by way of explanation, included the only fact of which he was certain, that there was heavy firing to the left of the camp. Gardner was not entirely satisfied with Pulleine's message and added a postscript. He mentioned that George Shepstone had come in for reinforcements, that the whole camp was turned out, that there was fighting about a mile away on the left flank and added, inexplicably, that the Zulus were falling back.

Pulleine was relieved to hear that Shepstone had sent the three Natal Carbineers from the advanced vedette straight down the escarpment to intercept Durnford. The Colonel would soon be back to take command; but in the meantime, here was one of his staff officers seeking help for his men on the plateau. Pulleine had promised to support Durnford if he got into difficulties: to demonstrate his good faith he decided to put another company of regular infantry on the plateau. Melvill carried the order to Captain Mostyn. 'F' Company was to go up the spur at the double. The order was relayed to Colour-Sergeant Ballard, and within seconds the men were on their way.

The sound of steady rifle fire to the immediate north of the camp could only mean that Cavaye's company had also engaged the enemy. Captain Edward Essex, Colonel Glyn's transport officer, who had been left in camp with no specific duties to attend to, offered to ride onto the plateau and assess the situation. On his way up he passed Mostyn who yelled out to him that Cavaye should look after his right as he was coming to take up a position on the left. Essex found 'E' Company in extended order, firing at a large body of Zulus moving westwards across their front. The warriors were nearly a thousand yards away, comfortably out of the range of all but the most skilled marksmen. As he started helping the infantry find the range for their rifles, Mostyn arrived and moved into the gap between Cavaye and Dyson. There were now one hundred and fifty guns blazing away at the Zulus, but they continued on their course undeterred. A few minutes later Captain Barry's NNC company appeared on their right front in disordered retreat, followed, in reasonable formation, by Captain Barton's horsemen. And advancing, steadily after them, came two huge Zulu columns.

There was a sound of galloping horses behind the infantry line on the plateau. The men who looked round saw George Shepstone leading Lieutenant Vause's troop of Native Horse up the spur; a short distance behind came Captain Stafford with the NNC company that had been escorting Durnford's wagons. The defending strength on the plateau now numbered almost five hundred men and included one hundred and fifty of the best armed blacks in Chelmsford's army. The weak link was Captain Barry's company. His men carried few guns and their assegaais and knobkerries were useless in a defensive action. The members of Number 5 Company, 2nd Battalion, 3rd NNC were equally aware of their limitations; they forsook the plateau in great haste.

In the camp, Pulleine listened to the growing volume of gunfire and waited for Essex to bring back information and for Durnford to return and release him from his responsibilities. Then he saw them – small figures on the plateau's edge, near the place where water ran off into the big donga. And as he watched, their numbers grew, until the skyline was a solid wall of warriors that stretched to the conical kopje and beyond. The 'Chest' and the 'Left Horn' were taking shape. He may have wondered whether Centane had been like this – a company of infantry and a troop of horse drawing a black army towards destruction. But Upcher and Rainforth, who would have known, were still in Helpmekaar. A few hundred yards from Pulleine, in front of 'H' Company, stood an officer who remembered Centane well: Lieutenant Charles Atkinson, watching the warriors mass on the plateau, must have estimated that they were as many as Sarhili had launched against Upcher's entrenchments; but with every passing minute his estimate would have needed revision. He would have seen that the empty veld in front of him offered little in the way of cover, and behind him were none of Upcher's prepared trenches. But like everyone else who had fought at Centane, he too, must have felt confident that the Martini-Henry and the drilled volleys of his battalion would win the day. There was no immediate move from the plateau to the plain, and for a while it seemed as if the enemy shared his view. The time was approaching 12:30.

Major Stuart Smith had left Pulleine to take charge of the two guns which Lieutenant Curling had earlier moved to a low rise some four hundred yards in front of the NNC camp. The position of the artillery determined the centre of Pulleine's line. 'A' Company was told to move up in support of the guns. With William Degacher commanding the battalion, Francis Porteous was its only officer, but his men were veterans of the Transkeian campaign and his sergeants, Brown, Clarkson and Heppenstall, were old soldiers. Porteous deployed his company on either side of the guns. On his right the line was continued by Wardell's company and the 2nd Battalion's 'G' Company, considerably enlarged by the addition of men from the 2/24th who, for a variety of reasons, had been unable to accompany the General's column. Lieutenant Pope commanded one hundred and seventy men and had Lieutenant Frederick

Godwin-Austen, younger brother of the former commander of 'B' Company, to assist him. The arrival of Dyer and Griffith had increased the officer complement of 'G' Company to four. Pope's right, which was unprotected, rested about a hundred yards from the big donga. A short distance in front of Wardell's and Pope's companies, squatted No. 9 Company of the 1/3rd NNC. It had been taken to that forward position, earlier that morning, for picquet duty and left there. On Porteous's left, extended towards the spur, stood the men of Captain Younghusband's 'C' Company. The soldiers, widely spaced, were deployed in two lines facing the plateau along a front almost a mile long. The front row knelt down, set their sights and prepared to fire. The flare of a rocket somewhere behind the conical kopje signalled that Russell's Battery had come into action – a reminder that Durnford, too, was somewhere out there.

From his position in front of the tents Pulleine had a good view of the plain, and through his fieldglasses saw a body of blacks heading towards the camp in great haste. Their red headbands identified them as the NNC company that had set out with the Rocket Battery. He estimated that they were about two miles away. Minutes later, Durnford's mounted troops came into view. They were retreating in creditable fashion, stopping now and again for an aimed volley to the rear. Behind the smoke and dust Pulleine could make out a Zulu regiment in full pursuit – the tip of the 'Left Horn' had swept down to the plain. It was about then that Pulleine heard that there were Zulus behind Isandlwana. The warriors who had passed in front of Cavaye and Mostyn were coming off the plateau a mile or so behind the camp. His immediate concern was for the troops on the plateau who were in danger of being outflanked. Melvill grabbed his horse and charged up the spur with orders for the infantry to retire. Captain Younghusband's company was detached from the line and moved further to the left in order to provide cover against an attack from the west while the men on the plateau made their withdrawal.

On the plateau, the Zulu corps which had been pursuing the Native Horse, had begun a wheeling movement towards the escarpment edge to cut off their path of retreat, while skirmishers probed the gap between Cavaye and Stafford which had been created when Barry's company fled. But as the range shortened the combined fire of the two 1st Battalion companies and the Native Horse began to have a more telling effect. The Zulu advance faltered and the front ranks drew back. The infantry used the hesitation to begin a withdrawal down the spur while keeping up a steady rate of fire. Four hundred yards below the plateau's edge they came into line with 'C' Company. Cavaye's men, who had descended first, moved to the right of Younghusband. Mostyn's company following closely behind, filled the space between them. The combination provided Shepstone's force with a good covering fire. His line of retreat brought his men into a crowded position between Cavaye and Porteous. The Zulus were in complete control of the plateau, but appeared reluctant to begin the descent onto the plain. For a while they seemed content to fire down the escarpment at the defending troops; and despite their indifferent marksmanship, gaps began to appear in the ranks of the defenders. The northern skyline, from the spur to the conical kopje, had become packed with warriors – the 'Chest' was in position. And then, as if to urge themselves on, there began a rattling of assegaais on cowhide shields; and with its subsidance a black tide started to well over the face of the escarpment.

Pulleine feared that Durnford and his fleeing men might be trapped between their pursuers and the warriors swarming down from the plateau. His thinly stretched infantry-line did not extend far enough to the right front to counter this threat to Durnford's line of retreat. What he could call a reserve consisted of Captain Krohn's NNC company and a motley collection of mounted men. The latter included thirty-four police, some fifty men from the volunteer units, and twenty-eight mounted infantry. He placed all the mounted men under the command of Captain Bradstreet of the Newcastle Mounted Rifles and ordered him to take up a position in the big donga to the right of Pope's company. The donga was wide enough to provide cover for Bradstreet's men and their horses, and the sudden fusillade from this new strongpoint threw Durnford's pursuers into confusion. It allowed his troops a respite long enough to scramble into the donga. Amongst the men who found their way into the muddy gully were two soldiers from the Rocket Battery. They described how Russell's force had been overwhelmed behind the conical kopje by a sudden Zulu advance, and how their mules and horses had bolted together with Nourse's natives after the first shots were fired.

The rifle-fire from the two hundred dismounted men in the donga seemed to devastate the packed ranks of the 'Left Horn'. Hundreds of figures dropped to the ground, some dead, some wounded, many seeking concealment in the long grass. Totally disregarding the danger, Durnford walked up and down the donga giving encouragement to the men and assisting with jammed guns. Time and again an induna would be seen urging his warriors to resume the charge, but the accurate shooting quickly brought them down. For the moment, at least, the tip of the 'Left

Horn' was blunted.

Further back, on Durnford's left, it was a similar story. The combined fire of infantry and artillery had halted the 'Chest'. The Zulus pouring down the escarpment were piling up on the plain, but the front ranks refused to advance. They dropped to the ground and crawled for cover. Every rock and every bush, no matter how small, became a place of refuge. Pulleine's perilously stretched line was holding its own against great odds. It was the front rank prone, the rear rank kneeling; load, present, FIRE! The Queen's soldiers knew they were giving of their best, and their morale was high. They joked, cheered and shouted taunts as they worked their rifles. It was the Martini-Henry and its rate of fire that dominated the battle just before one o'clock. The burning question was how long could they keep it up?

The fastest aimed rate of fire under ideal conditions with the Martini-Henry was twelve rounds per minute; but the thin-rolled brass cartridges were far from perfect. The expended cases frequently stuck in the overheated chambers and sometimes required prizing out with knives. Even greater delays occurred when the ejection claw ripped off the end-plate. But the soft lead slug was a bone-smasher and the littered veld in front of the infantry seemed to justify the faith the men had in their weapon. A critical observer, however, might have remarked that the number of supine warriors was perhaps greater than the accuracy of the shooting warranted.

There were no war cries now, no thumping on shields: only a low, angry, buzzing noise like 'a gigantic swarm of bees' that rose and fell, but never ceased. It was an ominous reminder from beyond the drifting black smoke of the rifles that the curtain of fire dared not be lifted. Even the men who had scorned the vaunted Zulu fighting reputation, no longer believed that the impi would break off the engagement. In the donga, Trooper Charlie Sparks of the Natal Mounted Police thought of the inspanned wagons on the Nek and fervently hoped that defences were being prepared in the camp; he knew that there was no reserve left to break the stalemate.

In the camp, all activities were directed at keeping the infantry line supplied with ammunition. No regular organisation existed for replenishing a firing line part of which was almost a mile from the ammunition wagons. It was the British Army's first major engagement since it was issued with breech-loading rifles and it had never occurred to anyone that the seventy rounds which every soldier carried into battle would be insufficient. The wagons held a reserve of half a million rounds packed in strong, mahogany boxes, secured with metal bands and brass screws. Even the small, sliding lids that gave access to the contents of the boxes were tightly screwed down. It was an arrangement that did not allow for the rapid removal of the paper-packaged cartridges. The Quartermasters of the 24th Regiment were experienced soldiers, skilled in their job, but nothing in their training had prepared them for a situation where they would have to maintain a flow of ammunition to such an extended firing-line so far from the wagons.

Cavaye's men had been in action the longest, and their pouches were becoming depleted. Captain Essex was asked to return to the camp and hurry the supply. The ammunition-wagon nearest 'E' Company was in the 2/24th camp. Quartermaster Edward Bloomfield had been in the army since the age of eleven, and with the 2nd Battalion since its inception. He had been described as 'upright, conscientious and intensely thorough', and he knew the rules – 2nd Battalion ammunition must be reserved for 2nd Battalion rifles. Lieutenant Smith-Dorrien, who had returned from Rorke's Drift shortly after 11 o'clock had been rounding up all the non-combatants he could find to act as ammunition carriers; but he was finding it impossible to persuade Bloomfield that he should release his ammunition to him. It took an officer of Captain Essex's rank to overrule the Quartermaster's misgivings about supplying ammunition to units other than 'G' Company. A mule-cart was finally loaded with cartridge packages and driven out to the 1st Battalion companies on the spur. Bloomfield's 'transgression' did not trouble his conscience for long. A stray bullet dropped him while he was assisting Captain Essex.

Many of the Zulus who had chased Durnford's men into the donga had crept into a nearby deserted kraal to escape the rifle fire. As more warriors came down the escarpment, they too squeezed in between the grass huts and the aloe-stockade. Durnford realised that he needed artillery help to break up the growing concentration, and sent one of his staff officers to Major Stuart Smith with a request for assistance. Smith skilfully took one of his muzzle-loading 7-pounders nearer to the donga and demolished the kraal with a few well-placed shells. The gun was back in its place within a matter of minutes. But in the donga, ammunition was becoming scarce.

Two runners, whom Durnford had sent to the rear for ammunition, had returned empty-handed. They had not been able to find the supply wagons belonging to Durnford's column in the confusion that was the camp, and the Quartermasters of the 24th had refused to issue ammunition to strange blacks. In desperation Durnford sent two white officers to the nearest supply point, which was in the camp of the 1/24th. James Pullen was as regulation conscious as Bloomfield. Only an order from Captain Degacher would have made him release his stock of ammunition for the use of black levies. He had witnessed the wild wasteful shooting of the Mfengu in the Cape Colony's war and was contemptuous of 'Kaffir' marksmanship. The officers returned to the donga with empty saddle bags and the distressing news that the camp was disorganised, that no attempt was being made to prepare defensive works, and that there were Zulus behind Isandlwana.

In front of Durnford the stalled 'Left Horn' was being reinforced by more and more warriors; but they were reluctant to advance against the rifles in the donga and had begun a wide circling movement towards the right of the camp. Durnford was being outflanked, and there was nothing he could do about it. It could only be a matter of time before the camp was surrounded. He decided to fall back on the camp and draw the line in after him. Pulleine was surprised to see Durnford withdraw his men and sent Captain Gardner to find out the reason. Durnford told him that the line was too extended and that it was his intention to concentrate the troops nearer the camp. The retirement of the mounted troops exposed the right flank of the infantry line at precisely the moment that Pope was attempting to close the gap between his company and the force in the donga. Seeing Durnford pull out, Pope wheeled his men to the right rear and took up a position on some low ground behind the donga. His manoeuvre shortened the line, but No. 9 NNC Company, which had been lying flat in the grass in front of him, saw the widening breach between 'H' and 'G' Companies, and fled to the rear.

Durnford left the mounted men in front of the 1/24th camp, and rode off to look for Pulleine. His path was obstructed by native troops and civilians pushing their way towards the Nek. Staff officers were milling about trying to keep some order in the camp. Bandsmen, orderlies, cooks and officers' servants were either attempting to load struggling mules with the vital brown-paper packages or dragging them towards the noise and smoke of the infantry line. Some of the transport drivers, obsessed beyond logic with rescuing their assets, were trying to inspan their bewildered oxen and contributed to the chaos. James Pullen was chasing after every straggler in sight in a desperate effort to assemble some kind of a force for the defence of the right flank. He too had seen the threat posed by the circling 'Left Horn' and had sent the column interpreter to Pulleine for reinforcements. Panic was minutes away. Privates Johnson and Trainer, the two survivors from the Rocket Battery, had returned to the camp with Durnford's men and discovered that Private Grant, a third member of their team, still had the horses he had been given to hold when the Battery went into action. The three men who had miraculously survived the destruction of the Rocket Battery, had had enough. They jumped on the horses and spurred their way across the Nek – the first soldiers from the 24th to leave Isandlwana.

The heavily engaged infantry line was oblivious of the confusion in the rear. 'E' and 'F' Companies, by then, had been in action for over an hour. The recoil of their guns had become progressively more vicious as the rifling fouled up. Many of the men had badly contused shoulders and some were holding their guns at arm's length. Others, with burnt hands, were attempting to wrap rags round the overheated barrels. One Zulu got the impression that the red-coats were using their feet in their haste to load their guns. Soldiers who had fought at Centane looked at the fallen warriors, and remembered how the Gcaleka advance had smashed itself to pieces on their guns; but the army of King Cetshwayo, in the face of continuous fire, retained every semblance of a disciplined force. The troops on the extreme left faced a regiment of white shields; 'E' and 'A' Companies were confronted by an array of black shields; while George Wardell's men were shooting at a wall of black shields spotted with red. Their plumes, animal-skin headbands, cow-tail collars and monkey-skin ear flaps, had the same purpose as the uniforms, facings and badges of Queen Victoria's regiments, and were based on a zealous military tradition – the very organisation of this primitive army made it all the more awesome. Even the artillery firing case shot seemed not to produce the customary chaos. Every time Lieutenant Curling raised his hand in signal for the lanyards to be pulled, the warriors would throw themselves flat on the ground and allow the shot to whiz harmlessly overhead. The last of the NNC infantry had deserted the line and in some sectors the firing had begun to fall off, when suddenly, a bugle sounded. It was the command to close ranks – Durnford had found Pulleine.

The infantry lines began to contract. The effect, for a few minutes, was an even more devastating concentration of fire. The Zulus dropped to the ground and waited. Then came a second bugle-call. The firing stopped and the soldiers began to retire onto the camp. Major Smith pulled out his guns which had been inspanned and limbered up throughout the action, and left a rent in 'A' Company. Shepstone's Native Horse pushed their way behind the infantry in an attempt to gain the western side of Isandlwana. Empty spaces were left in the line, gaps appeared between companies and platoons became separated. The Zulu front was less than three hundred yards from the retiring infantrymen when the buzzing stopped. A moment of utter silence was followed by one, great, drawn-out shout – the single word '*Usuthu!*' They came on at an awesome pace, those grandsons of Shaka: and to the men of the 24th it looked as if the very dead were springing out of the grass to join the rushing tide. The outcome was no longer in doubt to anyone in the camp.

ii

The first to foresake the camp had been the civilians connected with transport. They had begun slipping away about the time the impi formed up on the edge of the plateau. Next to make the move had been the black levies. As soon as they crossed the Nek they had shed every item that might identify them as collaborators with the white man. By the time Durnford fell back on the camp, the trickle to the rear had turned into a mass exodus. The mounted officers and the NCOs from the native contingents were out-distancing the men they had earlier tried to hold back. A purposeful authority might have marshalled these men and directed their desperate energies into creating a defensive laager; but in the absence of any positive direction, an irrepressible urge to fly from the hill of ill-omen overcame the men in the camp.

A horse became the passport to survival. They were chased after and fought over. Mounts, half-crazed by the noise of battle, shied away from desperate grasping hands and careered about the camp at will. Mules and oxen that had broken loose added to the pandemonium. The Rocket Battery survivors and some of the mounted volunteers, who had fled in the general direction of Rorke's Drift, escaped. but when Arthur Hall, the Lieutenant of Orderlies, made a break for it with an ambulance full of wounded, he was too late. The 'Right Horn' was sitting astride the road to Rorke's Drift. The only escape route lay towards the south-west – five gruelling miles to the Buffalo River.

Lieutenant Harry Davies of the Edendale troop quickly came to the conclusion that a mounted force riding together had the best chance of getting through to Natal. Lieutenant Henderson saw the wisdom of his reasoning. They rode over to the 1/24th camp to fill their ammunition pouches from Quartermaster Pullen's stock, and were told by a 1st Battalion drummer-boy to replace the cartridges forthwith. The black Sergeant-Major of the Edendale troop offered to take the boy away with him on his horse, but was contemptuously turned down. Some of Bradstreet's mounted troops, however, were not as fortunate as the Native Horse. When Durnford gave the order to retire from the donga, Trumpeter Stevens of the Natal Mounted Police, who had been holding their horses, released them too soon, and they had to return to the camp without their mounts and without hope of escape.

Coghill's injured knee had prevented him taking an active part in the battle. He had found himself an ineffectual cripple as order disintegrated in Pulleine's Headquarters. Unable to serve any useful function, he remembered that he was, after all, Colonel Glyn's orderly officer, and took it into his head to try and save the Colonel's personal effects. In the midst of the uproar he set out to look for Glyn's servants, and found his cook and groom. He ordered them to strike the Colonel's tent, load a wagon with his belongings and drive it to the Nek. A few minutes later, the artillery, with the limber gunners running behind, passed through the camp. They paused on the Nek long enough to confer with Coghill about what hope there was of making a stand, and decided it was futile. Major Smith, who was wounded, felt that his first duty was to save the guns.

The rock-strewn slope behind the stony kopje was near impossible for any wheeled conveyance; and the spectacle of the big guns in flight acted as an incitement to the warriors behind Isandlwana. Slowed by the broken ground and by stragglers clinging to the traces, the teams were quickly overtaken. Drivers were pulled off their horses and gunners from their seats. The unattended horses, crazed by noise and stab wounds, broke into a wild, headlong gallop that took them to their destruction over the edge of a boulder-strewn ravine. The only survivors were the two independently mounted artillery officers. Gunners and stragglers were hacked to pieces.

Coghill remained in the camp long enough to see his battalion falling back before the enemy and the other staff officers slipping away one by one. Melvill had ridden over to the 1st Battalion headquarters-tent to bring away the Queen's Colour (the green Regimental Colour with its twelve battle honours had been left at Helpmekaar). Nevill felt helpless on foot, but he was a good rider and well-mounted: the impulse to follow the other unattached officers was too compelling. Pausing just long enough to tell Colonel Glyn's groom to ride his master's horse to safety, he too, spurred his way across the Nek.

The mayhem behind the hill was even more horrifying than in the camp. A panic-stricken motley was running, stumbling and falling in a blind rush to Natal. Horses with saddles under their bellies, as if mocking the would-be riders who had been given the chance of survival and had lost it, were galloping aimlessly about. Half-naked warriors with poised assegaais, were chasing after terrified fugitives who could never hope to outstrip them on foot. Some men, beyond reason, were rushing blindly back towards the camp as if salvation was to be found in front of Isandlwana. Fingers reached for Coghill's stirrups, hands grabbed at his reins and men begged to be taken on the back of his horse. It was like a grotesque illustration from the *Inferno*, a murderous African saturnalia, to which only an artist who survived it might do justice. Band-Sergeant David Gamble, exhausted to the point of immobility, pleaded with mounted fugitives for a lift, and was ignored; on the fugitive trail it was everyone for himself. The Zulus caught up with him before he could find a generous hand. One survivor, who wisely chose to remain anonymous, later boasted how he had grabbed the reins of a passing horseman and jumped into the empty saddle after the horse reared and threw its rider. Acts of selflessness did, however, take place that afternoon behind Isandlwana: there were men who endangered their lives by chasing after riderless horses for a friend – the Hon. Standish Vereker handed over a saddled horse to an unlikely claimant, and thereby gave away his only chance of survival. Surgeon-Major Peter Shepherd, while galloping to safety, stopped to aid a wounded police trooper, and himself received a death thrust in his neck.

In his flight from the camp Coghill saw remnants of Shepstone's force fighting behind the hill and was grateful for the distraction they afforded the Zulus. The unfortunate wretches on foot, like so many clumsy rabbits drawing the warrior-pack after them, served the same purpose. Warriors from the 'Left Horn' were beginning to come round the stony kopje and had to be outraced. The path to safety was a deadly obstacle-course – a declivity dotted with spiny bushes, tall aloes, littered boulders and loose stones. It was a terrain that strained the skill and stamina of rider and horse, and sapped the breath from the man on foot. Fortunately for Coghill, who was wearing a blue patrol-jacket, the hunters seemed more interested in red coats and *Amacafula*. One of them did try his luck with a hurled assegaai. It missed Coghill and lodged, momentarily, in his horse's flank; but the wound failed to impede the animal's wild gallop. It was at a deep gully on the Manzimnyama that he had to rein in sharply.

The way down to the stream was steep, slippery and clogged with men leading their horses. Coghill was too impatient for such caution and yelled, 'this is no time to be leading a horse, get on with your horses you fellows in front then'. Once across, the fugitives were faced with a steep bush-covered hill. Scrambling up its slope Coghill's horse overtook Smith-Dorrien and caught up with Melvill, the cased Colour* across the front of his saddle. Behind them the sound of gunfire testified to the battle that was raging in the camp, and from below came triumphant Zulu calls mingled with the screams of their victims. This was no place to linger; after a few hurried exchanges the flight was continued. The top of the hill was flat and covered in part by lush green grass. But nothing that day was as it first appeared. The grass hid a marsh in which the exhausted horses sank, at times, up to their knees. The flat ground ended in a precipitous hundred foot drop to the Buffalo River. There they found the two artillery officers searching for a way down; Major Smith was bleeding profusely from the wound in his arm.

They eventually found a more gradual descent which had to be negotiated in single file through dense, thorny bush. Stumbling and sliding the fugitives reached the river bank with their uniforms in tatters. The fast flowing, muddy river was dotted with men and horses. A surprisingly large number had made it to the Fugitives' Drift; but the swollen condition of the Buffalo made the crossing a hazardous undertaking. Nor was the fighting over for the men who had reached the border. A few hundred yards upstream stood a party of Zulus taking pot shots at the men in the water. They had been discouraged from coming too close by members of the Edendale Horse who were returning their fire from the opposite bank. Most incongruous of all was the sight of a dazed trooper of the Mounted Police sitting on the Natal side carefully emptying water out of his boots. Coghill, leading the way, was already in the water when a mounted infantryman, blood streaming from his arm, staggered up. Smith-Dorrien climbed off his horse to help the soldier and blocked the way to the river. The next moment Major Stuart Smith was yelling, 'Get on

---

*The Queen's Colour was a four by three and a half foot flag of the realm fringed in gold with the numeral XXIV surmounted by a crown in the centre. It was rolled up on a heavy staff topped with the lion and crown of England.

man, the Zulus are on top of you'. The young transport officer plunged horseless into the water; seconds later the artillery officer and Private McDonald, a mounted infantryman from the 1/24th, were lying dead.

Coghill gained the Natal bank without mishap, but Melvill was in difficulties. The current had swept him off his horse. Still clutching the Queen's Colour, he was carried towards Lieutenant Higginson who was clinging to a large boulder in the river. Melvill yelled out to him to grab the staff, but Higginson lost his grip and both men were swept downstream. Coghill saw the man he was to have succeeded as adjutant battling to stay afloat while bullets spattered the water around him. He urged his horse back into the river and immediately drew the fire from the other side. As he neared the two men a bullet hit his horse, but he managed to reach Melvill and Higginson. After a frantic struggle the three men gained the river bank; but the Colour was lost.

Even on the Colony's side of the Buffalo they found no respite. Some warriors had forded the river and were making their way towards them. Higginson took off, ostensibly, to look for horses; and the two 1st Battalion officers tried to make a run for it. The climb out of the river valley at Fugitives' Drift is very deceptive. It looks gradual but it can exhaust even a rested man. Coghill, with his painful, swollen knee, had to cling to Melvill for support, and moving swiftly behind them, came the Zulus. They did not make it to the top. No officer of the 24th Foot, who had started the day in the camp at Isandlwana, was fated to see the sun set. Coghill and Melvill were killed shortly after two-thirty.

iii

At Isandlwana the battle had entered its last desperate phase. By then, all those who were to survive had fled. Two civilian drivers who had lingered too long and had attempted to disguise themselves by blackening their hands and faces, did not even make it out of the camp. The 'Horns of the Buffalo' had met behind the 'Sphinx'.

When the line began to fall back on the camp, Younghusband's company was pushed up the spur towards the northern slope of Isandlwana. He and Hodson formed their men into a tight square and kept the enemy at bay for a considerable time with well-placed volleys. Mostyn, Daly and

Anstey held the greater part of 'F' Company together in a fighting retreat through the NNC camp. But 'A' and 'E' Companies, isolated by the withdrawal of Shepstone's horsemen and the artillery, caught the full brunt of the 'Chest', and were overwhelmed a few hundred yards from the camp headquarters. With them died Paymaster Francis White, who had persisted in carrying ammunition to the firing line after the others fled. Wardell tried to keep his men in line with 'G' Company. Bunched together, the veterans of 'H' Company and Pope's short-service soldiers fought the hard-pressing horde with bayonets and rifle butts. Their retreat carried them towards the wagon-park and the position held by Durnford. But the Zulus came round the left of 'H' Company and cut off about fifty soldiers. They were forced to make their death struggle on the grassy slope in front of the camp. George Wardell and the Adjutant of the 2nd Battalion died in this stand.

More than half the infantry-line, however, did reach the camp line. The shooting, stabbing and hacking went on unabated between the tents and the wagons. Men who tripped over guy-ropes and other camp paraphernalia were pinned to the ground before they could crawl away. Some ducked under wagons to escape the spears, and firing between the spokes, continued the fight from behind the wheels until either their ammunition ran out or they were taken from behind. At close range, the bunched 'redcoats' were easy targets, even for the inexperienced Zulu sharpshooters, and many fell with gunshot wounds. The wounded, and those that got separated, were instantly surrounded and dispatched with helmet-shattering knobkerrie blows. Some, with no weapons left to defend themselves, 'covered their faces with their hands, not wishing to see death, some ran away, some entered the tents', but death followed all.

Of the troops who had been fighting on the left of the line, only 'F' Company stayed reasonably intact throughout its retreat. The men kept together over the obstacle-ridden passage between the foot of the Isandlwana and the tents. It was a fighting retreat without plan or purpose, motivated solely by an instinctive feeling that asylum was to be found by falling back to the road which had led them to Isandlwana the previous morning. They rounded the hill's southern face and took cover in the crevices and gullies of its eroded terraces.

'C' Company, which had been on the left flank of the line, was forced up the gradual northern slope of the hill. A wide terrace part-way up allowed them to move along the length of Isandlwana. It ended in a narrow ledge overlooking the Royal Artillery camp. Further retreat was impossible. High above the enemy, and a conspicuous target for their marksmen, Younghusband's men settled down to a defence that had to end when their ammunition ran out. Below them, the camp which Major Clery had so carefully laid out, was a sea of black, with here and there fast-disappearing islands of imperial red.

The largest surviving group was locked in battle between the 1/24th camp and the wagon-park. Durnford had been left with two officers and a group of some sixty police and volunteers. They formed a rallying point for those men, who out of honour, or because they saw no hope in flight, had remained in camp. Bandsmen, drummer-boys, cooks, clerks, and the stragglers James Pullen had rounded up, gathered around the engineering colonel. Pulleine and William Degacher may have been there too. What was left of Pope's and Wardell's companies fought their way to his side, and were placed on his right behind the 1st Battalion officers' tents. Some of the men managed to throw together a crude defensive position out of boxes and stones, but they were outnumbered by about a hundred to one.

On the other side of the Nek, behind Isandlwana, Mostyn's men were fighting desperately. From a shallow donga they 'kept up such a fire that no Zulu dared show his head over the Nek . . . Eventually their ammunition ran out. With bayonets fixed, 'F' Company began its last retreat, a slow, back to back course down the Rorke's Drift road. They did not get very far. The Zulus were waiting in overwhelming numbers. On this bloody path died William Mostyn, Edgar Anstey and James Daly.

It was a little after three, and next to the stony kopje Durnford was directing the fire of the only cohesive force left in the camp. Police troopers, volunteers and infantry were selling their lives dearly. 'We were unable to break their square until we had killed a great many of them by throwing our assegaais at short distances', was how one induna remembered it. But the numbers were dwindling fast and Durnford could do nothing to prevent the disintegration of his force. A Colour-Sergeant of the 1/24th was isolated with twenty men behind the officers' tents; they died in a close group. Within the next twenty minutes, all those men who had rallied round Durnford met their end. Lieutenants Pope and Godwin-Austen were amongst the last ones left standing. With revolvers in hand they began to walk towards the Nek, as though the time had come to return to Rorke's Drift.

On the ledge on Isandlwana, 'C' Company watched the last remaining whites being done to death. The camp had all but disappeared. Inspanned

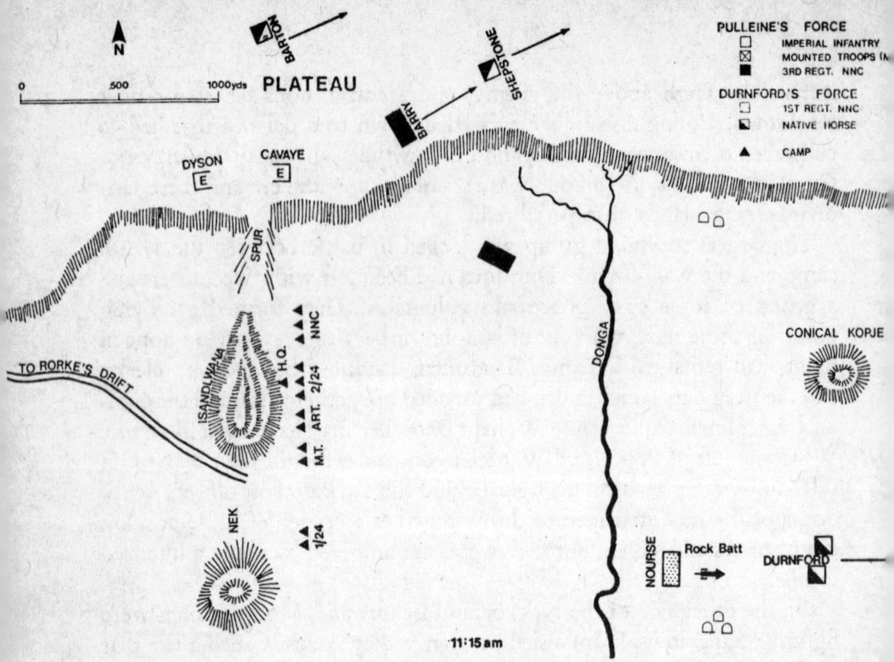
N
0
500
1000yds
PLATEAU
BARTON
SHEPSTONE
BARRY
PULLEINE'S FORCE
IMPERIAL INFANTRY
MOUNTED TROOPS
3RD REGT. NNC
DURNFORD'S FORCE
1ST REGT. NNC
NATIVE HORSE
CAMP
DYSON
CAVAYE
E
E
SPUR
DONGA
CONICAL KOPJE
TO RORKE'S DRIFT
ISANDLWANA
H.Q.
NNC
2/24
ART.
M.T.
NEK
1/24
NOURSE
Rock Batt
DURNFORD
11:15 am

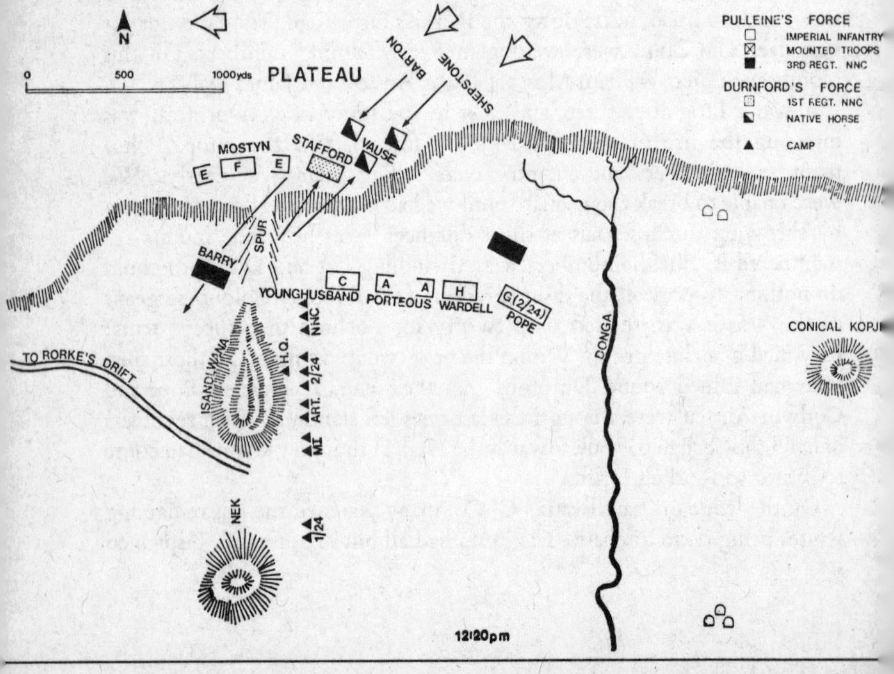
N
0
500
1000yds
PLATEAU
BARTON
SHEPSTONE
PULLEINE'S FORCE
IMPERIAL INFANTRY
MOUNTED TROOPS
3RD REGT. NNC
DURNFORD'S FORCE
1ST REGT. NNC
NATIVE HORSE
CAMP
MOSTYN
E
F
E
STAFFORD
VAUSE
SPUR
BARRY
C
A
A
H
G(2/24)
YOUNGHUSBAND
PORTEOUS
WARDELL
POPE
DONGA
TO RORKE'S DRIFT
ISANDLWANA
H.Q.
NNC
2/24
ART.
MI
NEK
1/24
12:20pm

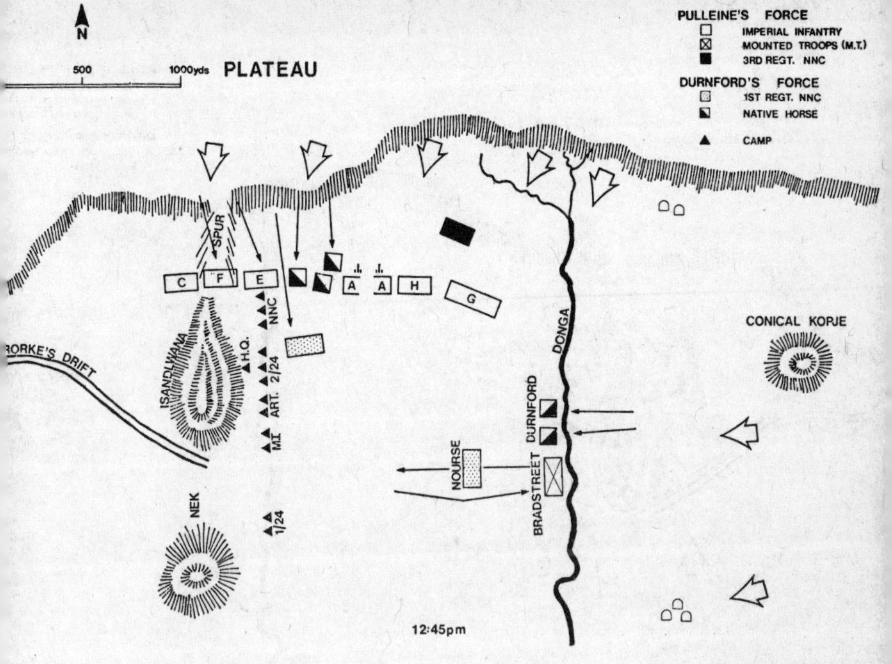
N
500
1000yds
PLATEAU
PULLEINE'S FORCE
IMPERIAL INFANTRY
MOUNTED TROOPS (M.T.)
3RD REGT. NNC
DURNFORD'S FORCE
1ST REGT. NNC
NATIVE HORSE
CAMP
SPUR
C
F
E
A
A
H
G
NNC
H.Q.
2/24
ART.
M.I.
ISANDLWANA
RORKE'S DRIFT
DONGA
DURNFORD
NOURSE
BRADSTREET
CONICAL KOPJE
NEK
1/24
12:45pm

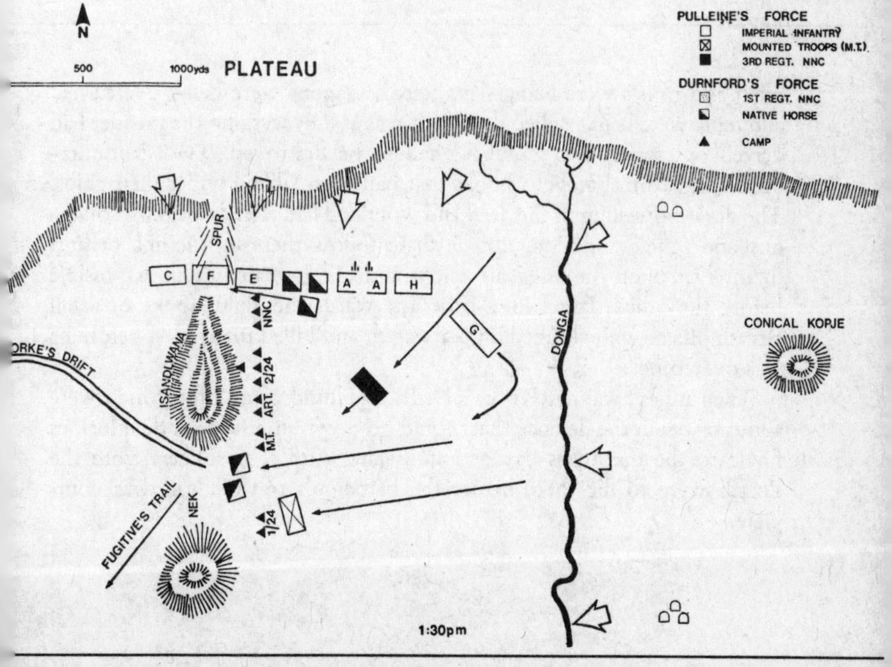
N
500
1000yds
PLATEAU
PULLEINE'S FORCE
IMPERIAL INFANTRY
MOUNTED TROOPS (M.T.)
3RD REGT. NNC
DURNFORD'S FORCE
1ST REGT. NNC
NATIVE HORSE
CAMP
SPUR
C
F
E
A
A
H
G
NNC
2/24
ART.
M.I.
ISANDLWANA
RORKE'S DRIFT
DONGA
CONICAL KOPJE
NEK
1/24
FUGITIVE'S TRAIL
1:30pm

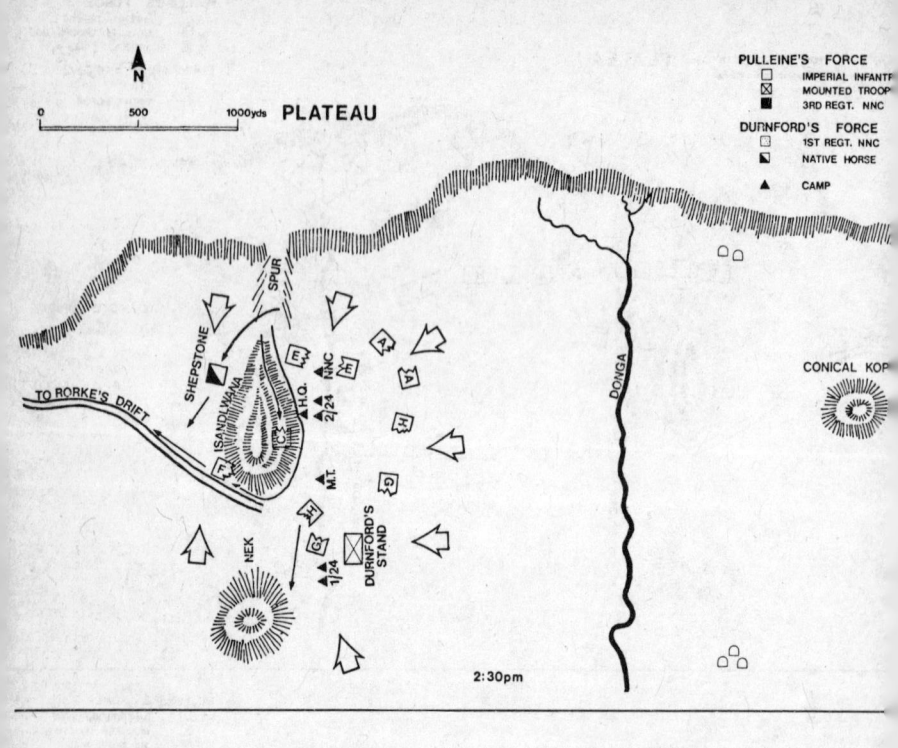

oxen and mules were being slaughtered, wagons were being overturned and tents were being pulled down – it was as if everything the invader had driven or carried into Zululand had to be destroyed. Two drummer-boys hung from butcher's hooks that had been jabbed under their chins. The disembowelling of the dead and wounded had already begun. Young-husband's men could wait for death to follow them up the hill, or hurl themselves upon the assegaais below and kill as many Zulus as possible before they died. For a long time afterwards the Zulus spoke of a tall British officer who climbed onto a wagon and killed many men before he was overcome.

Seven miles away, at Rorke's Drift, one hundred and forty men were about to begin the defence that would go down in history as the glorious finale to the disastrous day at Isandlwana. And four soldiers from the 1/24th were to die there before the battalion's roll of dead was complete.

iv

> Dead was the horse, dead, too, the mule,
> Dead was the dog, dead was the monkey,
> Dead were the wagons, dead were the tents,
> Dead were the boxes, dead was everything,
> Even to the very metals.*

Since nine-thirty that morning Lord Chelmsford had known that something was amiss at Isandlwana. His naval ADC had climbed a tree at one stage to study the camp through his powerful telescope, but had seen nothing unusual. After Dartnell's successful skirmish with Matshana's followers, the General had directed his energies to choosing a new camp site for the Central Column. He had heard the sound of artillery fire shortly after midday, but had not been unduly disturbed by it. At about two o'clock he received the note Pulleine and Gardner had written before the battle started, and a message from Hamilton-Browne, which by the time it reached him, had become a toned down paraphrase of the startling original. Hamilton-Browne had started with his battalion for Isandlwana in the late morning and had got to within six miles of the camp before he fully comprehended the gravity of the situation. His message had read: 'For God's sake come back with all your men; the camp is surrounded and must be taken unless helped'. The communication had passed through the hands of a few staff officers with the usual distrust of professionals for amateurs like the Commander of the 1/3rd NNC, and the verbal version that ultimately reached the General had lost all sense of urgency. Neither Hamilton-Browne's message nor Pulleine's restrained note had unduly alarmed Chelmsford, but he decided to return to Isandlwana with Russell and his mounted infantry. It was about three o'clock when he reached Hamilton-Browne's battalion. The black infantry had a shrewd idea of what had befallen the camp and were reluctant to return there, but the General insisted they accompany him. He had not gone far when an ashen-faced Rupert Lonsdale rode in from the direction of the camp. The Commander of the 3rd NNC had set out alone for Isandlwana earlier that afternoon, and was returning with the first eye-witness account of the massacre.

*Umsweanto, *A Zulu Boy's Recollections of the Zulu War and of Cetshwayo's Return*, tr. G. H. Swinny (London, 1884).

Colonel Glyn, at that time, was with the infantry and artillery at the new camp site in the Mangeni valley. Major Gosset was sent galloping back to bring him the news. It was six-thirty when Glyn's troops reached the General. By the time the silent column stumbled over the nearest Zulu dead, darkness had hidden the bloody testimony of the day's events. Colonel Harness was ordered to throw a few shells at the dark outline of the sinister hill. They merely served to release the pent-up feelings of the troops – the Zulus had returned to the Nqutu hills. Major Wilsone Black, shouting to his men to give them a taste of steel, took three companies of infantry in a rush that carried them through to the stony kopje.

It was on the Nek, among the anonymous dead that Chelmsford decided to spend the night. He had unwittingly chosen the place where the greatest number of corpses lay. 'You could not move a foot either way without treading on dead bodies', wrote a private in the 2nd Battalion. Henry Degacher, 'Offy' Shepstone and Trooper Scott, who had left brothers in the camp that morning, wanted to examine the bodies by lantern light; but everyone was forbidden to move beyond the bivouac. Degacher later told Major Gosset that he was afraid to stretch out his arm 'lest he strike his dead brother's face'. After midnight the clouds cleared, and the moonlit sky was sufficiently light to allow the serving of cold rations. But no one had an appetite for food; for the moonlight also revealed something of the horror that surrounded them. And even the grass was grisly to the touch: wet and slippery with the blood, spilled entrails and brains of the slain – 'we found that we had literally been lying in blood, for we were peeling cakes of it and mud from our mackintoshes'. And in the first light of morning they gazed out on a field of cadavers – 'cut up to pieces and stripped naked', with here and there a chinless face gawking at the sky.[*] But what remained longest in the memory of the men who spent the night of 22 January at Isandlwana, was the smell – 'like a sweet potato that has been cooked when it is just beginning to go bad', and the howling of the jackals in the nearby hills when they caught the scent of death.

---

[*] Some of the warriors, drunk on looted liquor, had disarticulated for trophies the lower jaws of men with luxuriant beards.

22

The final months

'I can't understand', said the dazed General, 'I left a thousand men there'. British arms had suffered its greatest defeat ever in a colonial war. The 24th Regiment lost twenty-one officers and five hundred and seventy-eight other ranks – sixteen officers and four hundred and eight men from the 1st Battalion. There were eighty-five known white survivors; thirty-six were regular army – ten from the 1/24th. They were: J. McCann, H. Davis, W. Parry and J. Power (Mounted Infantry); T. Bickley and E. Wilson (Band); J. Trainer, W. Johnson and H. Grant (Rocket Battery); and John Williams (Colonel Glyn's groom).

Confirmation of the massacre reached Pietermaritzburg forty-eight hours after the battle. Initial disbelief was followed by a panic that spread through Natal and touched the Transvaal. Only when it was realised that the impis were not about to descend on Natal, was a count of the missing undertaken. No one, at first, would believe that so many had died; everyone hoped that there were wounded who might still turn up or that some of the men had been taken prisoner. Anne Glyn would not accept that the gentle Pulleine was dead. She was reported to have remarked, with tear-filled eyes, 'he is hiding behind a wagon wheel or a big stone and must turn up'. James Sivewright, who had renewed friendship with some of the 1st Battalion officers in Pietermaritzburg, recalled in a letter he wrote on 8 February to Mrs Merriman:

Porteous who (with Coghill and a few others) dined with me the night before he marched out, was in high glee at having a chance of showing what an English Regt., taken through the musketry instruction as the 1/24th had been, could do ... Mostyn, Pat Daly and Anstey dined with me on New Year's night – two days before they left. As happy a trio as sat down to open the year – little Hoddy who danced his ballet dance in company with Coghill a night or two before he started until I fairly cried with laughter and Coghill himself one of the brightest, most dashing fellows that the English army possessed three weeks ago. Poor Coghill! He always comes first to my mind. I had seen much of him of late. I have a small cigarette case which he gave me the last night he was here – as we parted long after midnight never to meet again.

Forty-two 1st Battalion wives were widowed, and the suggestion was put forward that they stay on in South Africa as settlers. A fund was started in King William's Town for the bereaved families and £215 was collected in two weeks. On 2 February Reverend John Gordon conducted a memorial service in the Military Reserve on that other Buffalo River. The text he chose was: 'The beauty of Israel is slain upon thy high places'.

On 4 February Major Wilsone Black took out a patrol from Rorke's Drift and found the bodies of Melvill and Coghill. They were in a condition almost beyond recognition. Captain Parr removed the ring and bracelet Coghill used to wear, and a cairn of stones was built over their bodies. The water level of the Buffalo River had fallen considerably since the day of flight, and the Queen's Colour was found wedged between some rocks about five hundred yards downstream from the fugitives' crossing. It was handed over to an emotionally overcome Colonel Glyn at Rorke's Drift. A few days later it was ceremoniously escorted to Helpmekaar, where Captain Upcher, in command of the two companies that now constituted the Headquarters of the 1/24th, took charge of it.

The news of the disaster stunned a nation used to quick colonial campaigns that cost little in lives and paid high dividends in glory. The war in Afghanistan was pushed to the back pages. The Zulus were news. Unfamiliar African names, misspelt and mispronounced, came into common usage. Then the press, Parliament and the public started asking questions. For the first time since coming to office Disraeli had to give his full attention to the colonies on the southern tip of Africa. The Cabinet would have to find a scapegoat; but first the nation had to have its vengeance. Chelmsford was given all the reinforcements he wanted and three major-generals as well. 'The Noble 24th' was to be reconstituted as quickly as possible to avenge its fallen, and the regimental depots were turned inside-out for replacements. By the end of February, five hundred and twenty men from eighteen different regiments were assembled at Aldershot under the command of a lieutenant-colonel from the Grenadier Guards. They included Captain William Brander and Captain Farquhar Glennie of the 24th; the latter had commanded Pope's company in the Amatholes. They sailed for South Africa aboard the *Clyde* on 1 March.

A day after leaving Cape Town the *Clyde* ran aground on a reef near the mainland. She stayed afloat long enough for the troops to come ashore, then freed by the rising tide, went down with all the baggage. The shipwreck delayed the journey by only three days. On 11 April, the 'new 1/24th' landed in Durban. The march to Dundee, the nearest town to the assembly place of Chelmsford's Second Division, took the 'Fresh Lobsters' three weeks. They were joined later by the two 1st Battalion companies from Helpmekaar.

After Isandlwana, Chelmsford left the remnants of the Central Column on the Natal side of the Buffalo to stem the expected Zulu incursion into the Colony. A fort named in honour of Teignmouth Melvill was built at Rorke's Drift, and the Helpmekaar depot was fortified. Conditions in both garrisons were primitive in the extreme. The rains continued into autumn and the cold weather arrived early. There was a shortage of fresh food and medical supplies, and the clothing and blankets lost at Isandlwana were not replaced for weeks. Typhoid and dysentery moved in and took a heavy toll of the men who had missed death at the hands of the Zulus. Second-Lieutenant William Lloyd was himself ill when he wrote, 'the place is full of sick men and funerals are getting daily occurrences'. He also complained about the mud and the ever-present stench of fermenting corn in the commissariat sheds. But despite the misery of his condition, Lloyd found some consolation thinking about the prospect of rapid promotion in the 24th. He calculated that he might advance twenty-one steps, the equivalent of about ten or twelve years service: 'Such a thing has seldom happened before in the annals of history so the luck is simply extraordinary but how dearly bought'.

From Helpmekaar, it was possible, with the aid of a good telescope, to study the devastation around Isandlwana. At first the sky over the malevolent hill had been filled with circling vultures, and later the skeletons of the slain were seen bleaching in the sun. The bodies of Coghill and Melvill were ceremoniously interred on 14 April; but the regimental dead in Zululand lay unburied for another two months.

The reconstruction of the 1st Battalion took place in Dundee. Major William Dunbar became the new commanding officer. His field-officers were John Tongue and William Brander. Archer Morshead was promoted captain and Ralph Clements became the acting Quartermaster. William Lloyd was made a full lieutenant. Of the seven subalterns who in 1874 had sailed for Gibraltar aboard the *Peshawar*, only Wilfred Heaton and William Spring survived to benefit from the spate of promotions. The remaining vacancies in the battalion were filled, temporarily, with officers from the Guards and the Militia. Fred Carrington, who had been kept in the Transvaal to watch the Boers, wrote to remind Chelmsford that he was, after all, an officer in the 24th. He was given a brevet of major and told he would serve the more useful purpose where he was.

On 13 May, the 1st Battalion marched to Landman's Drift, a crossing on the Buffalo River some thirty miles upstream from Rorke's Drift. It was the place selected by Chelmsford for the assembly of the Second Division. He had given the command of the division to Major-General Edward Newdigate, an uninspiring man well past his prime who had been sent out on the recommendation of the Duke of Cambridge. The division's 1st Brigade, consisting of the 2/21st and the 58th Regiment, was given to Colonel Glyn. But the 1/24th was brigaded with the 94th Regiment under Colonel William Collingwood of the Royal Scots Fusiliers. Newdigate, supported by Glyn, had urged Chelmsford to include the 2/24th in the Second Division, a gesture that would have met with public approval. But the General, going against his declared practice of keeping regiments intact whenever possible, turned down the request. There were some who believed that his refusal was based on a fear that the 24th was for him an unlucky regiment. To Glyn's greater dismay, Chelmsford and his staff attached themselves to the Second Division for the march to Ulundi.

Immediately after Isandlwana, the General's staff had turned on Glyn in their search for a scapegoat. The fundamental error, they reasoned, had been the initial failure to entrench the camp. As commander of the Central Column it had been Glyn's responsibility to see that the work was carried out according to the printed instructions issued by Chelmsford before the invasion. But their attempt to inculpate Glyn had been quickly quashed by Major Clery's evidence. He had produced a note from Chelmsford which stated that the ground at Isandlwana was too rocky to dig trenches, and as the camp would soon be moved, it was hardly worth fortifying. At the official inquiry into the disaster, Glyn's testimony had been pointedly brief. He had refused to venture opinions as to where the blame lay. His personal thoughts remained a secret: but Mrs Glyn's feelings about the General were common knowledge in Pietermaritzburg.

After the massacre Richard Glyn became obsessed with keeping his troops at Rorke's Drift inside fortifications. Despite crowded, quagmire conditions he refused to allow anyone to pitch tents outside the fort. The word got around, during this period, that he had lost all drive and intiative. When the time came for Chelmsford's second round with the Zulus, he received command of an understrength brigade, while Evelyn Wood, the victor of the battle of Kambula, was allowed to act independently with a force of more than three thousand men. The objectives of the Second Division were the same as those of the Central Column, but Chelmsford chose to avoid all reminders of his first failure. The fortified bases at Rorke's Drift and Helpmekaar were by-passed, and new ones were established first at Conference Hill and then at Kopje Allein on the Blood River. His plan called for the Division to march north of the Nqutu Range before swinging south to gain the wagon-track to Ulundi, some fourteen miles beyond Isandlwana. A great deal of trouble was taken to avoid retracing the steps of the ill-fated Central Column.

Colonel Degacher's battalion was broken up into detachments for duty on Newdigate's lines of communications. At Itelezi Hill, near where the Prince Imperial was killed, a detachment of the 2/24th threw up an earthwork fort; it became the second one in South Africa to carry the name 'Fort Warwick'. Itelezi was about as far as the 2nd Battalion penetrated into Zululand; nor did the 1/24th make it to Ulundi. It was left to guard a base on the White Mfolozi River, some ten miles from King Cetshwayo's Great Kraal. Colonel Glyn, however, commanded his brigade at the Battle of Ulundi, and nearly lost another orderly officer. Eight officers from the old 1st Battalion were with him at the final showdown with the Zulus. They were William Dunbar, William Brander, Thomas Rainforth, John Tongue, Wilfred Heaton, Ralph Clements, William Lloyd and Edward Stevenson Browne. The latter commanded the 1st Squadron, Imperial Mounted Infantry, which had in its ranks twenty men from the 1/24th. They saw the 'Horns of the Buffalo' racing to encircle the 'Square' on the Mhlabatini plain; and saw them smashed to pieces by field-gun, Gatling and Martini-Henry.

For Lord Chelmsford and the 1/24th the war was over. The General was replaced by Sir Garnet Wolseley; and the battalion returned to Landman's Drift to await the order recalling it home. It arrived on 26 July. The route back to Durban lay through Helpmekaar, Greytown and Pietermaritzburg. The departure from Pietermaritzburg was a solemn affair. A 'war-battered drum and a couple of bugles' carried symbolically at the head of the battalion represented Carl Burck's once magnificent band. On 20 August, the 1/24th was joined at its encampment in Pinetown by

Captain Henry Harrison and the men who had spent the past twelve months in Port St. Johns. Two days later, at a brigade parade, Colonel Glyn presented the Victoria Cross to Surgeon-Major Reynolds for his part in the defence of Rorke's Drift and to Lieutenant Edward Browne for his conduct on Hlobane and at Kambula.

The losses suffered by the mounted infantry at Isandlwana had been made good with men from the 2/4th. In March, the 1st Squadron, Mounted Infantry, under Lieutenant-Colonel John Russell, had been sent to join Wood's column. They had arrived in time to take part, on 28 March, in the desperate retreat from Hlobane Mountain and the successful defence, the following day, of the camp at Kambula. On Hlobane Russell had galloped to safety with most of his men when he learnt that a huge impi was approaching, but Browne, Private Power and a few others had remained behind on the Hlobane lower plateau to assist Redvers Buller and his men as they fought their way down the narrow neck that connected the upper plateau to the lower one. It was never determined whether Russell's retreat had been the result of confusion or a deliberate misinterpretation of a message he had received from Colonel Wood. But Browne had accused him of cowardice, and had handed Wood a written denouncement of his commanding officer in which he stated that neither he, nor his men, would go into action under Russell again.

At Kambula, Browne had been with the mounted detachment that rode out of the camp to entice the 'Right Horn' to attack the defences. When the time came to turn back, one of the troopers was left behind with an unmanageable horse. The Zulus were a hundred yards away from him when Browne galloped back and held the horse until the trooper mounted. The man lost his stirrup in the process of mounting and the horse bolted in front of the advancing Zulu line. Browne chased after him, and with the Zulus less than thirty yards away, helped him control the horse. For his actions on 28 and 29 March, Browne was recommended for the Victoria Cross – the first soldier in the 1/24th to receive this decoration. Private Power, who had survived Isandlwana, was awarded the Distinguished Conduct Medal for his behaviour on the Gobatse Heights and Hlobane Mountain.

On 27 August, the 1/24th embarked on the hired transport *Egypt*. Its strength on departure was given as twenty-four officers, eighty-two NCOs and seven hundred and seventy-eight rank and file. Thirty-four men, too ill for the voyage home, were left in Natal. Two officers stayed behind; George Paton to deal with unresolved problems relating to the battalion's stay in South Africa, and Fred Carrington to assist Colonel Lanyon in the Transvaal. A week later, with wives, widows and orphans aboard, the *Egypt* left South Africa's shores, and Colonel Glyn could, at last, turn his back on the country whose problems had embroiled his battalion so deeply for five years.

An accident to the screw caused the *Egypt* to make a slow passage to England. The journey took a full month. The time was utilised by Mrs Glyn to repair the rents in the Queen's Colour. The battalion's short stopover in Simonstown had passed almost unnoticed in Cape Town; the surprise, therefore, was great when they saw 'Old Garge' and his entourage waiting on the jetty at Portsmouth. The Duke of Cambridge, who had been attending manoeuvres near Southampton, had decided that he was conveniently situated to examine the Colour which had cost Melvill and Coghill their lives and to meet Chard, Reynolds and Browne, the three Victoria Cross recipients on board the transport. In a short, restrained speech to the paraded men he expressed his regret that so few of the 'old soldiers of the 24th' had returned.

Epilogue

After Ulundi the War Office brought Chelmsford home to be honoured, fêted, and like his predecessor, shelved. Frere was censured by Parliament for the war, but allowed to remain in South Africa for a while longer. Disraeli's government, however, had barely recovered from the military setbacks and the embarrassment of the Prince Imperial's death, when Frere began to outline plans for new military adventures in the furtherance of confederation. The policy had never looked more realisable; but the price paid for victory in Zululand had left the Colonial Office little enthusiasm for confederation. Its South African policy became: curb Frere at all costs. Garnet Wolseley, who had succeeded Chelmsford as military commander, was made High Commissioner for South-East Africa, an appointment that effectively excluded Frere from the affairs of Natal, Zululand and the Transvaal.

Frere and Wolseley, two men of talent and reputation, working together, could have wrought great changes to the benefit of South Africa. Most of the tribes in the country had come under British hegemony and the time was ripe for a skilled statesman to guide the white-ruled states into a union in which the black man, his rights guaranteed by Westminster, could one day take his legitimate place. But political settlement had to be achieved quickly, before the Boer states, freed from the threat of black militancy, turned the situation into a denial of British sovereignty. Frere knew that Shepstone's maladministration of the Transvaal had contributed to an awakening national conscience amongst the Boers – 'Unless I had seen it, I could not have believed that in two years things could have drifted into such a mess'. Even before the Anglo-Zulu war was over, Frere had to defuse a dangerous agitation in the Transvaal, by promising concessions that would lead to self-government. But the British Parliament's censure of Frere and the division of the office of High Commissioner weakened his credibility among the Boers.

Shepstone had been eased into retirement, and through Major Lanyon, the new Administrator, effective control of the Transvaal passed into the hands of Wolseley. The very capable General, unhappily, was sensitive only to issues that furthered his personal ambitions. He had supported the choice of Frere as Carnarvon's Proconsul and secretly admired him as a courageous empire-builder, but what he judged to be beneficial for his own career, did not, at that critical juncture, coincide with either Frere's or South Africa's best interests. He promoted his military reputation and strengthened the Transvaal by a quick, decisive victory over Sekhukhune; but by ignoring the temper of the Transvaal Boers, prepared the ground for future strife in the land. In order to ingratiate himself with Westminster, he stifled all Frere's proposals for the settlement of Zululand and the Transvaal. With Sir Bartle's authority confined to the Cape Colony, confederation in South Africa ground to a standstill. Frere saw the Sprigg Government begin the disarmament of the Basothos (a step he viewed as a necessary civilising measure); he left South Africa as the Basothos went into rebellion. His recall came a year after the Zulu war ended, and just months before the Boers took up arms against the British. The subjugation of the black nations and the awakening of Afrikaner nationalism would be the only legacies of Carnarvon's dream. Frere spent his few remaining years writing a detailed defence of his policy.

Confederation died when its realisation was in sight. The advantages to be had from its implementation appealed to both Tory and Liberal Governments, but the cost in lives and money had proved too intimidating. Isandlwana had been the turning point in the confederation saga that began in 1874. The massacre had awakened Britain's exchequer to the price it was paying for effecting unity on South Africa's heterogeneous nationalities. On 22 January 1879, King Cetshwayo's impis postponed, by a few months, the downfall of the old Zulu Kingdom; but in doing so, permanently destroyed Frere's grand design and with it the black man's only chance, for a hundred years, to share in South African decision-making.

The fight to the death at Isandlwana, Melvill and Coghill losing their lives to save the Colour, the defence of Rorke's Drift – and in Afghanistan, Roberts's march from Kabul to Kandahar – all occurring within a space of eighteen months, rocketed Britain's army to unprecedented heights of popularity. War-correspondents and newspaper-artists accompanying the troops had sent home stories and illustrations that throbbed with shameless patriotism. The nation took a closer look at the men who filled the ranks of its army. Whereas before it had seen only drunkards and outcasts, it now saw loyal sons of Britain, a little rough on the outside, yet possessing the stubborn fortitude that forged great empires. Cardwell's brigade depots had become accepted within their communities, and as regional dialects and idiosyncrasies were incorporated into a regimental character, identification with the soldiers intensified. The bonds between regular army and counties were further strengthened when the impersonally numbered regiments were given territorial titles and militia units adopted the uniforms of their depot regiment. The 'Soldiers of the Queen' were in step with the age: the age which was launched in the rocky hills of Zululand and which inspired a generation of Britons with an ardent, evangelical imperialism.

The 1/24th spent a year at Gosport. During that time Burck formed a new band from musicians recruited from other regiments. The Act of Army Reform, passed in 1881, rescinded an old ruling which prohibited foreigners from serving as Bandmasters in the British Army; and in September 1882, he received recognition for his service in the 1st Battalion when he was made a warrant-officer. He remained Bandmaster of the 1/24th for another seven years.

In May 1880, Richard Glyn relinquished command of the battalion and took charge of the Brigade Depot in Brecon. Two years later he was promoted major-general. His successor as commander of the 1st Battalion was William Dunbar, who exercised office for exactly one month before retiring on half-pay. The officer next in line was Wilsone Black, C.B. During his tenure the 24th Foot was granted the right to add the words 'South Africa' and the dates '1877-78-79' to its Regimental Colour. In recognition of the deed that saved the Queen's Colour from falling into Zulu hands, Queen Victoria attached a silver wreath of immortelles to its staff. In July 1881, the Regiment was advised that its Welsh connection had been acknowledged by a change of name. The 24th Foot became the South Wales Borderers, and 'Men of Harlech' the regimental march. Two years later, the 1st Battalion, South Wales Borderers, was moved to Ireand. Lieutenant-Colonel Black was made Assistant Adjutant-General in Canada, and George Paton C.M.G. became the new commander of the battalion.

Six company officers of the old 1/24th had returned from South Africa in 1879. All of them attained the rank of major within three years. By 1885, William Brander, Henry Harrison, Thomas Rainforth and William Much had retired on half-pay with the honorary rank of lieutenant-colonel, leaving Russell Upcher as the senior field officer. In June 1886, he succeeded to the command of the 2nd Battalion, stationed at that time in Burma. For the next two years his battalion played an active part in the pacification of Upper Burma, and he received the Distinguished Service Order for his part in it.

On New Year's Day in 1879, the 1st Battalion's complement of subalterns was nineteen; there were ten left after Isandlwana. Archer Morshead, who was promoted captain immediately afterwards, retired as a major and honorary lieutenant-colonel ten years later. Edward Browne V.C. was promoted major in the 2nd Battalion in 1885, and became DAAG for Musketry in Bengal. He commanded the battalion for a short time in Aden, and was made a lieutenant-colonel in 1893. He later commanded the Brigade Depot at Brecon. Most of the subalterns killed at Isandlwana had been posted to the 1/24th in the years 1873 and 1874. The survivors from that group were William Spring, Wilfred Heaton and Ralph Clements. Spring died of natural causes in 1886. Heaton and Clements were promoted field officers in the 2nd Battalion in time to participate in the Burma campaign. Clements was twice wounded, and, like Upcher, received the DSO. In 1897 he was made lieutenant-colonel of the 2nd Battalion; and subsequently went on the Staff as a major-general. In December 1899, Clements found himself back in South Africa as commander of the 12th Brigade.

On a bitterly cold day in January 1900, the 2nd Battalion, South Wales Borderers, marched out of Aldershot to join the 15th Brigade embarking for Cape Town. The battalion was commanded by a man, who had campaigned in the Transkei as a junior subaltern: he was Colonel the Hon. Ulick de Rupe Burke Roche. And on the station platform, waiting to bid farewell to his troops, stood a short, bald old man: he was Lieutenant-General Richard Thomas Glyn, the Colonel of the South Wales Borderers.

Two other subalterns from the old 1/24th saw service in the Anglo-Boer War. Major George Palmes, who was stationed in India when the war broke out, obtained a transfer for special duties in South Africa. For his services in that war he was awarded the DSO. The other man was Frederick Carrington. As a brevet-major he commanded a wing of

Wolseley's mounted contingent in the last Sekhukhune campaign. Shortly afterwards he received a brevet of lieutenant-colonel and a C.M.G. For a time he commanded the Cape Mounted Rifles, the corps that replaced the much maligned Frontier Armed and Mounted Police. He fought for the Cape Colony in the Basotho Disarmament War and was seriously wounded. When Charles Warren took the British Flag into Bechuanaland, Carrington commanded the Second Mounted Rifles and later the Bechuanaland Border Police. He was Commander of the British Forces in South Africa when the Matabele rebellion broke out in Rhodesia. As Lieutenant-General Sir Frederick Carrington, he led the Rhodesian Field Force in the Anglo-Boer War. South Africa had well rewarded his decision to stay behind when the 1/24th returned home.

Richard Glyn died on 21 November 1900, at the age of sixty-nine. He was succeeded as the Colonel of the South Wales Borderers by Major General Henry Degacher, who died two years (almost to the day) after Glyn. His successor was Major-General George Paton.

Bibliography

Unpublished sources

Campbell, Doctor Killie, (comp.). Reminiscences of the Zulu War, 1879 (Africana Library, Johannesburg)

Carrington, Captain F. Letters (Regimental Museum, Brecon)

Coghill, Lieutenant N. J. A. Letters and Diaries (National Army Museum, London)

Crealock, Major J. N. Journal 1878-1879 (Cory Library, Grahamstown)

Heaton, Lieutenant W. Diary 1879 (Regimental Museum, Brecon)

Lloyd, Lieutenant W. Letters (Regimental Museum, Brecon)

Merriman, J. X. Letters (South African Library, Cape Town)

Molteno, Sir J. C. Letters (South African Library, Cape Town)

Morris, Private (610) G. B. Letters (Regimental Museum, Brecon)

Prior, C. E. Diary of the Griqua Campaign 1 June 1878 – 31 October 1878 (Kimberley Public Library)

Read, D. Diary of the Secocoeni War of 1876 (Africana Library, Johannesburg)

Symons, Captain W. P. Manuscript account of the Battle of Isandlwana (Regimental Museum, Brecon)

24th Regiment, 1st Battalion Monthly Returns 1874-1878 (Regimental Museum, Brecon)

Newspapers

Cape Argus 1875-1879. (Johannesburg Public Library)

Cape Town Daily News 1875-1878. (Johannesburg Public Library)

Cape Mercury 1877-1879. (Kaffrarian Museum, King William's Town)

Diamond Field Advertiser 1878. (Johannesburg Public Library)

Diamond News 1875. (South African Library, Cape Town)

Grahamstown Journal 1875. (Johannesburg Public Library)

Graphic 1878. (Johannesburg Public Library)

Illustrated London News 1878, 1879. (Johannesburg Public Library)

Kaffrarian Watchman 1877-1879. (Kaffrarian Museum, King William's Town)

Natal Mercury 1878, 1879. (State Archives, Pretoria)

Natal Witness 1878, 1879. (State Archives, Pretoria)

The Times 1879. (Johannesburg Public Library)

Official Papers and special publications

Cape Colony, Government House Papers (1875) relating to Griqualand West; Government House Papers (1877, 1878) relating to the Xhosa War (State Archives, Cape Town)

Correspondence, Memoranda and Minutes connected with the Dismissal of the Late Ministry, Cape Town: *Cape Times*, 1878.

Narrative of the Field Operations connected with the Zulu War of 1879. London: War Office, 1881.

Parliamentary Papers relating to South Africa (Blue Books) 1875-1879. London: H.M.S.O.

Journal articles

Bond, B., 'The effect of the Cardwell Reforms in Army Organisation, 1874-1902', *Journal of the Royal United Service Institution* 105 (620) 1960.

Campbell, J. W. B., 'The South African Frontier 1865-1885: A study in Expansion', *Archives Year Book for South African History* 1, 1959.

Chadwick, G. A., 'The Anglo-Zulu War of 1879 – Isandlwana and Rorke's Drift', *Military History Journal* 4 (4) 1979.

Gosset M. W. E., 'The Kaffir War 1877-78', *Journal of the United Service Institution of India* 8 (193) 1879.

Jackson, F. W. D., 'Isandhlwana, 1879: The Sources Re-examined', *Journal of the Society for Army Historical Research* 43 (173), (175), (176) 1965.

H.S. – An English Officer, (? Captain Henry Spalding) 'The Kaffir War', *Fraser's Magazine* February 1878.

Kinsey, H. W., 'The Sekukuni Wars', *Military History Journal* 2 (5), (6) 1973.

Lewsen, P., 'The First Crisis in Responsible Government in the Cape Colony', *Archives Year Book for South African History* 2, 1942.

Van Rooyen, T. S., 'Die Verhoudinge tussen die Boere, Engelse en Naturelle in die Geskiedenis van die Oos-Transvaal tot 1882', *Archives Year Book for South Africa History* 1, 1951.

Published books

Adams, J., *The South Wales Borderers*. London: Hamish Hamilton, 1968.

Agar-Hamilton, J. A. I., *The Road to the North: South Africa, 1852-1886*. London: Longmans, 1937.

Akehurst, R., *The World of Guns*. London: Hamlyn, 1972.

Atkinson, C. T., *The South Wales Borderers: 1689-1937*. Cambridge: University Press, 1937.

Aylward, A., *The Transvaal Today: war, witchcraft, sport and spoils in South Africa*. Edinburgh: Blackwood, 1881.

Barnett, C., *Britain and Her Army: 1509-1970*. London: Allen Lane, 1970.

Beet, G., *The Grand Old Days of the Diamond Fields: memories of past times with the diggers of Diamondia*. Cape Town: Maskew Miller, 1931.

Beet, G., and Terpend, T. L., *The Romance and Reality of the Vaal Diamond Diggings: being a sheaf of stories leading to the discovery of copper, diamonds and gold in Southern Africa, etc.* Kimberley: Diamond Field Advertiser, 1917.

Brookes, E. H., *The History of Native Policy in South Africa from 1830 to the Present Day*. Cape Town: Nasionale Pers, 1924.

Brookes, E. H., and Webb, C. de B., *A History of Natal*. Pietermaritzburg: University o Natal Press, 1965.

Brownlee, C. P., *Reminiscences of Kafir Life and History and Other Papers*. Lovedale: The Lovedale Press, 1896.

Brownlee, F., (comp.), *The Transkeian Native Territories: Historical Records*. Lovedale: The Lovedale Press, 1923.

Burton, A. W., *The Highlands of Kaffraria*, 2 ed. Cape Town: Struik, 1969.

Burton, A. W., *Sparks from the Border Anvil*. King William's Town: Provincial Publishing Co., 1950.

Chamberlain, M. E., *The Scramble for Africa*. London: Longman, 1974.

Clammer, D., *The Zulu War*. Cape Town: Purnell, 1973.

Coghill, P., *Whom the Gods Love ... A memoir of Lieutenant Nevill Josiah Aylmer Coghill, V.C.* (Private publication), 1966.

Colenso, F. E., and Durnford, E. C. L., *History of the Zulu War and Its Origins*, 2 ed. London: Chapman Hall, 1881.

Coupland, R., *Zulu Battle Piece – Isandhlwana*. London: Collins, 1948.

Cunynghame, A. T., *My Command in South Africa, 1874-1878*. London: Macmillan, 1879.

Curson, H. H., *The History of the Kimberley Regiment*. Kimberley: Northern Cape Printers, 1963.

Davenport, T. R. H., *South Africa: A Modern History*. Johannesburg: Macmillan, 1977.

De Kiewiet, C. W., *The Imperial Factor in South Africa*, 2 ed. London: Frank Cass, 1965.

De Watteville, H., *The British Soldier: his daily life from Tudor to modern Times*. London: Dent, 1954.

Doughty, O., *Early Diamond Days*. London: Longmans, Green, 1963.

Durnford, E. C. L., *A Soldier's Life and Work in South Africa 1872-1879: A memoir of the late Col. A. W. Durnford; edited by his brother*. London: Sampson Low, 1882.

Emery, F., *The Red Soldier. Letters from the Zulu War, 1879*. London: Hodder and Stoughton, 1977.

Ensor, R. C. K., *England 1870-1914*. Oxford: Clarendon Press, 1936.

Farwell, B., *Queen Victoria's Little Wars*. London: Lane, 1973.

Fenn, T. E., *How I Volunteered for "The Cape" and What I did There: being a short history of eight months service with the Frontier Light Horse etc*. London: Samuel Tinsley, 1879.

Fisher, J., *Paul Kruger: His Life and Times*. London: Secker and Warburg, 1974.

French, G., *Lord Chelmsford and the Zulu War*. London: Lane, 1939.

Froude, J. A., *Oceana or England and Her Colonies*, 3 ed. London: Longmans, Green, 1886.

Froude, J. A., *The Life of the Earl of Beaconsfield*. London: Dent, 1914.

Furneaux, R., *The Zulu War: Isandhlwana and Rorke's Drift*. London: Weidenfeld and Nicolson, 1963.

Glover, M., *Rorke's Drift – A Victorian Epic*. London: Leo Cooper, 1975.

Goodfellow, C. F., *Great Britain and South African Confederation 1870-1881*. Cape Town: Oxford University Press, 1966.

Gordon, R. E., *Shepstone: The role of the family in the History of South Africa 1820-1900*. Cape Town: Balkema, 1968.

Granville, A. K., *With the Cape Mounted Rifles: four years service in South Africa by an ex C.M.R.* London: Richard Bentley, 1881.

Grenfell, F., *Memoirs of Field Marshall Lord Grenfell.* London: Hodder and Stoughton 1925.

Hamilton-Browne, G., *A Lost Legionary in South Africa.* London: Werner Laurie, 1912.

Haresnape, G., *The Great Hunters.* Cape Town: Purnell, 1974. (Elisa Series Vol. 3)

Harford, H., *The Zulu War Journal of Colonel Henry Harford, C.B.*, ed. D. Child. Pietermaritzburg: Shuter and Shooter, 1978.

Harris, D., *Pioneer, Soldier and Politician.* London: Sampson Low, 1930.

Hart, H. G., *The New Annual Army List, Militia List and Indian Civil Service List for 1873, '74, '75, '76, '77, '78, '79, '80.* London: John Murray.

Haswell, J., *The British Army: A Concise History.* London: Thames and Hudson, 1975.

Herd, N., *The Bent Pine – The Trial of Chief Langalibalele.* Johannesburg: Ravan Press, 1976.

Holme, N., *Medal Rolls (1793-1889) of the 24th Regiment.* London: J. B. Hayward, 1971.

Holt, B., *Where Rainbirds Call: A Record of the Transkei.* Cape Town: H. Timmins, 1972.

Hutchinson, (Mrs.), *In Tents in the Transvaal.* London: Richard Bentley, 1879.

Jourdain, H. F. N., and Fraser, E., *The Connaught Rangers.* London: Royal Services Institution, 1924.

King, W. R., *Campaigning in Kaffirland.* London: Saunders and Ottley, 1853.

Laver, J., *The Age of Optimism: manners and morals 1848-1914.* London: Weidenfeld and Nicolson, 1966.

Lehman, J., *All Sir Garnet: A Life of Field Marshall Lord Wolseley.* London: Jonathan Cape, 1964.

Lehman, J., *The First Boer War.* London: Jonathan Cape, 1972.

Lewis, R., and Foy, Y., *The British in Africa.* London: Weidenfeld and Nicolson, 1971.

Lloyd, A., *The Zulu War 1879.* London: Hart Davies, MacGibbon, 1973.

Lorimer, E. K., *Panorama of Port Elizabeth.* Cape Town: Balkema, 1971.

Mackenzie, J., *The Papers of John Mackenzie*, ed. A. J. Dachs. Johannesburg: Witwatersrand University Press, 1973.

Mackinnon, J. P., and Shadbolt, S. H., *The South Africa Campaign, 1879.* (repr.) London: J. B. Hayward, 1973.

MacMillan, M., *Sir Henry Barkly: Mediator and Moderator 1815-1890.* Cape Town: Balkema, 1970.

Malherbe, V. C., *Eminent Victorians in South Africa.* Cape Town: Juta, 1970.

Martineau, J., *The Life and Correspondence of Sir Bartle Frere*, 2 vols. London: John Murray, 1895.

Mathews, J. W., *Incwadi Yami.* (repr.) Johannesburg: Africana Book Society, 1976.

McCourt, E., *Remember Butler.* London: Routledge and Kegan Paul, 1967.

McNish, J. T., *Graves and Guineas.* Cape Town: Struik, 1969.

McNish, J. T., *The Glittering Road.* Cape Town: Struik, 1970.

McToy, E. D., *A Brief History of the 13th Regiment (P.A.L.I) in South Africa during the Transvaal and Zulu difficulties, 1877-8-9.* Devonport: A. H. Swiss, 1880.

Meintjes, J., *Sandile: The Fall of the Xhosa Nation.* Cape Town: T. V. Bulpin, 1971.

Merriman, J. X., *Selections from the Correspondence of J. X. Merriman 1870-1890*, ed. P. Lewsen. Cape Town: van Riebeeck Society, 1960.

Mitford-Barberton, I. G., *Commandant Holden Bowker: an 1820 Settler book including unpublished records of the Frontier Wars*. Cape Town: Human and Rousseau, 1970.
Molema, S. M., *Montshiwa 1815-1896: Baralong Chief and Patriot*. Cape Town: Struik, 1966.
Molteno, P. A., *The Life and Times of Sir John Charles Molteno*. 2 vols. London: Smith Elder, 1900.
Molyneux, H. H., *Speeches on the Affairs of West Africa and South Africa*. London: John Murray, 1903.
Molyneux, W. C. F., *Campaigning in South Africa and Egypt*. London: Macmillan, 1896.
Mönnig, H. O., *The Pedi*. Pretoria: van Schaik, 1967.
Morris, D. R., *The Washing of the Spears*. London: Jonathan Cape, 1966.
Morris, J., *Heaven's Command: An Imperial Progress*. London: Faber, 1973.
Murray, M., *Union-Castle Chronicles 1853-1953*. Longmans, Green, 1953.
Murray, R. W., *South African Reminiscences . . .* Cape Town: Juta, 1894.
Myatt, F., *The Soldiers Trade: British Military Developments 1660-1914*. London: Macdonald and Janes, 1974.
Newnham-Davis, N., *The Transvaal under the Queen*. London: Sands and Co., 1900.
Nixon, J., *The Complete Story of the Transvaal*. London: Sampson Low, 1885; repr. Cape Town: Struik, 1972.
Noble, J., *Descriptive Handbook of the Cape Colony, its conditions and resources, etc.* Cape Town: Juta, 1875.
Norbury, H. F., *The Naval Brigade in South Africa During the Years 1877-78-79*. London: Sampson Low, 1880.
Norris-Newman, C. L., *In Zululand with the British Throughout the War of 1879*. London: W. H. Allen, 1880.
Parr, H. H., *A Sketch of the Kafir and Zulu Wars*. London: C. Kegan Paul, 1880; repr. Pretoria: State Library, 1970.
Parr, H. H., *Recollections and Correspondence of Major-General Sir Henry Hallam Parr . . .*, ed. C. Fortescue. London: T. Fisher Unwin, 1917.
Paton, G., Glennie, F., and Penn Symons, W., *Historical Records of the 24th Regiment from its formation in 1689*. London: Simpkin, Marshall, Hamilton, Kent and Co., 1892.
Paul, H., *The Life of Froude*. London: Pitman, 1905.
Phillips, L., *Some Reminiscences*. London: Hutchinson, (?) 1924.
Picard, H. W., *Grand Parade*. Cape Town: Struik, 1969.
Prichard, H. M., *Friends and Foes in the Transkei: an Englishwoman's experience during the Cape frontier war of 1877-8*. London: Sampson Low, 1880.
Roberts, B., *The Diamond Magnates*. London: Hamish Hamilton, 1972.
Robinson, R., and Gallagher, J., *Africa and the Victorians: the official mind of imperialism*. London: MacMillan, 1961.
Slade, F. G., *Prepared Notes extracted from My Diary during the South African War of 1878-1879*. Ordnance notes: No. 264, Washington, 10/3/1833.
Smith-Dorrien, H., *Memories of Forty Eight Years Service*. London: John Murray, 1925.
Smithers, A. J., *The Kaffir Wars 1779-1877*. London: Leo Cooper, 1973.
Soga, J. H., *The Ama-Xhosa: Life and Customs*. Lovedale: The Lovedale Press, 1927.
Soga, J. H., *The South-Eastern Bantu*. Johannesburg: Witwatersrand University Press, 1930.

Solomon, W. E. G., *Saul Solomon, 'The Member for Cape Town'*. Cape Town: Oxford University Press, 1948.

Stanford, W., *The Reminiscences of Sir Walter Stanford 1850-1881*, ed. J. W. Macquarrie. Cape Town: van Riebeeck Society, 1958.

Streatfeild, F. N., *Kafirland: A Ten Months Campaign*. London: Sampson Low, 1879.

Streatfeild, F. N., *Reminiscences of an Old 'Un*. London: Eveleigh Nash, 1911.

Theal, G. M., *History of South Africa From 1873 to 1884: Twelve Eventful Years*, 2 vols. London: Allen and Unwin, 1919; repr. Cape Town: C. Struik, 1964.

Trollope, A., *South Africa*, ed. J. H. Davidson. (repr. of 1878 ed.) Cape Town: Balkema, 1973.

Umsweanto, *A Zulu Boy's Recollections of the Zulu War and of Cetshwayo's Return*, tr. G. H. Swinny. London: George Bell, 1884.

Uys, C. J., *In the Era of Shepstone*. Lovedale: The Lovedale Press, 1933.

Walker, E. A., *A History of Southern Africa*, 3 ed. London: Longman Green, 1972.

Ward, H., *The Cape and the Kaffirs: A Diary of Five Years Residence in Kaffirland*, 4 ed. London: Henry G. Bohn, 1860.

Warren, C., *On the Veldt in the Seventies*. London: Isbister, 1902.

Webb, C., de B., and Wright, J. B., eds., *A Zulu King Speaks: Statements made by Cetshwayo kaMpande on the history and customs of his people*. Pietermaritzburg: University of Natal Press, 1978.

Williams, A. F., *Some Dreams Come True*. Cape Town: Timmins, 1948.

Williams, W. W., *The Life of General Sir Charles Warren*. Oxford: Blackwell, 1941.

Wilmot, A., *The Life and Times of Sir Richard Southey*. London: Sampson Low, Marston and Co., 1904.

Wilson, M., and Thompson, L., eds., *The Oxford History of South Africa*, 2 vols. Oxford: The Clarendon Press, 1969.

Wolseley, G., *South African Diaries (Natal) 1875*, ed. A. Preston. Cape Town: Balkema, 1971.

Wolseley, G., *South African Journal 1879-1880*, ed. A. Preston. Cape Town: Balkema, 1973.

Wood, H. E., *From Midshipman to Field Marshall*, 3 ed. London: Methuen, 1906.

Worsfold, B. W., *Sir Bartle Frere: a footnote to the history of the British Empire*. London: Butterworth, 1923.

Young, P. J., *Boot and Saddle: a narrative record of the Cape Regiment, the British Cape Mounted Riflemen, etc.* Cape Town: Maskew Miller, 1955.

[Anonymous] *Life at the Cape a Hundred Years Ago . . . by a Lady*. Cape Town: Struik, 1963.

Index

Aborigines Protection Society, 88
Abyssinian Expeditionary Force, 21
Act of Army Reform (1881), 258
Act No. 3 of 1874, 51-52
Aden, 259
Adendorff, Lt. James, 223
Afghanistan, 186, 195, 250, 257
Africa, 21
Afrikaner Bond, 168
Aldershot, 147, 250, 259
Alice (Ciskei), 158, 159
Amacafula, 176, 189, 201, 205, 209, 240
Amathole Mountains, 72, 133, 142, 147
  eastern, 149, 151, 163
  Ngqikas driven from, 93
  war in the, 152 *et seq.*
Amatwala ndwe, 106
Amiel, Maj. Charles Frederick, 85
Annexation
  of Griqualand West, 32
  of Transvaal, 83
  of Port St. Johns, 169
Anstey, Lt. Edgar Oliphant, 17, 65, 249
  at Centane, 132
  at Isandlwana, 215, 219, 222-224, 242-243
  mentioned in despatches, 183

Army
  British,
    after Zulu War, 257-258
    in 1874, 22
    reforms after 1868, 18-19
  of the Transkei, 124, 164
  of the Vaal, 44, 48
    at Barkly, 58
    in the Karroo, 44-45
    return to Cape Colony, 60-61, 64
  Zulu, 184, 199, 204, 219
    at Isandlwana, 217, 218, 223 *et seq.*
    at Kambula, 254
    organisation of, 185
    at Ulundi, 253
    warnings about, 197, 210
Artillery
  in the Amatholes, 155, 159
  of Army of the Vaal, 43
  at Centane, 135
  of the Central Column, 205, 207
  on Gwadana Hill, 103
  at Ibeka, 105
  at Isandlwana, 213, 223, 230, 234, 236, 238
  Rowland's, 178
Ashantiland, 21
'Ashanti Ring', 20
Atkinson, Sub-Lt. Charles John, 17
  at Centane, 132, 136, 137

at Isandlwana, 230
mentioned in despatches, 139
Australia, 20
Ayliff, James, 98, 99, 144
   in Amatholes, 156
   on Gwadana Hill, 103
Aylward, Alfred, 36, 42, 46, 60
   and the 'Black Flag', 38
   and Cunynghame, 88
   in Lydenburg Volunteer Corps, 74
   rebel army of, 43

Bailie's Grave, 152, 157
Bain's Kloof, 44
Ballard, Col.-Sgt. James, 214, 229
Band of the 1/24th, 30
   in the Amatholes, 155, 159
   artillery drill for, 121
   after Isandlwana, 253
Bapedi people, 69, 178
Barkly (Griqualand West), 49, 58
Barkly, Sir Henry
   and annexation of diamond fields, 32, 55
   and conference despatch, 54-57, 62
   and expedition to Kimberley, 41-42
   on intervention in the Transvaal, 72
   in Kimberley, 59-60
   and Langalibalele debate, 50, 53, 54
   purchases Vooruitzicht, 47
   retirement of, 81
Barolong people, 173
Barracks
   Buena Vista (Gibraltar), 22
   Main (Cape Town), 27, 28, 43, 66
   in Pretoria, 87
Barry, Capt. A. J., 222, 225, 229
Barton, Capt. W. 226, 229
Basotho people, 85, 257

Basotholand, 35, 50
Batlhaping people, 171
Battle
   of Centane, 12, 135-139
   on Gobatse Heights, 174-175
   of Gwadana Hill, 103-104
   of Ibeka, 105-106
   of Isandlwana, 12, 228-246
      1/24th survivors of, 249
      confederation and, 257
   of Kambula, 253
   at Msintsana stream, 118-119
   at Nyumaga, 130-131, 140
   of Ulundi, 253
Beaufort West (Cape Colony), 53
Bechuanaland Border Police, 260
Bellairs, Col. William, 114, 120, 142
Bengough, Maj. H. M., 211, 216, 221, 226
Bennett, Sgt. George, 227
Bickley, Pvt. J., 227
Bismarck, Prince Otto von, 68
Bikitsha, Chief Veldman, 99, 102
   at Centane, 133
   at Ibeka, 104-106
   at Nyumaga, 131
'Black Flag', the, 38, 39
   Rebellion, 11
Black, Maj. Wilsone, 258
   in the Amatholes, 163
   in attack on Sihayo's kraal, 209
   finds bodies of Melvill and Coghill, 250
   return to Isandlwana, 248
Bloemhof (Transvaal), 171
Bloomfield, Q.M. Edward, 234
Boers, the, 32, 69, 109, 200
   British view of, 86
   and Burgers, 67
   and confederation, 55
   Froude's opinion of, 55
   in the Karroo, 45

reaction to a Zulu war, 201
and sale of guns to blacks, 33
and Shepstone, 83
and Wolseley, 257
and the Zulus, 187
Bolo Drift, 142
Boma Pass, 104
Bomvanaland, 96, 114, 123, 165, 168
Bomvana people, 93
Boundary Commission, 191, 194, 198
Bourne, Inspector, 118
Bowker, Cmdt. Bertram, 113, 115
Brabant, Cmdt. Edward Yewd, 116, 152-157
Bradstreet, Capt. R., 232
Brand, President J. H.
  background, 68
  and conference despatch, 62
  and diamond fields dispute, 33
  at London conference, 74
Brander, Capt. William Maxwell, 65, 259
  return to South Africa, 250, 251
  at Ulundi, 253
Brecon (Wales), 19, 23, 149, 258, 259
British Kaffraria, 92, 96
Bromhead, Lt. Gonville, 161, 212
Brown, Col.-Sgt. Thomas P., 230
Browne, Lt. Edward Stevenson, 66, 84, 170, 255, 259
  in Army of the Vaal, 44
  at Christiana, 173
  commands mounted infantry, 171, 172, 175
  at Helpmekaar, 206
  at Hlobane and Kambula, 254
  at Isandlwana, 215, 216
  and Maj. Russell, 254
  at Ulundi, 253
Brownlee, Hon. Charles Pacalt, 102, 141
  dismissal of, 144
  and Xhosa disarmament, 116, 117
Buffalo Border Guard, 204
Buffalo Poort, 151 *et seq.*
Buffalo Range, 151
Buffalo River, *see* Rivers
Bull, Dr Frank, 215
Bullard, Bandmaster Harry T., 150, 219
Buller, Maj. Redvers Henry, 147, 201
  in the Amatholes, 158-161, 165
  commands F.L.H., 156
  on Hlobane, 254
  in the Transvaal, 177
Bulwer, Sir Henry, 185, 190, 191, 194, 201
Burck, Bandmaster C. G., 11, 30, 77, 91, 197, 258
Burgers, President Thomas François
  attitude of Cape newspapers to, 71, 74
  background, 67-68
  and the Bapedi, 69-70
  and the Sekhukhune war, 74
  and Shepstone, 82
  and the Volksraad, 69, 83
Burley, Drummer G., 174
Burma, 149, 259
Burness family, the, 172
Burnshill Mission, 157
Bushman's River Pass Affair, 51, 52
Bushmen, 32
Buthelezi, Chief Mnyamana, 189, 199
Butterworth (Transkei), 96, 102

Calico Ball, the, 73
Cambridge, George, Duke of ('Old Garge'), 252, 255
Canada, 20
Cape Colony, the, 22, 55, 97

fears of black uprising in, 71, 74
Langalibalele and, 52
Transkei links with, 93
Cape of Good Hope, 21, 27
Cape Mounted Rifles, 260
'Cape Smoke', 59
Cape Town, 22, 28-30, 52, 55, 56, 66, 78, 255
Christmas in, 27, 77
and the diamond fields, 31, 32, 41
President Brand in, 68
winter in, 68, 73
Wolseley in, 53, 62, 64
Cardwell Edward, 19, 65
army reforms of, 18-20, 258
Carnarvon, Henry Howard Molyneux, 4th Earl of, 20, 42
and Act No. 3 of 1874, 51, 53
and President Burgers, 68
and Canadian confederation, 55-56
and conference despatch, 54-56
at London conference, 74
offer to Frere, 79
and the Permissive Bill, 78
resignation of, 145
and Shepstone, 75
Carrington, Lt. Frederick, 77, 170
in Army of the Vaal, 44, 45
at Centane, 133, 135-137, 139
after Isandlwana, 252
mentioned in despatches, 183
and mounted infantry, 46, 84, 170
as musketry instructor, 20
organises F.L.H., 121
as Shepstone's escort, 190
subsequent career, 259-260
in the Transvaal, 156, 177, 178, 255
Carrington's Horse, 121, 170
Castle (Cape Town), the, 27-28
Cathcart (Ciskei), 149
Cathcart, Gen. Sir George, 93

Cattle
as bait, 153
in Griffith's offensive, 114
in the Pirie bush, 151
as reparations, 176, 198
Sihayo's, 208
Xhosa killing of, 94
Zulu, 186-187
Cavaye, Lt. Charles Walter, 65
in Army of the Transkei, 124, 129
at Isandlwana, 227, 229, 231, 232, 234
at Nyumaga, 130
pursues Makinana, 117
Centane, 164
the battle at, 135-139
the camp at, 133
comments on, 139-140
recalled, 230
Central Column, the, 247, 253
assembles at Helpmekaar, 203
camp at Isandlwana, 213
Chelmsford splits, 219
crosses the Buffalo, 207
at Rorke's Drift, 206 et seq, 251, 252
Cetshwayo kaMpande, King, 64, 109, 184, 195, 201, 221, 257
appoints diplomatic agents, 190
and the Boers, 187
and the disputed territory, 189
and military tradition, 185
and missionaries, 187
and Shepstone, T., 188, 190
Chalmers, Inspector, 99
on Gwadana Hill, 103
Chambers, Sgt. George, 204
Chard, Lt. John Rouse Merriott, 255, 207, 224
Charters, Q. M. William, 18, 91
Chelmsford, Lord *see* Thesiger
Chermside, Assist. Commissary R. A., 206

Chillianwala, 131
  recalled, 206
Christiana (Transvaal), 172, 173, 175
Churchill, John, Duke of
    Marlborough, 17
Ciskei (Cape Colony), 117, 139
Clarke, Capt. Marshall, 176
Clarkson, Sgt. John, 230
Clements, Lt. Ralph Arthur Penrhyn,
    77
  in Army of the Transkei, 124, 131
  commands mounted infantry, 109
  after Isandlwana, 251
  later career, 259
  moved to Natal, 184
  at Ulundi, 253
Clery, Maj. Cornelius Francis, 205
  evidence of, 252
  at Isandlwana, 212, 218, 221
Cochrane, Sub-Inspector, 103
Coghill, Lt. Nevill Josiah Aylmer,
    17, 73, 77, 84, 150, 205,
    249-250
  ambition of, 66
  appointed ADC to Cunynghame, 76
  appointed ADC to Frere, 184
  in attack on Sihayo's kraal, 209
  background of, 65
  body of, 250, 251
  death of, 241, 257
  diary entries, 115, 120, 145, 146
  follows Khiva, 122
  fox-hunting, 68
  on the fugitives' trail, 239-241
  at Gibraltar, 23
  injures knee, 114
  at Isandlwana, 221, 222, 238
  in Kimberley, 88
  letters home, 66, 72, 77, 78,
      88, 184, 186, 198
  mentioned in despatches, 183
  at Nyumaga, 131

  in Pietermaritzburg, 193-194
  returns to England, 146
  at Rorke's Drift, 207
  in the Transvaal, 85-88
Colenso, Frances Ellen, 84
Colenso, Bishop John William
  and Frere, 194
  and Langalibalele, 51
Colesburg (Cape Colony), 47, 61
Collingwood, Col. William Pole, 252
Collins, Pvt. Michael, 158
Colonial Office, 167, 186, 192, 194,
    256
  and Act No. 3 of 1874, 50, 53
  and dismissal of Southey, 60
  hostile to Frere, 195, 256
  and Port St. Johns, 169
  prohibits war with Zulus, 199
Colonial Secretary, the
  of the Cape Colony, 32
  of Natal, 51
Colours of the 24th Regt.
  Queen's, 240, 255, 258
    in Buffalo River, 241, 250
    at Chillianwala, 18
    at Isandlwana, 238, 250
  Regimental, 17, 238, 258
    thrown into sea, 18
Commando(s)
  Burgers', 70, 74
  in frontier wars, 107
Commissariat
  on the eastern frontier, 112
  Imperial, 121, 125, 132
  Merriman's opinion on, 112
Commission by purchase, 65
Confederation, 12, 52, 55, 61, 63,
    71, 179, 256, 257
Conference despatch, the, 54 et. seq.,
    68
Conference Hill, 190, 253
Cooper, Sgt. Thomas, 214

271

Cowie, William, 38
Cradock (Cape Colony), 61, 152
Craven Club, the, 59
Crealock, Maj. John North, 147
Cunynghame, Lt.-Gen. Sir Arthur Thurlow, 64, 66, 68, 76, 79, 84, 109, 122, 144, 146, 148, 150, 167
 background, 42-43
 and colonial defence, 71
 commands on Eastern Frontier, 107
 comment on battle of Centane, 139-140
 and expedition to diamond fields, 41, 43, 48, 49, 60
 and hunting, 87
 Kei offensive of, 129
 and Makinana affair, 117
 and Merriman, 107, 111, 117
 opinion of the Boers, 86
 opinion of the FAMP, 108
 opinion of Frere, 80
 recall of, 145
 in the Transvaal, 85-88
 and Wolseley, 53
Curling, Lt. H. T., 230, 236
Currey, John Blades, 34
Currie (Donald) Line, the, 22, 31
Curteis, Lt. Edward Witherden, 43

Dalasile, Chief, 134, 135
Daly, Lt. James Patrick, 17, 68, 77, 249
 in Army of the Vaal, 43
 at Isandlwana, 215, 224, 241, 243
Danielskuil (Griqualand West), 172
Dartnell, Maj. John, 201, 206
 at Isandlwana, 214, 215
 on Mangeni River, 217-219, 228
Dassen Island, 76
Davies, Lt. Harry D., 227, 237
Deane, Sub-Lt. Richard Grenville, 67
 death of, 78
Debe Nek (Ciskei), 157, 159
Defence Commission, the, 71, 101
Degacher, Maj. Henry James, 22, 41, 65, 149, 166, 248
 in Amathole campaign, 153, 154, 161
 in Army of the Vaal, 43
 in attack on Sihayo's kraal, 209
 commands 2/24th, 91
 death of, 260
 departure from Isandlwana, 219
 joins Central Column, 205
 in King William's Town, 150
 returns to England, 66
Degacher, Capt. William, 21, 149
 in Army of the Vaal, 144
 in attack on Sihayo's kraal, 209
 in Cape Town cricket team, 65
 commands 1/24th, 205
 at Helpmekaar, 205, 206
 at Isandlwana, 223, 227, 230, 243
 returns to England, 66
 returns to South Africa, 183
Delagoa Bay, 68, 69
Desertions from 1/24th
 in Cape Town, 31, 64, 73
 during frontier war, 183
 in Kimberley, 60
Diamond Field Horse
 on Gobatse Heights, 174
 returns to Griqualand West, 172
 in skirmish at Debe Nek, 157
Diamond fields, the, 31, 32, 61, 175
Diamond Light Infantry, 174
Diamonds, 22, 58, 61
 at Christiana, 173
 discovery of, 32
 stolen, 35
Dickinson, Lt. John Douglas, 44, 66
Diggers Protection Association, the, 36, 37, 46

Dingane kaSenzangakhona, King, 185
Dinkwahyanc, Chief Johannes, 69, 70
Disputed Territory, the, 121, 187, 189
Disraeli, Benjamin, 20, 250
Doyle, Drum-Major, 79, 91
Draaibosch (Ciskei), 127
Drought, 77, 186
  end of the, 197
  in Kaffraria, 99
  and Rowland's campaign, 178
  in Sekhukhuneland, 176
  in Zululand, 186-187
Dsjate (Sekhukhuneland), 74, 177, 179
Dunbar, Maj. William Mathew, 204, 210, 258
  commands 1/24th, 251
  at Isandlwana, 217
  at Sandile's funeral, 166
  at Ulundi, 253
Dundee (Natal), 251
Dunne, Asst.-Commissary Walter Alphonsus, 204
Durban (Natal), 84, 251
Durnford, Col. Anthony William, 13, 84, 224
  as boundary commissioner, 191
  and the Bushman's River Pass affair, 51, 52
  character of, 225, 226
  as commander of 1st NNC, 202
  at Isandlwana, 224-226, 232
  plans for a native army, 201
  reprimanded by Chelmsford, 211
  at Rorke's Drift, 208, 211, 221
Durnford's Native Horse, 202, 211, 226, 240
  at Isandlwana, 224, 227, 229, 231, 237, 238
Dwessa Forest, the, 125, 165
Dyer, Lt. Henry Julian, 228, 231, 242
Dyson, 2nd Lt. Edwards Hopton, 184
  at Isandlwana, 227, 229

East London, 91
  landing of 2/24th at, 150
  landing of 88th at, 121
Eastern Frontier, the, 71, 72, 84, 91
Eastern Province, 42, 55, 84
Edmund kaSandile (Gonya), 166
Edwards, Sgt. John, 227
Eland Kraal (Natal), 211, 216, 221
Elliott, Maj. Henry George, 123
  leads Thembu contingent, 113
  in Mpondoland, 168
Ellis, Pvt. Owen, 203, 210
Essex, Capt. Edward, 205
  at Isandlwana, 227, 229, 230, 234
Eustace, Col. John T., 98, 99, 102, 103
Exeter Hall, 168, 187

Farmers Defence Union, the, 168
Fay, Sgt. Thomas, 227
Field, Cook-Sgt. Alfred, 203
Fitzmaurice, Sgt. J., 170
Fort
  Beaufort (Ciskei), 76, 147, 148, 158
  Black (Amatholes), 163
  Buffalo (Kei valley), 127
  Burgers (Sekhukhuneland), 176-178
  Cunynghame (Ciskei), 111, 121
  Evelyn (Amatholes), 163
  Glamorgan (East London), 148
  Glyn (Transkei), 124
  Linsingen (Kei valley), 127, 128
  Melvill (Rorke's Drift), 251
  Merriman (Amatholes), 152, 166
  Napier (Pietermaritzburg), 193, 195
  Nixon (Transkei), 126, 164
  Peddie (Eastern Province), 97
  Warwick (Ciskei), 127, 128

Warwick (Zululand), 253
Weeber (Sekhukhuneland), 176
Fortifications
  Chelmsford's attitude to, 210, 217, 252
  Glyn's view, 210
Frankfort (Ciskei), 155, 165
Frere, Sir Henry Bartle Edward, 12, 79, 101, 167, 186, 191
  and annexation of Port St. Johns, 168-169
  background of, 80-81
  and the Boers, 256
  and boundary award, 191-192
  and Britain's prestige, 179
  censured by Parliament, 256
  comment on Centane, 139, 140
  and disarmament of blacks, 117, 257
  fear of a Zulu victory, 218
  and Griqualand West, 175
  and Indian Mutiny, 80, 107, 143
  in King William's Town, 102 et seq.
  meeting with Sandile, 111
  and Molteno, 83, 141-144
  need for a Zulu war, 191, 194
  in Pietermaritzburg, 194, 208
  retirement of, 257
  ultimatum to Cetshwayo, 198
  view of Cetshwayo, 191
  view of FAMP, 108
  view of Sarhili, 103
  visit to Transkei, 102-103
Frontier Armed & Mounted Police (FAMP), 77, 88, 96, 260
  in Army of the Transkei, 124
  in Butterworth, 99
  at Centane, 135-137
  commanded by Griffith, 103
  on Gwadana Hill, 103-104
  history of, 108
  at Ibeka, 105
  at Msintsana stream, 119
  at Nyumaga, 130
Frontier Light Horse (FLH), 121, 129, 169
  in the Amatholes, 156, 157, 161
  at Centane, 135, 137
  in Rowland's campaign, 177, 178
  in Zulu War, 201, 208
Frost, Cmdt. John, 142, 143, 153, 155, 156
Froude, James Anthony, 55, 60, 61, 80
  and Barkly, 55-57
  and Molteno, 55, 56, 63
  in Natal, 61-62
  returns to London, 61
  at Uitenhage, 62
  view of the Boers, 55
  and Wolseley, 57, 62
Fynn, Henry Francis, 215, 216

Gallwey, Michael Henry, 191
Gamayana valley, 173
Gamopedi valley, 172
Gamble, Band-Sgt. David, 196
  at Isandlwana, 239
Gardner, Capt. Alan, 205
  at Isandlwana, 228, 229, 235
Garrison(s)
  Cape Town, the, 30
  in Durban, 192
  in Greytown, 149
  at Helpmekaar, 251, 253
  Mediterranean, 19
  at Rorke's Drift, 253
  in Stutterheim, 149
Gasebonwe, Chief Botlhasite, 171, 172, 185
Gcaleka people, 88, 92, 169
  at Centane, 133-136
  on Gwadana Hill, 103

at Ibeka, 105-106
and the Mfengu, 92, 96-97
at Msintsana stream, 118-119
at Nyumaga, 130-131
and the Thembu, 96
and Wodehouse, 96
General Order No. 142, 120
German settlers, 96
Germany, 21, 68, 83, 169
Gibraltar, 17, 21-22
Gladstone, William Ewart, 20
Glennie, Capt. Farquhar, 250
Glyn, Anne, 69, 252, 255
  on Pulleine's death, 249
Glyn, Col. Richard Thomas, 22,
      41, 92, 102, 156, 192, 197, 248,
      254
  and Army of the Vaal, 43, 45
  attitude to Chelmsford, 216-217
  awarded C.B., 183
  background of, 119-120
  as Colonel of South Wales
    Borderers, 259
  as Commandant of the Castle, 28
  as Commandant of the Ciskei, 108
  commands Central Column, 200,
    205, 207, 210
  commands Eastern Districts, 103
  death of, 260
  and disarmament of Xhosas, 116
  and fox-hunting, 68
  at Helpmekaar, 205
  at Isandlwana, 215, 217, 219, 221
  leaves South Africa, 255
  after the massacre, 250, 252-253
  and Molteno, 99
  at Nyumaga, 130-131
  promoted Maj.-General, 258
  at Sihayo's kraal, 209
  in the Transkei, 114, 119, 123,
    124, 129, 133, 163, 164
  at Ulundi, 253

Gobatse Heights, 174, 175, 254
Godwin-Austen, Capt. Alfred, 161, 212
Godwin-Austen, Lt. Frederick, 231, 243
Gold Coast, 20
Gold fields, the, 61
Gongqo valley, the, 158, 160
Gordon, Rev. John, 196, 250
Gosport (Hampshire), 258
Gosset, Capt. Matthew, 146, 155, 248
Government
  Cape Colony, 257
  responsible, 52, 53
  Tory, 21, 53
  Whig, 20
Grahamstown, 152
Grant, Pvt. H. 236
Gray, Cmdt. George, 120
Grenfell, Capt. Francis, 66, 146, 193
  at Centane, 135, 137, 139
Grey, Sir George, 93-94, 96
Greytown (Ciskei), 142, 149
Greytown (Natal), 195, 197, 253
Griffith, Cmdt. Charles Duncan,
    88, 108, 119, 142, 149
  accused by Bowker, 113
  as Cmdt.-General, 143
  commands FAMP, 102
  Gcalekaland campaign of, 114-115
  at Ibeka, 105
Griffith, Sub-Lt. Thomas Llewelyn
  at Isandlwana, 228, 231
  at Sandile's funeral, 166
Griqualand East, 97
Griqualand West, 30, 31, 41, 54-56, 60
  the Administration of, 33, 54, 171
  expedition to, 42
  rebellion in, 38
Griqua people, 32, 59, 171-175
Griquatown, 172, 173

Gungubele, Chief, 143
Gwadana Hill, 103
Gwili Gwili Range, 151, 153, 156

Hall, Lt. Arthur William, 237
Hamilton-Browne, Cmdt. G., 204, 217, 224
  in attack on Sihayo's kraal, 209
  return to Isandlwana, 247
Harness, Maj. Arthur, 195, 205
  in the Amatholes, 158
  at Isandlwana, 219, 248
Harrington St. (Cape Town), 29
Harrison, Capt. Henry Albert, 254, 259
  in Army of the Vaal, 44
  at Port St. Johns, 169
  in the Transkei, 164
Hayne's Mill, 153, 156, 161, 219
Heaton, Sub-Lt. Wilfred, 17, 78, 251, 259
  at Helpmekaar, 228
  in the Transkei, 164
  at Ulundi, 253
Helpmekaar (Natal), 210, 253
  conditions at
    after Isandlwana, 251
    before the invasion, 203-204, 207
Henderson, Joseph, 82, 83
Henderson, Lt., 227, 228
Heppenstall, Sgt. Christopher, 230
Hicks-Beach, Sir Michael, 145, 186
Higginson, Lt. Walter
  at Fugitives' Drift, 241
  at Isandlwana, 224-227
Hintsa kaKawuta, Chief, 97
Hlazakazi Hills, 213, 214
Hlobane Mountain, 254
Hlubi people, 50-52
Hodson, Lt. George Frederick, 17, 68
  at Isandlwana, 222, 241
  mentioned in despatches, 183
  at Nyumaga, 129
  as orderly officer, 120, 129
Holela (Gcalekaland), 113, 125
Holland, 68
Holland's Shop, 118
Hopetown (Cape Colony), 45, 46, 61
Hopton, Maj. Edward, 124, 129, 203
Horse sickness, the, 85, 177, 179, 203
Hotels
  at Breede River, 44
  at Draaibosch, 127
  in Hopetown, 45
  in Kimberley, 59
  in Newcastle, 85
  in Wynberg, 77
Hunting, 22
  the fox, 69
  in the Transvaal, 86-87

Ibeka (Transkei), 99-121
  the battle at, 105-106
  as 'Fort Glyn', 124
  fortifications at, 104
Idutywa, 96, 97, 104, 113
Imperial Command, the, 128
Impi(s), 72, 86, 199, 210, 215, 257
  the big, 218, 219, 222, 226, 228
India, 22, 149
Indian Mutiny, the, 18, 65, 201
  Frere's experiences in, 80, 107, 143
Isandlwana Hill, 212, 251
  the battle at, 228-246
  the camp at, 213, 242, 243
  Durnford's arrival at, 224
  Pulleine takes command at, 221
  the flight from, 238-241
  the night of the 22nd at, 248
  solar eclipse at, 228
Itelezi Hill, 253
Izeleni Post, the, 153

Jali, kaMkayi, Chief, 157
Jingo Song, the, 196-197
Johnson, Pvt. W. 236
Joubert, Acting-President Petrus, 70

Kaffrarian Vanguard, the, 196
Kalahari Desert, the, 174
Kama clan, the, 157
Kambula, 253
Karroo, the, 44
Keate Award, the, 171
Kei Mouth, 116
Keiskamma Hoek, 152, 156
Khiva, 126
  at Centane, 133, 134
  and Mapasa, 116, 139
  at Moordenaar's Kop, 122
  at Nyumaga, 130
Kimberley, 22, 33, 41, 58-59, 167
King William's Town, 65, 84, 88, 102, 147, 158, 196, 210
  past history of, 91-92
  the war and, 110, 150
Koegas (Griqualand West), 172
Kokstad (Griqualand East), 169
Komga (Ciskei), 77, 99, 111, 121, 122
Kopje
  Allein, 253
  conical, 213
  stony, 212, 239
Korana people, 32, 172, 173
Krohn, Capt., 223, 224, 232
Kruger, Stephanus Johannes Paulus
  and Burgers, 70
  in Pietermaritzburg, 197
  and Shepstone, 82
Kumasi (Gold Coast), 20
Kuruman (Tswana territory), 172, 173
Kwa-Centane, 130, 132

Labour for diamond mines, 175
Laing's Nek, 85
Lambert, Col. W., 127-129
Land Court, the, 171
Landman's Drift, 252, 253
Langalibalele, Chief, 21, 185
  debate on, 54
  rebellion of, 50-53
Langeberg, the, 173, 175
Lanyon, Maj. William Owen, 60, 171, 255, 257
  and Griqua rebellion, 172-173
Likatlong (Tswana Territory), 173
Livingstone, David, 21
Lloyd, 2nd Lt. William Whitelock, 184
  after Isandlwana, 251
  at Ulundi, 253
Logan, Maj. Walter Bernardino, 120
  at Ibeka, 124
  retirement of, 197
London Conference, the, 74
Lonsdale, Cmdt. Rupert La Tour, 201
  in the Amatholes, 152, 154, 157, 165
  commands 3rd Regt. NNC, 204, 209
  at Isandlwana, 214, 215
  in Mangeni valley, 215, 217, 219, 228
  reports fall of camp, 247
Lotutu Bush (Amatholes), 157-159
Luneburg (Transvaal), 190, 196
Lydenburg (Transvaal), 69, 87, 179
Lydenburg Volunteer Corps, 74, 87

McDonald, Pvt. Miles, 241
Macdowel, Lt. Francis Hartwell
  at Isandlwana, 222, 228
  at Rorke's Drift, 207, 210
Maclean, Insp. Allan, 105

McNaghten, Capt., 161
Magogo Hills, 214, 215
Magumdana, Chief, 215, 216, 224
Makabalikele Ridge, 159
Maki, counsellor, 98
Makinana kaMhala, Chief, 117, 118
Malakatha Hills, 213-215
Malan, Maj. C. H., 125
Malgas, Donker, 172
Mankurowane, Chief, 171, 173
Mansell, Inspector G., 213, 214
Manubi Forest, the, 125
Mapasa kaBuku, Chief, 98
  and disarmament, 116
  and Fort Linsingen, 128
  and Khiva, 139
  and Sarhili, 98
Maqoma kaNgqika, Chief, 76, 110, 147
Market Square
  in Kimberley, 33, 37, 48
  in Pretoria, 82
Matanzima kaSandile, 149, 156, 166
Matshana, Chief, 228
  stronghold of, 211, 214
Mauritius, 53, 200
Mazeppa Bay (Transkei), 121
Melbourne (Australia), 29
Melvill, Lt. and Adj. Teignmouth
  body of, 250, 251
  death of, 241, 257
  at Fugitives' Drift, 241
  hunts Sarhili, 165
  at Isandlwana, 217, 221, 223, 224, 226, 229, 231, 238, 240
  kept in South Africa, 184
  returns to Cape Colony, 150
  returns to England, 67, 120
  shipwrecked, 76
  in the Transkei, 99

Merriman, Hon. John Xavier, 78, 141, 148
  background of, 101-102
  becomes 'Minister of War', 107
  and the Commissariat
  and Cunynghame, 107, 112, 117
  dismissal of, 144
  and Froude, 62
  and Gungubela, 143
  and Makinana affair, 117
  and raid on Ngqika Reserve, 142
Mfecane, 97, 172
Mfengu people, 88
  levies, 123, 223, 235
    in the Amatholes, 152, 154, 156-158, 160
    at Centane, 135, 136, 139
    desertion of, 103, 129
    at Ibeka, 104-106
    at Nyumaga, 130
    and Sandile, 165, 166
    soldiers' attitude to, 125
  relationship with Cape Colony, 167
  relationship with Gcalekas, 92, 96-97
  and Wodehouse, 96
Mfenguland, 97
Mhlakaza, 94
Middle Drift (Ciskei), 158
Middle Drift (Natal), 211
  1st NNC at, 202
  surveyor incident at, 194
Military Reserve, the, 92, 121, 140
  church service in, 196, 250
Militia, 19, 199
Mining Board, the, 39
Missionaries, 187, 206
Mnyameni Bush, the, 132-134, 137
Moderate Party, the, 39, 43, 49
Moffat Institute, the, 172
Molteno, Hon. John Charles, 79, 97, 101, 113, 119, 167

and Act No. 3 of 1874, 51, 53, 54
background of, 53
and confederation, 54
and conference despatch, 54, 55, 62, 63
and Cunynghame, 43, 71, 112, 118
on disarmament, 117
dismissal of, 144
and Frere, 80, 83, 141-143
and Froude, 55, 62
and Griqualand West, 33, 63
in King William's Town', 141
at London Conference, 74
and the 'Permissive Bill', 78
and regular troops, 99, 107, 144
Molyneux, Capt. William C. F., 146
Moni, Chief, 114
Montgomery, Col. Robert Blackall, 84
Moordenaar's Kop, 122
Moore, Maj. Hans Garrett, 122, 126
Morris, Pvt. George, 184, 204
Morshead, Lt. Archer Anderson, 137, 259
   dist. adj. in Greytown, 203
   dist. adj. in the Transkei, 120
   at Nyumaga, 129
   promoted, 251
Mostyn, Capt. William Eccles, 149
   at Isandlwana, 215, 229, 231, 232, 241, 243
   at Manzimnyama camp, 214
   in Pietermaritzburg, 197
   returns to Brecon, 64
   sent to Fort Beaufort, 148
'Mount Ararat', 38
Mount Kempt, 151, 155, 156
Mounted Infantry, 77, 109
   in Army of the Vaal, 43, 48
   disbanded, 60
   at Christiana, 172
   commanded by
      Browne, 171, 253
      Carrington, 170
      Clements, 109
      Newnham-Davis, 173
      Russell, 178
   on Gobatse Heights, 174
   Imperial
      1st Squadron, 178
         at Helpmekaar, 206
         on Hlobane, 254
         at Isandlwana, 213, 215, 219, 247
         at Kambula, 254
         at Ulundi, 253
      2nd Squadron, 184
   at Newcastle, 170
   at Nyumaga, 131
Mpande kaSenzangakhona, King, 185
Mpetu, 116
   Brownlee at, 117
   fort at, 127
Mpondo people, 93, 168
Mpondoland, 93, 168
Mqikela kaFaku, Chief, 169
Much, Bt. Maj. William Thomas, 149, 227, 259
   at Fort Glamorgan, 148
   at Helpmekaar, 204
Murray, Capt. O. E., 218
Napier, Gen. Sir Robert, 21
Natal Carbineers, 204, 229
Natal, Colony of, 55, 97, 191, 256
   labour from 35
   and the Langalibalele rebellion, 51
   settlers of the, 21, 195
      and Froude, 62
      and Wolseley, 52
      and the Zulu war, 195
Natal Mounted Police, 82, 201, 204, 233, 238
Natal Native Contingent (NNC), 224
   formation of, 201

First Regt. of the, 202
   Chelmsford's plans for, 208, 211
   at Isandlwana, 224, 227, 229, 232
   Rocket Battery of, 224, 227, 232
Third Regt. of the, 206
   in attack on Sihayo's kraal, 209
   at Isandlwana, 213, 215, 217-219, 232
   No. 5 Co., 1st Batt., 222, 229, 230
   No. 9 Co., 2nd Batt., 222, 231, 235
   at Sandspruit, 204-205
Native Policy, 55, 68, 75
Naval Brigade, the, 132, 198
   in the frontier war, 121, 123, 124
   in Pearson's column, 198
Ndimba kaMhala, Chief, 117
Ndlambe clan, the, 157
New Kei Drift, 99
'New Rush' Mine, the, 31, 35, 47, 48
New Zealand, 20
Newcastle (Natal), 85, 170
Newcastle Mounted Rifles, 204, 232
Newdigate, Maj.-Gen. Edward, 252
Newnham-Davis, Lt. Nathaniel, 173, 175
Newspapers
   Cape Argus, 41, 53, 144
   Cape Mercury, 99, 102
   Cape Times, 150
   Cape Town Daily News, 42
   Diamond Fields, 36, 37
   Diamond News, 41
   Eastern Star, 112, 117
   Gibraltar Chronicle, 22
   Grahamstown Journal, 41, 53
   Kaffrarian Watchman, 227
   Mining Gazette, 47

   Times of Natal, 208
Ngangelizwe, Chief, 102, 113
Ngcayichibi, 98
Ngqika people, 93
   in the Amatholes, 152 *et seq.*
   at Centane, 137, 139
   rebellion of, 126 *et seq.*
Ngqika Reserve, the, 111, 168
   Makinana's flight to, 117
   Frost's visitation of, 142-143
Ngubo, 98, 105, 106
Ngxitho, 134
Nongqawuse, 94
Nourse, Capt. C., 227, 232
Nqutu Range, 209, 212, 215, 225, 226, 253
Nkqwiliso kaNdamase, Chief, 168, 169
Ntaba-ka-Ndoda Hill, the, 153, 157, 159, 161
Ntsonyana clan, 134, 139

'Old Colonists', the, 168
   and annex. of diamond fields, 32
   and annex. of Transvaal, 83-84
   and Barkly, 81
   and Burgers' war, 71-72
   and the conference despatch, 56
   and Molteno, 83
Orange Free State, 83
Ordinance 10, 35
Oskarberg *see* Shiyane
Owen, Maj. A. A., 129, 130

Palmer, Col. Henry Wellington, 146, 148, 150
Palmes, Sub.-Lt. George Champney, 77, 259
   at Centane, 132
Parliament of the Cape Colony, the, 60
   defence debate in, 71

Frere and, 101
Langalibalele debate in, 50, 54
laying foundation stone of, 43, 44
liberal lobby in, 55
special session of, 62-63
Parr, Capt. Henry Hallam, 205, 250
  at Isandlwana, 221
Paterson, John
  and conference despatch, 54, 56
  land syndicate of, 35
  and Vooruitzicht, 47
Paton, Capt. George, 149, 196
  in King William's Town, 120, 255
  later career, 258, 260
Peace of Amiens, 27
Pearson, Col. Charles Knight, 184, 200
Perak, 120
Percy, Insp. Gilbert, 37
'Permissive Bill', the, 78
Phillips, Lionel, 48
Phillips, Sub-Insp. F. L., 214
Pietermaritzburg (Natal), 50, 65, 208
  after Isandlwana, 249
  departure of 1/24th from, 197, 253
  Frere in, 193-195
Pine, Sir Benjamin C. C., 50-53
Pinetown (Natal), 254
Pirie
  Bush, 151, 153 et seq.
  Mission, 153, 161
Pope, Lt. Charles D'Aguilar, 219, 230-232, 235, 242, 243
Port Elizabeth (Cape Colony), 55, 61, 76, 101
Port St. Johns (Transkei), 168, 254
Porteous, Lt. Francis Pender, 183, 206, 227, 249
  at Helpmekaar, 203
  at Isandlwana, 230, 231
Power, Pvt. John, 249

on Gobatse Heights, 175
on Hlobane, 254
'Pramberg Kaffirs', the, 172, 173
Pretoria (Transvaal), 70, 87, 175
Prichard, Mrs
  flight to Blythswood, 104
  at Idutywa, 99
Primrose Square (Cape Town), 29
Prince Alfred Guard, the, 118
Proclamation
  of Merriman, 113
  of Shepstone, 83
  of Southey, 37
Prophets (Xhosa), 94, 105, 106
Province of Utrecht, 70, 189, 190
Pulleine, Brev. Lt.-Col. Henry Burmester, 23, 84, 91, 149, 211
  character of, 13, 225
  commands Cape Town garrison, 44, 64
  commands Durban garrison, 192
  commands in King William's Town, 66
  commands Pietermaritzburg garrison, 195-197
  commands in the Transkei, 165
  at Isandlwana, 221 et seq.
  mentioned in despatches, 183
  messages from, 223, 228-229, 247
  popularity of, 92
  and volunteers, 108, 110, 120
Pulleine's Rangers, 120-121, 129, 137, 201
Pullen, Q.M. James, 19, 20
  in Army of the Vaal, 44
  at Isandlwana, 235, 243
  promoted Q.M., 91

Queenstown, 76
  district, 93, 96
  volunteers, 143, 148

Railroad, 43, 56, 69
Rainforth, Capt. Thomas, 64, 65,
 149, 259
 in Army of the Transkei, 124, 164
 at Centane, 132, 135
 at Greytown, 203
 at Helpmekaar, 215, 230
 at Ulundi, 253
Rabula Heights, 153, 156
Raw, Lt. Charles, 226
Rebellion
 Digger (Black Flag), 11, 37 *et seq.*
 Griqua, 171-175
 Ngqika, 166 *et seq.*
Regiments (British)
 3rd (The Buffs), 2nd Batt., 200
  in Mounted Infantry, 170
  at Tugela Mouth, 192
 4th (King's Own Royal), 2nd
  Batt., 199, 210
 13th (Prince Albert's Light
  Infantry), 1st Batt., 23, 84,
  200
  in Mounted Infantry, 171
  moved to Pietermaritzburg, 65
  in Pretoria, 87
  in Utrecht, 190
 21st (Royal Scots Fusiliers), 2nd
  Batt., 252
 24th (2nd Warwickshire), 2nd
  Batt., 149, 200, 212
  in the Amatholes, 152-155, 158
  in attack on Sihayo's kraal,
   209-210
  comments on, 150, 166
  in Greytown, 195
  at Helpmekaar, 204, 205
  at Isandlwana, 213, 219, 223,
   230 *et seq.*
  after Isandlwana, 253
  at Middle Drift, 192
  moved to Natal, 166

 58th (Rutlandshire), 252
 80th (Staffordshire Volunteers),
  85, 190
  in Mounted Infantry, 171
  moved to Transvaal, 177
 86th (Royal County Downs), 27
 88th (Connaught Rangers), 91, 109
  in Cape Town, 196
  landing at East London, 121
  at Nyumaga, 131
 90th (Perthshire Light Infantry),
  144, 200
  comment on, 148
  at Fort Beaufort, 148, 149
  at Kokstad, 169
  on Makabalikele Ridge, 159-160
 94th Foot, 252
 99th (Duke of Edinburgh's), 199
 South Wales Borderers, 258, 259
Reynolds, Surgeon-Maj. James
 Henry, 254, 255
Rhodesian Field Force, the, 260
Rifles
 breech-loading, 19, 106
  in defeat of Xhosas, 167
  in NNC, 205
 Martini-Henry, 12, 20, 140, 253
  at Centane, 140
  comments on, 140
  from horseback, 46
  for hunting, 22
  at Isandlwana, 230, 233, 236
 muzzle-loading, 106, 158
  at Nyumaga, 131
 Snider-Enfield, 46
  in colonial defence, 109
  at Ibeka, 106
  for mounted infantry, 46
Rivers
 Assegaai, 187
 Bashee (Batse), Transkei, 93, 96,
  113, 114, 123, 125, 165

Bashee (Batse), Zululand, 210
Blood (Ncome), 187, 189, 198, 253
Breede, 44
Buffalo, Ciskei, 92, 150, 153
Buffalo, Natal, 187, 189, 190, 203, 206, 212, 237, 250, 252
   Central Column crosses, 207-208
   fugitives in, 240
Cwengwe, 153, 155
Gamayana, 173
Gcina, 98
Gonubie, 148
Harts, 171, 172
Izeleni, 153
Kabousie, 88, 122
Kei, 29, 93, 96, 122, 127
Liesbeeck, 78
Limpopo, 64
Mangeni, 211, 213-221, 226, 228
Manzimnyama, 212, 214, 215, 222, 240
Modder, 48
Msintsana, 118, 119
Mtamvuma, 93
Mtata, 93, 96, 114
Mzimvubu, 168, 169
Nahoon, 127
Nondweni, 221
Nqabora, 124, 125
Nyumaga, 130
Olifants, 178
Orange, 45, 47, 61, 172
Pongola, 190
Qolora, 133, 137
Qora, 99, 104, 124, 125
Rabula, 157
Shixini, 125, 164
Spekboom, 69, 177
Steelpoort, 178
Thomas, 148, 149, 166
Tugela, 191-194, 197, 200, 211
Tutura, 133

Vaal, 49, 58, 85, 172
Waterfall, 176
White Mfolozi, 253
Robben Island, 51, 53
Roberts, Lt. J. A., 226
Robinson, Capt., 133
   at Centane, 137
   at Ibeka, 104
   at Nyumaga, 130
Robinson, Joseph Benjamin, 33, 44, 60
   and Moderate Party, 39, 40
   and Vooruitzicht, 47
Roche, Lt. Hon. Ulick de Rupe Burke, 77, 169
   in Anglo-Boer war, 259
   at Port St. Johns, 169
Rocket Battery, the, 202, 211
   at Isandlwana, 224-225, 227, 231, 232, 236, 237
Rorke, Cmdt., 143
Rorke, James, 206, 212
Rorke's Drift, 200, 203, 210, 212, 217, 224, 237, 246
   Central Column at, 206, *et seq.*
   after Isandlwana, 252, 253
Rowland, Col. Hugh, 177, 194, 200
   the reconnaisance in force of, 178
Royal Commission, 83
Royal Engineers, 207
Royal Marines, 123, 130
Royal Warwick Lodge, 73
Royal Warwick Theatre, 73
Russell, Brev. Maj. Francis Broadfoot, 202
   at Isandlwana, 224, 227, 232
Russell, Maj. John Cecil
   and Browne, 254
   commands mounted infantry, 178
   on Hlobane, 254
   at Isandlwana, 219, 247
   unpopularity of, 206

Saltmarshe, Lt. Arthur Harry, 160
Sandile kaNgqika, Chief, 12, 76, 93
    139, 185
  in the Amatholes, 151, 156-158,
    163
  background of, 110-111
  and Brownlee, 118
  burial of, 166
  at Centane, 133, 134
  death of, 165
  decision to fight, 126
  meeting with Frere, 111
Sandspruit (Natal), 204
Sarhili kaHintsa, Chief, 96-99, 126,
    139, 164, 185
  and the 'Cattle-Killing', 94
  at Centane, 133, 134
  deposed, 113
  eludes pursuers, 165
  fate of, 168
  and Frere, 102-103
  at Ibeka, 105
  and Mapasa, 98
  sends peace emissaries, 104, 113,
    123
  and Wodehouse, 97
Sawbridge, Capt. Edward Bridgman,
    43, 66, 149
Schermbrucker, Cmdt. Friedrich
  in Amatholes, 152, 155, 156, 165
  in Natal, 196
  at Sandile's funeral, 166
Second Division, the, 252, 253
Sekhukhune, Chief, 109, 175, 185,
    190, 194
  background of, 69
  and President Burgers, 70
  and Rowland's reconnaisance,
    178, 179
  and Shepstone, 176, 177
  Wolseley defeats, 257
Sekhukhuneland, 69, 70, 176

Sekwati, Regent, 69
Sentries
  in the Amatholes, 154
  at Isandlwana, 213-217, 222
Siphezi Hill, 213, 215, 216, 222
Shaka kaSenzangakhona, King, 97,
    103, 184
Shepherd, Surgeon-Maj. Peter
  death of, 239
  at Helpmekaar, 204
Shepstone, Capt. George, 226-229,
    237, 239
Shepstone, Henrique, 171, 172
Shepstone, John Wesley, 191, 198
Shepstone, Sir Theophilus
    ('Somtseu'), 50
  and annex. of the Transvaal,
    81 *et seq.*
  background of, 75
  and the Boers, 83, 176-179,
    188-190, 256
  and the Boundary Commission,
    198
  and Cetshwayo, 82, 176, 188, 190,
    191, 198
  character of, 186, 188
  and the Disputed Territory, 189
  and Durnford, 84-85
  and Frere, 177
  and Langalibalele, 51
  at the London Conference, 74
  retirement of, 257
  and Sekhukhune, 177
  shipwrecked, 76
Shepstone, Capt. Theophilus, Jr.
    ('Offy'), 204, 248
Ships
  Active, H.M.S., 109, 121, 150, 169
  African, R.M.S., 81
  Bahiana, warship, 79
  Balmoral Castle, 79
  Clyde, troopship, 250, 251

Egypt, SS, 254-255
Elizabeth Martin, SS, 22, 27
European, R.M.S., 61, 65-66
Florence, SS, 76, 121
Himalaya, troopship, 23, 27, 150
Orontes, troopship, 91
Peshawar, SS, 17, 251
Simoon, troopship, 22-23, 27
Teuton, SS, 84
Walmer Castle, 55, 67
Windsor Castle, 76, 103
Shiyane Hill, 206
Short-service
  enlistment, 19
  soldiers, 149
Sigcau kaSarhili, 116
  at Centane, 134
  at Ibeka, 105
  war party and, 98
sickness
  in the Amatholes, 166
  'camp fever', 60
  at Fort Burgers, 179
  heat stroke, 124
  at Helpmekaar, 204, 251
  in Hopetown, 46
  in King William's Town, 150
Sidenge Range, the, 149, 151, 154, 155, 165
Sihayo, Chief, 198, 208
  attack on kraal of, 209-210
  family vendetta of, 194
Simonstown (Cape), 30, 66, 200, 255
Sitshaka, Chief, 103
Sivewright, James
  on the Disputed Territory, 197-198
  on the officers of the 1/24th, 249
Siyolo, Chief, 157-160, 165
Smith, Brev. Maj. Stuart
  death of, 240-241
  at Isandlwana, 228, 230, 234, 236, 238

Smith-Dorrien, Lt. Horace Lockwood
  at Fugitives' Drift, 240
  at Isandlwana, 221, 234
Sokexe (Sihayo's kraal), 208
Solomon, Saul, 53
'Somtseu's Column', 210
South Africa, 21-22, 29
Southey, Sir Richard
  and Army of the Vaal, 48
  arrests rebels, 49
  as Colonial Secretary, 32
  and Cowie affair, 38
  dismissal of, 60
  and enrolment of blacks, 42
  on the Griqua rebellion, 175
  and the Land Court, 59
  as Lt.-Governor, 33 *et seq.*
  proclamations of, 37, 39
  views on racial prejudice, 36, 55
Spalding, Brev. Maj. Henry, 205
Sparks, Trp. Charles, 233
Sprigg, Hon. John Gordon, 168
  becomes Prime Minister, 145
  chairman of defence commission, 71
  in King William's Town, 117
  as opposition leader, 101
Spring, Sub-Lt. William Edward Day, 17, 112, 169, 252, 259
Staff College, the, 120, 184
Stafford, Capt. W. H., 229
Standerton (Transvaal), 85
Steam transportation
  in defeat of Xhosas, 167
  in moving troops, 91
Stevens, Trumpeter Richard, 238
Stockenström, Judge Andries, 171, 194
Stratton, Sgt. A., 160
Streatfeild, Cmdt. Frank, 152, 153, 157, 160

Strickland, Maj. Edward, 112
Stutterheim (Ciskei), 149
Suez Canal, 21, 22
Sullivan, Commodore Francis
    William, 121, 185
Supply lines, 127, 199
Sutu, Regent, 110
Swazi people, 70

Table Bay, 27, 67
Tala Ridge, 130, 132
Takoon (Tswana territory), 172
Taung (Tswana territory), 173
Taylor, Drum-Major Robert, 91
Theatre Royal, the, 193
Telegraph, the, 32
    defeat of the Xhosas and, 167
    failure to cut, 127
    in King William's Town, 110
Thembu people, 144
    driven across the Kei, 93
    and the Gcalekas, 96
Thesiger, Lt.-Gen. Frederic Augustus,
    (Lord Chelmsford), 145, 149,
    163, 167, 178, 195, 256
    attack on Sihayo's kraal, 209
    background of, 146
    Buffalo Range offensive, first,
        153-155, 219
    Buffalo Range offensive, second,
        156
    Buffalo Range offensive, last, 161
    and colonial troops, 147, 156
    and Durnford, 208, 211, 221
    and Glyn, 205, 210, 252
    at Helpmekaar, 205
    at Ibeka, 164
    at Isandlwana, 214 *et seq.*
    Lotutu offensive, 158-161
    after massacre, 249, 250, 252, 253
    messages for, 247
    and 2/24th, 166, 252
    splits Central Column, 219
    superseded, 253
    Zulu War preparations, 186, 192,
        195
    Zulu War strategy, 199-200, 211
Tini kaMaqoma, Chief, 148, 149
    capture of, 165
    in Lotutu Bush, 159
Tongue, Capt. John Moore Gurnel,
    166, 251, 253
Trainer, Pvt. J. 236
Transkei, the, 29, 55, 92, 97, 164,
    167
    Frere's visit to, 102-103
    Melvill's visit to, 99
    Thesiger's visit to, 164-165
    tribal divisions in, 93
Transvaal, the, 55, 64
    annex. of, 83
    Carrington in, 183
    Cunynghame and Coghill in,
        85-88
    labour from, 35
    Rowland in, 177-179
    Sekhukhune and, 69-70, 176
    Shepstone and, 81 *et seq.*
    trouble in, 69, 70, 81, 176
Transvaal Executive Council
Transvaal Mounted Infantry, 170
Transvaal Mounted Volunteers, 178
Trollope, Anthony, 28, 29
Tsatsu clan, the, 143
Tswana people, 32
Tucker, Henry, 36, 37, 60
    arrested, 49
    in Cowie affair, 38-39
Tugela Lower Drift, 198
Tyala, Counsellor, 118, 126
Tyityaba valley, 127, 142

Uitenhage (Cape Colony), 62
Ukukhafula, 134

Ukuyolela, 105, 134
Ultimatum (Frere's), 198, 199, 206
Ulundi (Zululand), 191, 199, 215, 253
Union Line, the, 31, 65
United States of America, 21
Upcher, Capt. Russell, 91
  in Army of the Transkei, 124, 129
  commands at Centane, 132-137, 139
  at Helpmekaar, 215, 230, 250
  at Nyumaga, 129-130
  recommended for C.B., 183
  subsequent career, 259
Upton, Sgt. George, 214
Utrecht (Natal), 85, 187, 200

Vause, Lt. Wyatt, 225, 229
Vereker, Lt. Hon. Standish William P., 223, 225, 239
Victoria Cross, the
  of Browne, 254, 255
  of Chard, 255
  of Moore, 127
  of Reynolds, 254, 255
  of Wood, 147
Volksraad, the, 69, 70, 74, 82, 83
Volunteers, 201
  at Isandlwana, 218, 219
  from Kimberley, 145, 172
  in Ninth Frontier War, 109, 148, 154, 156
Von Linsingen, Cmdt. Wilhelm Carl Ferdinand, 158-160
Von Schlickmann, Conrad, 37, 38
  arrested, 49
  in Lydenburg Volunteer Corps, 74, 87
Vooruitzicht, 35
  purchase of, 47, 59

Wales, 19
Walker, Lt.-Col. Forestier W. E., 76, 146, 184, 193
Walsh, Lt. Henry Alfred, 218
War
  Anglo-Boer, 259, 260
  Anglo-Zulu, 207-254
    causes of, 186-192
  Crimean, 18, 42, 65
  First Opium, 42
  Franco-Prussian, 19
  Frontier
    Sixth, 75
    Seventh, 111
    Eighth, 49, 76, 93, 111, 147
    Ninth, 12, 104, 115, 166-168
      causes of, 98, 186
  'Kaffir', 22
  Second Sikh, 18
  Sekhukhune, 167, 186
War Council, the, 107, 109
War-mark, the, 134
War Office, the, 64, 71, 256
Wardell, Capt. George Vaughan, 63, 149
  commands Ft. Warwick, 127-128
  at Isandlwana, 230, 231, 236, 242
Warren, Col. Charles, 172, 260
  in the Griqua Rebellion, 173, 174
Waterboer, Nicolaas, 32
Waterkloof, the (Ciskei), 148, 149, 151, 158, 165
Wedding-feast, the, 98
Wellington (Cape Colony), 43
White, Paymaster Francis Freeman, 18
  at Isandlwana, 242
Williams, Pvt. J. (Glyn's Groom), 227, 238, 239
Wilson, Pvt. G., 227
Witchdoctors
  and Sir George Grey, 93

at Ibeka, 106
in Zululand, 187
Wodehouse, Sir Philip, 96, 97
Wolseley, Maj.-Gen. Sir Garnet
Ashanti campaign of, 20
in Cape Town, 53, 62, 64
and Frere, 80, 257
and Froude, 62
as High Commissioner, 256
at London Conference, 74
mission to Natal, 52, 53, 56, 188
opinion of Shepstone, 75, 189
opinion of the Zulus, 64, 185
succeeds Chelmsford, 253
in the Transvaal, 257
Wood, Col. Henry Evelyn, 146, 151
in Buffalo Poort offensives, 150, 153-156, 161
commands 90th Regt., 158
at Kokstad, 169
in Lotutu offensive, 157, 159
in Zulu War, 200, 208, 253

Wynberg (Cape), 77

Xhosa people, the, 77, 93
and the 'cattle-killing', 94
consequences of defeat, 168
and the Mfengu, 97
reasons for defeat, 167

Younghusband, Capt. Reginald, 73, 149, 197
at Isandlwana, 231, 232, 241, 243, 246
misses Transkei campaign, 120
returns to South Africa, 183

Zanyokwe valley, 158, 159, 160
Zulu people, 52, 64, 70, 140, 208, 184, 224, 250
Zululand, 191, 192, 200, 203, 256
drought in, 186-187
invasion of, 207-208
labour from, 35